THE DJ WHO "BROUGHT DOWN" THE USSR

THE LIFE AND LEGACY OF SEVA NOVGORODSEV

MODERN BIOGRAPHIES

THE DJ WHO "BROUGHT DOWN" THE USSR

THE LIFE AND LEGACY OF SEVA NOVGORODSEV

MICHELLE S. DANIEL

BOSTON
2023

Library of Congress Cataloging-in-Publication Data

Names: Daniel, Michelle, 1986- author.
Title: The DJ who "brought down" the USSR: the life and legacy of Seva Novgorodsev / Michelle Daniel.
Description: Boston: Academic Studies Press, 2023. | Series: Modern biographies | Includes bibliographical references.
Identifiers: LCCN 2022043640 (print) | LCCN 2022043641 (ebook) | ISBN 9781644696477 (hardback) | ISBN 9798887190990 (paperback) | ISBN 9781644696484 (adobe pdf) | ISBN 9781644696491 (epub)
Subjects: LCSH: Novgorodsev, Seva. | Disc jockeys--England--Biography. | Russians--England--Biography. | Radio in propaganda--Great Britain--History. | International broadcasting--Great Britain--History. | Cold War--Music and the war. | BBC Russian Service--History--20th century. | BBC Russian Service--History--21st century. | Radio programs, Musical--Soviet Union. | Radio programs, Musical--Russia (Federation) | Rock music--Political aspects--Soviet Union. | Rock music--Political aspects--Russia (Federation)
Classification: LCC ML429.N74 D36 2023 (print) | LCC ML429.N74 (ebook) | DDC 791.44092 [B]--dc23/eng/20220913
LC record available at https://lccn.loc.gov/2022043640
LC ebook record available at https://lccn.loc.gov/2022043641

ISBN 9781644696477 (hardback)
ISBN 9798887190990 (paperback)
ISBN 9781644696484 (adobe pdf)
ISBN 9781644696491 (epub)

Book design by PHi Business Solutions
Cover design by Ivan Grave

Published by Academic Studies Press
1577 Beacon St.
Brookline, MA 02446, USA

press@academicstudiespress.com
www.academicstudiespress.com

Contents

Foreword

This is not just a book of excellent, eccentric Cold War history—this book is vital for the present. We all need to understand the phenomenon of Seva Novgorodsev if we want to start thinking seriously about how to challenge the likes of Russia and China in the information space. Seva, as readers of this book will discover, is one of the great hidden heroes of the Cold War, wielding a weapon as potent as any missile: rock music. A Soviet dissident, he became a DJ on the Russian Service of the BBC. He introduced the most underground music to his loyal audiences. It transformed their minds, inspiring them with the dream of being as free as the music Seva played. Dictators know that culture is crucial, that is why they seek to control, fund, and censor it. Seva was, in his own way, as important as Gorbachev or Reagan in ending the Cold War.

—Peter Pomerantsev

Preface

In his 1946 "Long Telegram," American diplomat and historian George Frost Kennan cited the infamous words of Red Terror mastermind Joseph Stalin from nearly two decades earlier: "In [the] course of further development of international revolution there will emerge two centers of world significance: a socialist center . . . and a capitalist center."[1] As the atomic dust of World War II settled and relations between the East and West turned frosty, the communist-capitalist split Stalin foretold became reality.

Hoping to erode heathen socialism, Western radio broadcasters such as the Voice of America (VOA), Radio Free Europe and Radio Liberty (RFE/RL), Deutsche Welle (DW), and the British Broadcasting Corporation (BBC) tuned their agendas to the holy crusade, launching Western music, culture, and ideas to reach the unreachable. For decades, invisible air wars raged over the breadth of the USSR and Eastern Bloc with the Soviet authorities aggressively jamming transmissions. Despite such earnest obstruction, the West ultimately appeared to conquer all as the Soviet system collapsed at the end of 1991.

Understandably, as the West's focus shifted to the Middle East during the Gulf War, international broadcasting came under financial scrutiny and underwent subsequent cutbacks by governments.[2] Nevertheless, by failing to maintain a diplomatic voice in the former Soviet sphere, decades of fastidious Western diplomacy have been undone in the current age of information and cyber warfare.[3] Perhaps, *soundcraft* in general, which here means the strategic use of aural media

---

1 "George Kennan's 'Long Telegram,'" February 22, 1946, History and Public Policy Program Digital Archive, National Archives and Records Administration, Department of State Records (Record Group 59), Central Decimal File, 1945-1949, 861.00/2-2246, https://digitalarchive.wilsoncenter.org/document/116178.

2 The high costs of funding Radio Free Europe and Radio Liberty, for example, are delineated in a number of Cold War-era US congressional reports. Notably, according to Senate Committee on Foreign Relations Report No. 92-851 dated June 12, 1972, the bill S. 3645 "is to amend section 703 of the US Information and Educational Exchange Act of 1948 to authorize an appropriation of $38,520,000 in fiscal year 1973 for continued government funding of [RFE/RL]."

3 The Western broadcasters' Russian services all terminated shortwave broadcasting by 2011 (VOA earlier than the BBC, though both switched to and have maintained an online presence that, while being essential, is not necessarily reaching the audiences that were once reached during Cold War operation levels). RFE/RL remains strong, but as a surrogate operation.

and mediums like radio in statecraft and warcraft, so easily fell to the wayside because international broadcasting was never fully appreciated, much less understood, by the general public. What exactly did the catch-all phrase "win hearts and minds" mean and look like in practice? To what extent did Western radio diplomacy impact broader society in communist spaces and how did this impact change government policies and politics? Naturally, it is easier to examine the relationships between those who govern rather than to understand the intricacies and the countless micro-interactions of everyday citizens. But the most influential, change-making group in any international relations setting is the citizenry itself—listeners are the reason radio was so successful as a mechanism of change and reconstruction during the Cold War.[4] Radio carried out *perestroika* in listeners long before Gorbachev's *perestroika* became a policy. Former VOA Russian Service director Mark Pomar articulated that what made the Soviet listener—and even more so the Russian listener—different from others during the Cold War was the desperate need to connect with those beyond the Iron Curtain: "It didn't matter what station it was, it was a Voice from out there."[5]

This study attempts to unpack the developed intimacy between the listeners and the "voices" themselves, including those émigrés who were wrangled into a pair of headphones for the all-consuming purpose of driving back communist ideology with Western music and culture. The DJs who broadcast to the USSR had, in many ways, the most impact on the erosion of the Soviet mentality, for they had the ear of the younger generations who in turn made the difference in the twilight years of the USSR.

Among the many DJs who broadcast to the USSR, two personalities stand out due to their prolificacy as broadcasters and ability to capture the imagination of Soviet youth. The first and earlier of the two DJs, American Willis Conover, was the beloved host of the jazz hour on VOA starting in 1955. Despite broadcasting in English, he became a "father" figure to young Soviets, influencing government-persecuted *stilyagi*—Russia's first hipsters and consumers of American jazz and fashion.[6] The second is the BBC's Seva Novgorodsev,[7] who like VOA's

---

4 Just one anecdotal example: a VOA listener named Roman moved to America because he'd been listening to rock DJ Bill Skundrich in the mid-'80s and felt so compelled by this "voice" that he left the USSR as soon as he could (Bill Skundrich in conversation with author, January 2021).

5 Mark Pomar in discussion with author, February 6, 2019.

6 Charles Paul Freund, "The DJ Who Shook the Soviet Union with Jazz," *Newsweek*, August 9, 2015, https://www.newsweek.com/dj-who-shook-soviet-union-jazz-360935#:~:text=Voice%20of%20America%20DJ%20Willis,The%20Wall%20Street%20Journal%20notes.

7 Per Seva's preferred transliteration.

Conover is little known in the West but legendary in the USSR. Bearing greater significance for his impact on the youth towards the end of the Cold War, Seva himself grew up listening to Conover's voice religiously and undoubtedly built his own style with the baritone "voice of jazz" in mind. But while much has been documented about Conover's life and legacy,[8] few in the West have studied Novgorodsev's BBC career and more importantly his prominent role in the cultural education and spiritual edification of Russian youth as a Soviet émigré, jazz musician, *stilyaga,* and member of the Russian intelligentsia.[9]

Born in Leningrad on July 9, 1940, Seva Novgorodsev served as presenter for the BBC Russian Service for nearly four decades from 1976 until his retirement in September 2015. Considered a sage of rock 'n' roll,[10] Seva introduced banned Western popular music and culture into the Soviet Union and, according to international relations scholar Paul Sheeran, was *very* influential in the pre-*perestroika* era particularly.[11] Seva developed a unique style of presenting that satirized Soviet technical verbiage, subverting the USSR's carefully constructed defense systems with untranslatable-to-English wordplay while largely avoiding politicisms. The Central Committee of the Communist Party viewed him as an ideological saboteur and spent millions of rubles jamming his signals and undermining him in state-controlled media. Despite the 1978 murder of fellow BBC presenter Georgi Markov[12] and KGB *rezidenty* in London monitoring him, Seva remained on the air for thirty-eight years, garnering well over twenty-five million

---

8 See Terry Ripmaster's *Willis Conover: Broadcasting Jazz to The World* (Lincoln: iUniverse, 2007), as well as several other books on VOA that include Conover, such as Alan Heil's *Voice of America—A History* (New York: Columbia University Press, 2003). Chapter 13 is devoted to Conover and his jazz hour.

9 Seva has been written about by Russians in Russian, but in the West there are very few books or articles. See the very notable piece by Kristin Roth-Ey—"Listening out, Listening for, Listening in: Cold War Radio Broadcasting and the Late Soviet Audience," *The Russian Review* 79, no. 4 (October 2020), https://onlinelibrary.wiley.com/doi/epdf/10.1111/russ.12285—about Seva's impact on Soviet youth. A great contribution to understanding the Russian intelligentsia of the postwar generation is Vladislav M. Zubok's *Zhivago's Children* (Cambridge, MA: Harvard University Press, 2009), assessing the cultural aesthetics of the 1950s and '60s under Khrushchev's Thaw, and the way in which Khrushchev created confusion among the Soviet apparatchiki, the *stilyagi* (who were labeled cultural "deviationists"), and the intelligentsia (both the official Soviet variety and anti-Stalin "beatnik" variety) with his rollercoaster attitude towards art and artists of all kinds.

10 In many interviews given in recent years, Seva openly admits to not liking rock music. Fans were aware of his preferences.

11 Paul Sheeran, *Cultural Politics in International Relations* (Farnham: Ashgate Publishing Ltd., 2001), 94.

12 A DJ for the BBC's Bulgarian Service, Markov hotly slandered his government over the air from London. See "Ricin and the Umbrella Murder," CNN.com, October 23, 2003, http://www.cnn.com/2003/WORLD/europe/01/07/terror.poison.bulgarian/.

listeners worldwide and fostering the growth of the Russian community in the UK from a mere forty at his arrival in London to four hundred thousand by 1991. He was awarded the Member of the British Empire in 2005 by Queen Elizabeth II for his services to broadcasting and retired from the BBC on September 4, 2015.

Having wisely saved all of his listener letters, he donated the vast sum to the Hoover Institution in 2015.[13] Despite postal unreliability and KGB censorship, the volume of this mail from the USSR is staggering and speaks to, as RFE/RL's audience research director R. Eugene Parta put it, "the Hidden Listener" behind the Iron Curtain.[14] Using these invaluable letters in addition to articles, interviews, videos, radio transcripts on seva.ru courtesy of the BBC, an incredible catalogue of membership cards from the rock information fan club NORIS,[15] and Seva's own autobiography, this book explores the far-reaching impact of Seva's broadcasts and the music he popularized through the BBC Russian Service, which operated on a miniscule budget in comparison to its competitors Radio Liberty and VOA Russian Service.[16] But most important are the interviews conducted with late Soviet-era listeners who willingly shared their stories either in person during 2019 or through email. A representative selection of these listener responses is included in this book as their stories are vital to understanding the cultural and spiritual value of radio—and Seva himself—to former Soviet citizens.

Seva did not aim to topple any regime or otherwise propound the righteousness of capitalism.[17] For the majority of his audience, Seva provided perspective, experience, and camaraderie, speaking to listeners on their level and

---

13 Because Seva was in fact interested in the intellectual and spiritual nature of his audience, he collected all the letters from his listeners and accumulated so many that they took up an enormous amount of space in his apartment. "When the management . . . asked me, 'what would be the best name to give this huge collection of letters,' I recommended calling it 'The evolution of the Soviet youth's mentality during the '70s and '80s'" (Dmitri Tolkunov, "Seva Novgorodsev," *All Andorra*, April 29, 2019).

14 R. Eugene Parta's *Discovering the Hidden Listener* (Stanford: Hoover Institution Press, 2007) contains surveys and interviews conducted in the Soviet from 1972–90, which gauge the effectiveness of Western broadcasters, with emphasis on Radio Liberty for which he worked.

15 NORIS stands for (in Russian) Independent United Rock Information Syndicate.

16 Per the BBC Russian Service's own purview, Radio Liberty was its primary competitor, not so much VOA's Russian Service. *The Sunday Times* reported in 1985 on the grim financial situation of the BBC, stating that VOA had ten times more money than all of the other sections of the BBC World Service put together. Despite this resource imbalance, Soviets who listened to VOA and Radio Liberty on a normal basis would listen religiously to Seva because, as one Russian émigré in the late '80s put it, his was the only program that felt "genuinely Russian" (Nick Higham and Nigel Horne, "Bloc-buster Tactics," *The Sunday Times*, November 3, 1985).

17 Roth-Ey, "Listening out," 576.

extemporaneously, as if with a friend. As will be shown in the previously unheard recollections of listeners, a distinct commonality surfaced in their accounts, which points to a shared experience of the late Cold War generation[18]—those who felt alienated and unable to express themselves discovered in Seva's programs comfort, entertainment, and most importantly spiritual liberty. Seva circumvented what seemed so permanent and monumental—the Soviet Union, the American threat, the bipolar world order—and opened a bright public space for discourse, connection, and change.

18 The majority of contributing respondents are born in the 1960s and early '70s.

Introduction: Radio, Rock 'n' "Role"

"It all started with 'Rock Around the Clock,'" recalls Seva Novgorodsev with a smile, alluding to the moment the 1955 quintessential hit by Bill Haley & His Comets crackled from shortwave radios all over the Soviet Union. This is early rock 'n' roll; this is the West. And *this*, Seva implies, is where the fall of the USSR really began: on the air, one voice, one song, one word at a time, presenting an incorporeal threat to the regime, to the Soviet way of life.[1]

As with the USSR's demise, there is no single explanation for why Seva made the substantial impact he did. Seva was not a career radio man as VOA's Willis Conover was, nor did he enter the studio with a voice curated for the microphone. He was raw. Untrained. Of course, talent and hard work factored into his quick rise to popularity; however, with the airwaves drowning in voices, talent and hard work alone were not enough to vault him to the top. Historian Kristin Roth-Ey candidly questions why Seva and his programs on BBC, particularly *Rok-posevy*, even drew the audiences that they did:

> After all, by the time the show hit the airwaves in the late 1970s, Soviet mass culture had struck its own cautious *modus vivendi* with Western popular music. The state-owned record label, *Melodiya*, released compilation albums of Western pop and rock artists. Central Soviet radio and television ran shows that featured them, and the Komsomol organized dances with their music. The Soviet press carried some current information about the Western music scene; the most important and popular source was the Komsomol monthly, *Rovesnik*, but it was possible to find informed commentary in other publications as well. Between official, state-sanctioned sources, cross-border leakage from other countries, and the black market, Soviet music fans in the late '70s and early '80s were not starved of sustenance.[2]

---

1 Radina Vučetić, *Coca-Cola Socialism: Americanization of Yugoslav Culture in the Sixties* (Budapest: Central European University Press, 2018), 109.

2 Roth-Ey, "Listening out," 567.

Hence, there had to be other lubricating factors—environmental, cultural, and political—that made Seva's programs *and* him, as a personality, resonate.

The first factor was timing. Like Conover, who had entered the ether at a tumultuous time for the Soviet people—right after the death of Stalin and during the peak of jazz's popularity—Seva went on air just as rock permeated the Soviet space and inspired government censorship. Information about rock music was such a valuable commodity in Russia that Western radio—and thereby Western voices—became an intrinsic and integral part of people's everyday lives.

The second factor was the Cold War-era BBC itself, which had accumulated credibility with listeners worldwide as a trustworthy source of news and programming that, by and large, strove to be free of bias. Anecdotal evidence suggests that even at the height of the Cold War, the corporation was considered by Soviet people of varying persuasions as acceptable to listen to (i.e., not anti-Soviet) while other Western broadcasters, particularly Radio Liberty, were not. This trust made the BBC a somewhat neutral space on the airwaves where Seva could gather a diverse and broad range of listeners—party members and leather-fetishizing metalheads alike. Moreover, the BBC's austere editorial policies forced Seva to craft the esoteric kind of Bolshevik-speak that made him so popular in the first place, understood by the Soviet masses but lost on the *apparatchiki*—and the BBC censors.

The third factor was the political fluctuations in the Soviet Union in the 1970s and '80s, which bore a direct relationship to the use of radio frequency interference to obstruct reception, commonly referred to as jamming. Jamming—the intangible force that affected virtually every Soviet citizen, though not evenly—was a powerful determiner of who listened to whom. Not merely the obstruction of a signal, jamming was a felt presence. It was an indicator of the Kremlin's mentality, the vicissitudes of international relations, and the vagaries of Soviet domestic politics. RFE/RL, then, received most of the attention while the BBC for years dwelt near the bottom end of the Comintern's spectrum of concern, though a favorite written complaint from Seva's listeners was how difficult it was to hear him, at least before all jamming ceased near the end of the '80s. But Seva wasn't jammed ubiquitously—nor could he have been—and oftentimes merely shifting the radio from one side of the room to another yielded the desired results.

Lastly, the fourth factor for Seva's popularity was the widespread "masculinity crisis" following Stalin's death and triggered by the Thaw. Nikita Khrushchev's 1956 excoriation of Stalin's cult of personality—until which, for all his faults and heinousness, Stalin had been viewed as the quintessential father role model—left a hole in society. Fathers of the Long Sixties, in general, went from being men of action and iron to filling office chairs and scientific roles. The motif of the wandering man, who knows neither his purpose nor how to be masculine in this new, commodity-rich, technologically driven society, permeated Soviet movies, music, and writing. As in the film *Moscow Doesn't Believe in Tears,* men were often portrayed as poor fathers untrained in communication and lacking the ability to show empathy. Consequently, marginalized youth, in need of strong fathers, sought solace, guidance, and information from elsewhere as the Cold War progressed—and even more so as the economy crashed in the 1980s.[3] Seva's life and broad experiences in Soviet Russia predisposed him to be the sort of paternal role model that fit the needs of a disenfranchised generation hungering for spiritual and emotional edification. Soviet men could point to Seva as a shining example of a real Russian *muzhik* who went off to do something unusual, off the beaten path, speaking directly and honestly to his homeland with his own words. And the BBC provided him the platform to do so.

A Very British Sort of Broadcasting

No other Western broadcaster could have been better matched to Seva Novgorodsev's style, listenership, and methods than the British Broadcasting Corporation.[4] By the time Seva was first heard on air in 1977, the BBC had accrued an amazing reputation with global audiences as a broadcaster committed to speaking peace and truth to nations. A 1982 article in *Christian Science Monitor* (*CSM*) quoted an editor at the World Service, Barry Holland, regarding the BBC's commitment to delivering truth. Holland said, "There's a kind of gas in this building," referring to Bush House, the BBC's iconic former headquarters. "Invisible, but very much present. It's an atmosphere, if you like, the ethos of a balanced view."[5] As journalist Peter Pomerantsev wrote concerning this exact statement:

---

3 "The '60s masculinity crisis was sort of a precursor or a staged rehearsal for the masculinity crisis in the Soviet Union of the '80s, which was much more dire because the economic situation was much more dire." See Marko Dumančić, "'Frozen by the Thaw': The Soviet Masculinity Crisis of the Long Sixties," in *The Slavic Connexion*, October 9, 2021, podcast, https://www.slavxradio.com/marko.

4 See Andrew Crisell, *An Introductory History of British Broadcasting* (London: Routledge, 2002).

5 Peter Pomerantsev, *This Is Not Propaganda: Adventures in the War Against Reality* (New York: PublicAffairs, 2019), 112.

> This gas was a means of gaining credibility. Trust. To project the image of Britain as the sort of place that you could rely on for the BBC trinity of "accuracy, impartiality, and fairness," which in turn was meant to promote what the founder of the BBC, Sir Reith, had called the British values of "reasonableness, democracy, and debate," which in turn was meant to make Britain more admired globally.[6]

The BBC shoved political considerations to the back of the line for this "trinity," never resorting to pillorying and never yielding to editorial pressures. For instance, when VOA started to include two-minute editorials featuring the opinion of the US government, the BBC and its culture shunned the idea for the UK.[7] Despite its relatively miniscule budget, the BBC had the greatest international audience overall at the height of the Cold War: "One Soviet estimate was as many as 40 million regular listeners, but even the VOA itself claim[ed] only 12 million."[8]

One Moscow-based listener appreciated all the Western stations for the provision of "information" but complained about the "unintelligent propaganda" of VOA's programming. In contrast, the BBC was a favorite with her whole family, "loved for its 'balanced approach and objectivity.'"[9] And while this objectivity has resulted in criticism of the BBC for the absence of clear reproof of reprehensible acts and events,[10] the BBC has an undeniable worldwide appeal. As David Willis wrote for the *Christian Science Monitor,* "In many parts of the world, it is easier for the BBC to be accepted than the voice of the United States superpower, although sometimes it works in reverse: Soviet dissidents, for instance, tend to prefer VOA precisely because it is American and thus anti-Soviet."[11]

According to one former staffer who also worked at Radio Liberty, the BBC's structure, selection of staff, and manner of delivery contributed greatly to the corporation's appeal:

---

6 Ibid.

7 David K. Willis, "How the British Broadcasting Corporation Keeps Its Balance," *Christian Science Monitor,* August 17, 1982.

8 Ibid.

9 Donald J. Raleigh, *Soviet Baby Boomers: An Oral History of Russia's Cold War Generation* (New York: OUP USA, 2013), 149–50.

10 The BBC was accused by some of being so infuriatingly fair it would give the devil an interview should it have offered God the microphone. See Pomerantsev, *This is Not Propaganda,* 112.

11 Willis, "How the British Broadcasting Corporation Keeps Its Balance." The idea of *American* and *anti-Soviet* being one and the same no doubt influences people's radio dials and biases.

> The BBC had no elaborate hierarchy of pay grades and positions. . . . I was struck by the importance the Russian Service accorded to the selection of staff. . . . Programs were made by experts in their field: Seva Novgorodsev made broadcasts about music, Dr. Edik Ochagavia covered medicine, Valery Lapidus, an engineer by training, made programs about technology. . . . Another difference in the way the stations worked. At Liberty the scripts were read on air by presenters with trained voices. At the BBC we read our own scripts and, as we didn't have any voice training, we just spoke in our usual manner, as if we were talking to friends. . . . Real human voices burst onto the Soviet airwaves. They were instantly recognizable and trustworthy.[12]

Aural recognizability dates back to wartime. One of the BBC's big takeaways from WWII was that creating larger-than-life personalities was vital, not for commercial purposes but to help boost the morale of the troops and the nation.[13] Thus, in the Cold War, this practice continued, and the World Service got into the habit of recruiting and elevating well-educated and eloquent-in-their-native-tongue émigrés. Seva was a quintessential example: "Living in England your English is never good enough, no matter who you are . . . [but] I wasn't working for Barclays Bank or something like that, I was working for the World Service and rather than being a second-rate Englishman I became a first-rate Russian."[14]

Radio Diplomacy (and Propaganda)

From its inception, the BBC fundamentally differed from every other "wireless" network in the world. While it was a legally independent creation, the BBC was not autonomous, particularly during World War II when it became essentially an ambassador for the British Empire to peoples everywhere. The BBC's official motto itself—"Nation shall speak peace unto nation"—attests to the corporation's sense of duty in promoting internationalist cooperation and

---

12 Igor Golomstock, *A Ransomed Dissident: A Life in Art Under the Soviets* (London: Bloomsbury Publishing, 2018), 170–71.

13 The program *BBC Variety* was boosted post-May 1940 by imported American stars. See Siân Nicholas, "The People's Radio: The BBC and Its Audience, 1939–1945," in *Millions Like Us?: British Culture in the Second World War*, ed. Nick Hayes and Jeff Hill (Liverpool: Liverpool University Press, 1999), 81.

14 Seva Novgorodsev, interview by Adriana Alexander, Museum of London, October 25, 1999.

harmony. Broadcasting created a much more informed citizenry in democratic and nondemocratic countries, which meant that policymakers and state actors had to not only *consider* the public in other countries, they had to also *speak* to those people directly. Even the BBC's board of governors confirmed the new level of concern at Bush House in a white paper to Parliament early in the Cold War: "Wireless has given to governments direct means of access to audiences overseas which enables them to influence foreign governments by and through direct contact with the masses."[15] It was no doubt this sense of responsibility at the highest echelons that led to the BBC seeking "close consultancy" with the Foreign Office (FO) on content as early as the 1930s. Through both the nesting of stalwart diplomats into key positions at Bush House and sharpening struggles between the BBC and Foreign Office, the corporation took on the role of intermediary in the war, particularly once the Nazis invaded the USSR in 1941, thereby birthing a new phase in the evolution of broadcasting—radio diplomacy.[16] Radio diplomacy combined the "mass-produced" aspect of propaganda[17] with traditional state-to-state diplomacy for the purpose of persuading, maintaining, or otherwise crafting public opinion and discourse to achieve certain goals.

The creation of radio diplomacy during the 1940s was crucial because it established a set of behaviors and practices for the BBC that continued into the Cold War, even if the aim was no longer to forge or keep alliances but rather "winning hearts and minds." As a result, when the BBC launched its Russian Service (RS) in 1946, it had a major advantage over other Russian-language broadcasters such as VOA Russian, which launched in 1947, and Radio Liberty, which launched in 1953. However, the RS's position was not always secure and was not exempt from criticism and government pressure largely because of its obvious power as a direct voice to the Russian people. Time and again the service came under fire from the British establishment and placed the BBC's objectivity and editorial autonomy in jeopardy. One very notable incident occurred at the time of Stalin's death in 1953 when a subdivision of the FO accused the RS of permitting the

---

15 Michael Nelson, *War of the Black Heavens: The Battles of Western Broadcasting in the Cold War* (Syracuse: Syracuse University Press, 1997), 87.

16 In Gary D. Rawnsley's *Radio Diplomacy and Propaganda* (New York: St. Martin's Press, 1996), he argues for the importance of radio as a tool of foreign policy, but disputes W. J. West's assertion that radio rendered conventional diplomacy redundant, calling it an overstatement.

17 Paul M. A. Linebarger, *Psychological Warfare* (New York: Hauraki Publishing, 2015), 39. Linebarger defines propaganda as "the planned use of any form of public or mass-produced communication designed to affect the mind and emotion of a given group for a specific public purpose whether military, economic or political."

airing of content that was "damaging to the Free World." One official dared to say that "the definition of the role of the BBC's broadcasts to Russia is primarily a matter for the Foreign Office."[18] A bitter row followed, and the head of the RS at the time, Anatol Goldberg, was targeted.[19] Goldberg, who had been with the BBC since 1939, defended the choice to be temperate in approaching the Soviet Union at this delicate juncture because Stalin's death represented a chance to create new connections and dialogue. Finally in 1958, though the BBC refused to fire Goldberg, it replaced him as head of the RS but kept him on as the host of the long-running program *Notes by Our Observer*, a show that certainly benefited from the BBC's hard-earned reputation.[20] Many Russian listeners tuned in to Goldberg for the precise reason that he, like Seva in the years to come, understood the audience and its needs: they wanted information.[21]

As American sociologist W. Phillips Davison stated in his 1960s book on international political communication, a broadcaster must have the ability and willingness to provide people "useful" information.[22] And what was deemed "useful?" Entertainment for one and "instrumental" information for another. Furthermore, concerning propaganda and propagandists, Richard Crossman, a member of a joint Anglo-American psychological warfare team during the war, stated in 1952 that a good propagandist is not in fact a "brilliant liar," but rather someone who is able to establish "empathy" with the target audience. "The central substance of propaganda . . . was 'hard, correct information.' Therefore 'news must take priority over views, facts over preaching.'"[23] Is it any wonder, then, that the BBC, which indeed placed emphasis on facts, education, balance, and objectivity, would rise to the top, and that all those presenters who kept with BBC editorial standards *and* established empathy with the audience would also rise? It's therefore the BBC that served as the proper vessel for Seva, and Seva

---

18 David Wedgewood Benn, "How the FO tried to stifle the BBC," *New Statesman*, December 6, 1999, https://www.newstatesman.com/long-reads/1999/12/how-the-fo-tried-to-stifle-the-bbc. Whether the BBC is in partnership with the FO seems to be unclear. John Tusa (a WS director) says that it was "never an arm of" the Foreign Office, but clearly from time to time the FO thinks that the WS and BBC Monitoring are obligated to work with the FO.

19 Ibid.

20 Nelson, *War of the Black Heavens*, 31.

21 John Tusa, "BBC World Service Celebrates 75 Years on Air," *Daily Telegraph*, December 16, 2007, https://www.telegraph.co.uk/news/uknews/1572672/BBC-World-Service-celebrates-75-years-on-air.html.

22 See W. Phillips Davison, *International Political Communication* (New York: Praeger, 1965).

23 Quoted in David Wedgewood Benn, "Winning Hearts and Minds," *Gulf News*, December 4, 2004, https://gulfnews.com/uae/david-wedgwood-benn-winning-hearts-and-minds-1.340549.

who became the ideal navigator for the enormous target audience: lovers of rock 'n' roll.

"Rock the Seva Way"

Rock music was like war fought on stages rather than battlefields, with the enemy being any obstruction of arbitrary "freedom" and "self-expression." The very word "rock" implies foundation-shifting strength and immovable courage, and so, when the genre carried over into the Eastern Bloc and the USSR, it reflected both the greater struggle between the people and the government and an individual's internal struggle—love for the nation, but anger towards the regime. In the context of the USSR and its sphere of influence, rock was revolution itself, partly because it came from the West and partly because it dissolved the existence of the USSR in the minds of the youth.[24] Could it be entirely coincidental that once this genre took hold of the youth that revolutionary things happened—and happened so suddenly?[25]

Russian rock was an overwhelmingly male-dominated genre with women embracing the music as well but mainly as spectators rather than performers. One possible explanation for this gender disparity was that rock music helped young men in all stations of life enter an area that could be masculine in expression without stooping to the stereotypical idea of the strong Soviet male. Per Marko Dumančić's *Men Out of Focus: The Soviet Masculinity Crisis of the Long Sixties,* men in Russia experienced difficulty adjusting to life after World War II, especially following the death of Stalin, the ultimate male model and father figure, when Khrushchev began to institute many changes. Positive though they were, these changes put mental strain on men who began losing their sense of place and authority in an increasingly complex and female-oriented society.

---

24 For youth culture and social movements, see Alexei Yurchak's *Everything Was Forever, until It Was No More* (New Jersey: Princeton University Press, 2005), a seminal work that exposes the nuanced depth and richness of the USSR. Additionally, Padriac Kenney's *A Carnival of Revolution* (Princeton: Princeton University Press, 2003) offers the argument that social movements cropping up across Eastern Europe (but not Russia) were the harbinger of death for communism. However, this study proves that Russia also experienced kinetic social energy, though it was not so easily observable to the West.

25 For studies on rock and its social and emotional impact on Soviet youth, see Sergei I. Zhuk, *Rock and Roll in the Rocket City* (Baltimore: Johns Hopkins University Press, 2010), which covers Ukrainian youth in Dnipropetrovsk and Radina Vučetic's *Coca-Cola Socialism* (Budapest: Central European University Press, 2012), which focuses on Yugoslav culture in the 1960s.

Whereas during the war there were metal factories in which to work and battlefields on which to fight, after Stalin the state shifted its focus to technology and goods and services, and science prevailed over the sword, as did offices over bunkers. Such jobs were not restricted to men or designated as masculine occupations, but were equally—and in many cases more so—held by women.

As it became clear that a sort of aimlessness and hopelessness was developing amongst men and was causing their lifespan to decrease and alcoholism to rise, Brezhnev tried "to turn the clock back and reintroduce the Stalin tropes" through the tried-and-true erection of great statues of past male heroes.[26] But even though the public was tired of men being "lost" and indolent or aimless, people didn't "buy into this Stalinist superhero" anymore.[27] Why? This archetype didn't suit the needs of the generations looking to be more integrated with the world rather than guard *against* the world. In contrast, rock music was exotic and full of "pathos." It was hard and phallic, producing adrenaline, imbuing men with exciting purpose and liberating them to be masculine on their own terms.[28]

Rock in the 1970s and '80s offered what jazz did during the Thaw: it provided men (and certain women) a way to express themselves and creatively step out of the shadows of established war heroes and authority figures while still embracing their country and culture.[29] Jazz, although more cerebral and less explicitly "aggressive" as rock, was also a male-dominated genre and arena of performance.[30] Playing a rock or jazz instrument carried masculine associations. Seva's choice of instrument was the tenor saxophone, itself the embodiment of jazz in

---

26 Dumančić, "'Frozen by the Thaw.'"

27 Ibid.

28 Seva has pointed out that alcoholism is a sort of ritualistic habit that defines manhood in Russia, but that by leaving the country he was liberated of such influences and could become a man on his own terms, not those dictated by society. "The Russian style of life with its permanent stress, drinking crazy amounts of vodka with your friends—by refusing to do it you are not a man and nobody will trust you—is very self-destructive." Tolkunov, "Seva Novgorodsev."

29 This sense of duty can be seen in the fact that few Russian rock stars emigrated even when they could and never expressed any need to leave. It was as if they saw themselves as the vanguard of Russian culture (rather than of the state) and societal progress. Seva never wanted to leave Russia either, but he did so at the behest of his wife and son.

30 For studies on jazz in the USSR and jazz diplomacy, see S. Frederick Starr's *Red and Hot: The Fate of Jazz in the Soviet Union* (New York: Limelight, 2004), Alexei Batashev's *Sovetskii dzhaz* (Moscow: Muzyka, 1972), Penny M. Von Eschen, *Satchmo Blows up the World* (Cambridge, MA: Harvard University Press, 2006), William Minor's *Unzipped Souls: A Jazz Journey through the Soviet Union* (Philadelphia: Temple University Press, 1995), and Lisa E. Davenport's *Jazz Diplomacy: Promoting America in the Cold War Era* (Jackson: University Press of Mississippi, 2009). Others written from the USSR perspective include János Gonda's *Who's Who in Hungarian Jazz* (Budapest: Magyar Zeneművészek, 1974).

that it was complex, sexualized, gendered, and risqué, if not outright amoral; it was also the only instrument banned by Stalin's cultural police post-World War II. If Seva had played any other instrument, perhaps he would not have earned the same level of respect from his young listeners. After all, what did his audience eventually give him? A Selmer Mark VI tenor saxophone, the most iconic and sought-after model. It was a symbolic gift, whether or not anyone was fully aware of the meaning behind the choice.

Through his *Rok-posevy* and *Sevaoborot* programs, Seva became a cult figure by inadvertently creating a new Russian male paradigm for the cosmopolitan age, one that was nonthreatening, hopeful, and devoid of the usual power dynamic. Cultured, educated, worldly, and nimble in life and love, he shaped and embodied the idea of the "true gentleman," as his listeners came to call him—a British-influenced model certainly, but one that appealed to the late Cold War generation's West-curious sensibilities. He created a "powerful alternative socio-cultural space" that modeled an "authority and community" both different from and antithetical to Soviet norms:

> Seva as media personality stood at the center: authoritative—expert, in fact—but democratic with a small "d"; individualistic, but altruistic, communitarian; emotionally expressive and open-minded, but also, always, ineffably cool. The structure of the program itself [*Rok-posevy*] matched Seva's persona and reinforced these values.[31]

By broadcasting information, humor, and music, Seva stepped into the role of father, friend, and mentor for a generation of Soviet youth and émigré Russians, neither dissuading them of their beliefs nor persuading them into any particular political or ideological view. Through his fastidious work on-air and correspondence with the many young men and women who wrote to him, Seva was able to tool and formulate the "True Gentleman" persona. Because the conditions were ripe for his style and personality, and because he understood his audience as the West never could, Seva forged an enduring relationship with the Soviet people, resulting in a revolution of the soul that set the stage for the relatively peaceful end of the USSR.

---

31 Roth-Ey, "Listening out," 576–77.

Part One

1917–76

CHAPTER 1

The Great Wireless Experiment

> Totalitarian regimes have always dealt pitilessly with political opposition, refusing to permit the development of civil society, crushing any intellectual dissent and censoring freedom-loving culture. Any manifestations of subcultural energy are similarly unwelcome: there is only one leader, one nation, one style, one music.[1]
>
> —Artemy Troitsky

Amidst the terror of the First World War, 1917 stands out as a red-letter year for Russia with one dramatic, punishing event after another: the abdication of Tsar Nicholas II in February, the weak-kneed Provisional Government collapsing into the hands of Vladimir Ilyich Ulyanov, the Bolsheviks executing a questionable coup d'état under Ulyanov's belligerent banner on October 25.[2] But Ulyanov's seeming success is not without opposition, both within the party and without, and a full year of revolution turns into more than three years of "chaos, strife, and savagery."[3] The resistance is substantial, submerging the new state—if it can be called such—into a fractious and volatile civil war, resulting in horrific death numbering in the millions between 1917 and 1922.[4] Undeterred, Vladimir Ulyanov, fresh from Germany to where he'd been banished, uncharitably deals with "counter-revolutionaries," rallying the country and leading the new Russia towards an authoritarian government rather than the communist

---

1 Artemy Troitsky, *Subkultura* (London: Cornerhouse Publications, 2017), 85.

2 Whether or not the Bolsheviks actually executed this coup is controversial, though they did mobilize the people in St. Petersburg and then subsequently filled the power vacuum. See S. A. Smith, *Russia in Revolution* (Oxford: Oxford University Press, 2017), 161.

3 Ibid.

4 Ibid., 161–62. "The population on Soviet territory (within 1926 borders) fell from its 1917 level by 7.1 million in 1920 . . . and by 12.7 million in early 1922."

utopia he trumpets. Although, to be fair, socialism must come first and then communism organically follows—per Marx and Engels.[5] The Soviet age thus commences with contradictions, confusion, and a severe lack of communication. It doesn't take long for the West to recognize that Russia, as they have known it for ages, is no longer, and that instead she is evolving into a turbid beast of a different variety—a Bolshevik Dragon at which they can only gape in horror and burgeoning fear.

Changing his name—wisely at that—Vladimir *Lenin* begins crushing resistance to his socialist experiment through inventive but "unsystematic"[6] imprisonment of the "bourgeois" and "class enemies"—the inception of the eventual Gulag system[7]—and seizing private property, including farms from so-called wealthy peasants, kulaks.[8] To assist him in gaining control of the now-volatile country, he creates the ruthless Cheka—the secret police precursor to the KGB that conducts the arrests—and establishes the Red Army (in opposition to the White Army), leaving its leadership to fellow revolutionary Leon Trotsky.[9] Lenin surely knows that building a communist nation requires more than just violence and oppression and chaos. Information about what is happening is limited and slow to reach every part of the sprawling nation, and while that helps to delay and deter bad publicity, with the situation changing so rapidly, any information is old information. But with the high rate of illiteracy, especially in the most rural and remote places, how can Lenin possibly explain to everyone what he's trying to do, much less the concept of communism itself? It seems clear that something more than just printed media is necessary, something more than newspapers. How can he harness the masses who had suffered under the tsarist regime, tap into their pain, and persuade them to buy into this change?

Having spent years abroad as an émigré revolutionary, Lenin witnessed the West developing the telegraph into a thing called wireless radio that could transmit audible voices—an invention credited to Guglielmo Marconi though Marconi used the patents of Serbia-born Nicola Tesla. A genius with no professional savvy, Tesla had made the ground-breaking Tesla Coil and formulated

---

5 See Karl Marx and Frederich Engels, *The Communist Manifesto* (1848).

6 Anne Applebaum, *Gulag: A History* (New York: Doubleday, 2003), 7. A Moscow newspaper printed that the Red Guards, whom Lenin and Trotsky had formed, "unsystematically arrest hundreds of people every day, and then don't know what to do with them."

7 Ibid., 13.

8 Ibid., 6.

9 Ibid., 4–5. The Cheka was founded by Feliks Dzerzhinsky in December 1917.

plans for wireless communication years before Marconi.[10] However, Marconi the charismatic opportunist commercialized wireless radio and as a result of his efforts, the technology exploded in many parts of the world as if in answer to a state of exigence—though not in Russia. Not yet.

While Tsar Nicholas II may have had no particular use for a technology that could potentially help him speak to remote parts of the nation, Lenin perceives things quite differently. Despite his cruelties and delusions, he is unquestionably a visionary and able disrupter. Having pulled the rug from under the long-established monarchy, he cunningly surmises that radio is exactly what the bloodied, eviscerated country needs. Moreover, he recognizes what the West, even money-minded Marconi, does not readily see: radio is the medium of mass messaging, an unparalleled conduit for instantaneous propaganda.[11]

Zealously, even as violence becomes its own kind of stability and the Red Terror engulfs the nation, the goateed conductor of revolution sets the gears in motion to *wire* the USSR for sound. He establishes a radio laboratory in Nizhny Novgorod and channels funds towards radio research shortly after the Bolshevik takeover. Reportedly, some Russians who did rather like listening to the "stuttering of Morse code" (nascent radio-heads) suddenly hear, without warning, voices. Real voices.[12] It is in February 1919 that for the first time a clear statement over the airwaves is heard, spoken by Russian engineer and scientist Mikhail Alexandrovich Bonch-Bruyevich. Famously, he is heard by people in Moscow saying, "Hello, this is the Nizhny Novgorod Radio Laboratory speaking."[13]

Emboldened by this success, Lenin proudly and boldly declares that the future of the Soviet Union is communication "without distances"—specifically a paperless newspaper.[14] A short time later his wireless dreams come true. On November 7, 1922, the Comintern radio station, "the most powerful in the world," commences formal broadcasting within the USSR, eventually

---

10 W. Bernard Carlson, *Tesla: Inventor of the Electrical Age* (New Jersey: Princeton University Press, 2013), 315.

11 Stephen Lovell, *Russia in the Microphone Age* (Oxford: Oxford University Press, 2015), 43. See also Lovell's "How Russia Learned to Listen," *Kritika* 12 (2011): 592. Lowell states that radio was a distinct boon to the Bolsheviks because it was an instant disseminator of propaganda, a collective organizer with a huge reach, and a modern accelerator of progress.

12 Nelson, *War of the Black Heavens*, 1. See also Thomas Guback and Steven Hill, *The Innovation of Soviet Broadcasting and the Role of V. I. Lenin* (Urbana: University of Illinois, 1972).

13 Lovell, "How Russia Learned to Listen," 592.

14 V. I. Lenin, *Collected Works*, vol. 35, *Letters* (Moscow: Progress Publishers, 1973), 437. Letter to M. A. Bonch-Bruyevich, February 5, 1920.

expanding its reach to the rest of Europe.[15] But this national and international reach takes time to develop—over a decade, in fact. Still, radio becomes, as Lenin desired, a powerful tool for the administration, as a means for education and cultural dissemination, and as one of the only available and effectual methods to achieve Sovietization.[16] Radio aids in obliterating "one of the darkest heritages of Tsarism, the greatest obstacle to cultural development."[17] Before being forced out of the Communist Party, Leon Trotsky, in a speech given on March 1, 1926 to the Friends of Radio in the USSR, remarks:

> The conquest of the village by radio is a task for the next few years, very closely connected with the task of eliminating illiteracy and electrifying the country, and to some extent a precondition for the fulfilment of these tasks. Each province should set out to conquer the countryside with a definite programme of radio development. Place the map for a new war on the table! [. . .] It is necessary that by means of the radio the peasant shall be able to feel himself a citizen of our Union, a citizen of the whole world.[18]

In other words, no Soviet left behind.

A parallel development alongside radio, particularly crucial when thinking of the future of the Soviet Union, is the new political attention given to a demographic that has never before been targeted: the youth. Young people with their immense potential and limited or nonexistent memory of life before prove to be an especially important sector of the population for the Bolsheviks. Accordingly, a union-wide organization known as the *Komsomol* springs into existence,

---

15 Nelson, *War of the Black Heavens*, 2.

16 In Lovell's *Russia in the Microphone Age*, he argues that radio in the interwar period was not as beneficial to Lenin as it was to Nazi Germany as a propaganda tool. He references Stefan Plaggenborg: "[P]arty and state agencies bemoaned their inability to harness radio as a significant force for cultural construction" (8–9). While Lovell is correct, what other technology or method of communication during the interwar period could possibly have done better constructing a political and social consciousness than radio given the lack of resources, extreme poverty, and illiteracy of the Russian people? Lovell does concede: "The fact remains . . . radio was a major technological innovation that coincided with, and underscored, social change" (10).

17 "Soviet Cultural Progress," *Soviet Union Review* 12, no. 1 (January 1934): 12.

18 From Trotsky's inaugural address at the First All-Union Congress of the Society of Friends of Radio, Moscow. First published in the *Collected Works of L. D. Trotsky* (1927). As appears here, taken from *Labour Review* 2, no. 6, November–December 1957.

interestingly conceived by two Jewish young men, to attract, train, and educate youth all across the USSR:

> Young people . . . represented the most mobile, and at the same time, the most problematic, section of society. On the one hand, young men and women are more easily influenced, which is good; on the other, they are more susceptible to free-thinking, to frustration, and to the dangerous habit of asking unwanted questions. . . . [A]nd the organization that was responsible for constructing and managing the Communist consciousness of young people was the Komsomol . . . sometimes translated as the Communist Youth League. . . . Komsomol rhetoric reflected the idealistic, educational character of the organization.[19]

Membership in the Komsomol exponentially increases as the years wear on, because of both social and political pressure. Education is the watchword for the Komsomol; thus, if a young person isn't a member, it seems more a sign of delinquency than political defection. As a result of both the harnessing of the youth's energies and the drive towards a radio revolution, the nation gradually—though not without extreme bloodshed—yields to this new regime, to Lenin, and to the "Great Socialist Experiment."

Komsomol Pioneers listening to radio in Tomsk Oblast (Siberia), 1930 (credit: Library of Congress)

---

19 Troitsky, *Subkultura*, 85.

But nothing—and no one—lasts forever. Upon Lenin's unexpected death in 1924, the USSR gains a new, albeit familiar, general secretary: the brutal, well-read, and highly insecure Joseph Vissarionovich Stalin. Having served as Lenin's "big stick" for years, Stalin takes the reins of power, evicting Leon Trotsky from the nation and then executing him in August 1940 in Mexico City.[20] While Adolf Hitler shifts all of Germany into a veritable war machine, using state radio to align the public mindset, Stalin similarly embraces the technology, though he himself does not take the microphone in fist—unlike his German counterpart—preferring instead to leave the business of oration to others.[21] With the aid of radio, Stalin's power and reach at home and abroad magnifies, and a cult of personality unlike any other burgeons. The idea of the New Soviet Man and Woman[22] emerges, and the Kremlin's mouthorgans propound Soviet successes in inverse proportion to Soviet reality. And reality is bleak indeed. Famines have been devastating the people in many parts of the barely solidified nation, and Stalin himself subjects Ukrainians to severe cruelty during the interwar period in part to correct resistance:[23]

> Stalin had developed an interesting new theory: that resistance to socialism increases as its successes mount, because its foes resist with greater desperation as they contemplate their final defeat. Thus, any problem in the Soviet Union that could be defined as enemy action could be defined as evidence of progress.[24]

Consequently, in line with Stalin's theory, problems such as starvation are viewed as resistance, and such resistance can only be a "sign of victory."

Stalin demands massive, often unnecessary projects, which kill millions, and expands the Gulag system. Only *rumors* of what really happens in these isolated labor camps find their way down the long bread lines. Otherwise, the people officially hear of only greatness, charity, and the successes of each Five-Year Plan, or *piatiletka*. The second of these especially aims to build upon the improved

---

20 Robert Conquest, *The Great Terror: A Reassessment* (Oxford: Oxford University Press, 2018), 418.

21 Yuri Levitan is a prime example. See Craig R. Whitney, "Soviet Star Radio Announcer Recalls Great Moments in History," *New York Times*, November 1, 1977.

22 The New Soviet Man/Woman was an invention of Stalinist propaganda during this period. It projected the ideals of, amongst other things, hard work and selfless collectivism. See B. R. Myers, *The Cleanest Race* (Brooklyn: Melville House Publishing, 2010), 81.

23 See Timothy Snyder's *Bloodlands* (New York: Basic Books, 2010), 21–57 for an account of the famine that killed millions of Ukrainians in 1933.

24 Ibid., 41.

conditions of life for the peasantry, which collectivization—the giving up of individual farmlands in exchange for a "collective"—presumably granted. "And so," as Lenin said, "all the prerequisites have been created to make the collectives truly Bolshevist and to make their members cultured and prosperous. . . . Thus, finally, the many millions of peasants will live as human, civilized beings."[25] Grand words that don't, and unfortunately never will, match the individual's lived experience.

Clearly, such dissemination of misinformation through radio is a form of state repression; after all, most citizens have little understanding of how they are being manipulated and reoriented by mass media and have few to zero alternative sources to contradict the "facts" as presented. However, in this particular time and space the pros of Soviet radio propaganda arguably outweigh the cons, especially as World War II spreads like a shroud over Eurasia. Stalinist radio actually saves the Soviet Union—the people *and* the Socialist Experiment.

Soviet Radio and the Arts

Ironically, during the late tsarist period in particular, the arts were diverse and enjoyed the liberty to develop, generally speaking, with very little interference from the Romanov dynasty, which had the confidence of hundreds of years of staying in power not to bother itself with coded messaging. The Soviet government, however, is infantile by any measure and seeks to align all aspects of everyday life and living with the new order to help establish the regime and indoctrinate the populace to think, speak, and behave Bolshevik.[26] This brainwashing, no doubt, also helps to solidify the Soviet authorities' own ideas of what the fledgling union should stand for—it is certainly not the case that Lenin and company knew to the letter what exactly the government should look like. In fact, it took over a decade for policies to become cogent, but by the early 1930s, the Soviet leadership expects "the public to be obedient and identical."[27] Hence, entertainment for the masses finds itself in an unfortunate, directly proportionate relationship with the political and economic fluctuations of the state.

---

25 Vyacheslav Molotov, "The Second Five-Year Plan," *Soviet Union Review* 12, no. 2 (February 3, 1934).

26 Stephen Kotkin coined the phrase "speaking Bolshevik" in his book *Magnetic Mountain* (Berkeley: University of California Press, 1995).

27 Troitsky, *Subkultura*, 85.

In 1921, with the dawn of the New Economic Policy, musical entrepreneurs are encouraged or at least permitted to operate with some degree of freedom, but then with the first *piatiletka* commencing in 1928, this liberty is severely rescinded due in part to Stalin's controlling nature and concern about the appearance—however small—of disunity across the nation. His paranoia extends naturally, necessarily, to popular music, which, in order to receive official sanction, must reflect party ideology, propagate the mother tongue, and promote the message of one nation under socialism. No longer do private music publishers or agencies exist, with every sector of entertainment becoming consolidated and branded by state-owned enterprises such as Gosestrada for theater productions and Goskontsert, Roskontsert, and the "All-Union Tour Concert Association" Soyuzkontsert for all things music.[28] Consequently, music development itself is constrained.

In the earlier part of the interwar period, jazz is strictly forbidden, and the possession of any music paraphernalia banned. Following the first *piatiletka,* the government, however, eases restrictions in the '30s, but reverses this cultural détente by the end of the decade only to sharply shift course yet again as political necessity demands an alliance with America—and therefore American jazz. Hence, the painful birth of the USSR also signals the contrived emergence of ideologically correct music, popularized or made ubiquitous through radio broadcasting. And both popular music *and* radio broadcasting become important actors in Soviet politics and international relations in the twentieth century, setting the stage for a yet unestablished occupation, the radio DJ as a purveyor of the popular, to become an effective influencer of the most fluid and fictile portion of the population, Soviet youth.

---

28 Peter J. Schmelz, *Such Freedom, if Only Musical: Unofficial Soviet Music during the Thaw* (New York: Oxford University Press, 2009), 90.

CHAPTER 2

The Sounds of War

With the definitive resurgence of the German threat in the 1930s, popular music takes to the battlefield. By degrees, the world submerges into a conflict more terrifying than the last, with the advanced military technology of Hitler's Wehrmacht at the head. Still, despite Panzer tanks and bombers, the most consequential and comprehensive new player in the global conflict is radio, bringing an experimental dimension to warcraft. Foreseeing this potential, Hitler's minister of propaganda, Joseph Goebbels, had stated years earlier in 1933: "what the press was to the nineteenth century, radio will be to the twentieth."[1] But radio does not just relay news from the front or blast propaganda across borders: it broadcasts music. Wartime songs meant to boost the morale of combatants and civilians alike crackle from speakers across Europe, Asia, and North America, bringing the talents of Glenn Miller, the Andrews Sisters, and Duke Ellington to cozy kitchens and frozen dugouts alike, providing a soundtrack in defiance of reality. But along with the music rise "Voices"—radio presenters, who by virtue of their reach, however imperfect or limited, hold instant, intimate, and ephemeral power, capable of both liberating and destroying the soul of the listener.

Radio becomes ubiquitous, and the medium's utility is so great as a supplier of news, entertainment, and connection that, as the global conflict intensifies, radio does not feel like an intrusion. Proving Joseph Goebbels quite correct, by 1940 Europe's airwaves drown in war chatter—from the BBC to Vatican Radio to the OWI's (Office of War Information) precursor to Voice of America—seeking to sway the ambivalent and convince the uncommitted of the righteousness of the collective Western front. Naturally, well-spoken Nazi radio presenters, having defected from their own countries, have much to say in return, susurrating in their native tongues to the underappreciated working classes of Europe. "[L]ife has been a round of . . . intermittent moments of hovering over

---

1 Horst Bergmeier and Rainier E. Lotz, *Hitler's Airwaves: The Inside Story of Nazi Radio Broadcasting and Propaganda Swing* (New Haven: Yale University Press, 1997), 6.

the radio and trying to reconstruct something of the truth from the waves and waves of lies and boasts and prevarications which reverberate back and forth across Europe," grumbles George Kennan in his diary on April 15, 1940, venting his grievance as an American Foreign Service member in wartime London.[2] But everybody quickly grows accustomed to these propaganda wars in the ether, not necessarily aware that the battle for hearts and minds is just as vital to the outcome as the kinetic campaigns.

It is into this hostile environment, in Leningrad's *Aleksandrovskaia bol'nitsa* (Alexander hospital), that a future radio personality is born on July 9, 1940. His mother, Lyudmila Mikhailovna, perhaps due to a surge of patriotism, initially dubs her newborn son Valery—a name from the Latin root meaning brave or valorous. However, as it happens, a mere conversation with an old, cultured lady four days later causes Lyudmila to revoke the appellation. The babushka says she knows of many who bear the name of Vsevolod and they are all "extremely intelligent people."[3] Thus, Lyudmila, anxious to heed the old woman's wisdom in the event that she is some sort of soothsayer, at once changes her Valery to Vsevolod, a moniker that not-so-humbly means "to rule all." As the young wife of the vice chairman of the Baltic Shipping Company—Boris Levenstein—Lyudmila arguably suffers less than others under Stalin's reign, but the war will bring tribulations for her family as well.

Indeed, less than a year later, Adolf Hitler thrusts eastward towards the USSR, soon penetrating into Soviet territory. Operation Barbarossa tears the Levenstein family asunder along with countless other Russian clans. The prolonged tragedy that follows is something no amount of on-air braggadocio or Five-Year Plan can possibly fix.

Stalin Sounds Sad

> It's not easy being a prophet in our days, and I don't want to resort to tea leaves. I'll merely note that the beginning of the 1941 war season differs significantly from that of the season of 1940.
>
> —I. M. Maisky, Soviet Ambassador to England, April 6, 1941

"Comrades!" booms the dictator of the USSR, crackling over the airwaves across thousands of miles of Soviet lands. On this day, July 3, 1941, Joseph

2 George Kennan, *The Kennan Diaries* (New York: W. W. Norton & Company, 2014), 136.
3 Seva Novgorodsev, *Integral pokhozh na saksofon* (Saint Petersburg: Amphora, 2011).

Stalin's commanding tenor distorted by a certain humanizing warble charges from the speaker and assaults the ears of the people who gather around radio sets and loudspeakers in seemingly frozen silence. The news is grim: Germany has attacked; Russia's western border has been breached.

"Citizens!" Stalin bellows, demanding the individual's whole love and attention. "*Brat'ia i syostry!*" Brothers and sisters—terms of endearment he's never used before. And yet, children with their mothers and fathers and aunts and uncles and grandmothers and grandfathers attune to their leader in captive urgency and accept his every word, drinking it like water. *Stalin,* they think, *is talking to us. Stalin is talking to* me.

"He sounds really sad," notes one grim *otets* from the kitchen of his communal apartment, worry lacing his voice as he harkens keenly to their self-styled "Man of Steel."[4] Later, this perceptive listener will be arrested for his empathetic comment, but for now, he's making an astute judgment.

On the night that the Nazis executed Operation Barbarossa, Stalin suffered a mental break and hid in his Moscow dacha, likely reflecting on the warnings of a Hitler offensive he'd deliberately ignored, including from Churchill himself, and the messengers he'd rewarded with death).[5] The Soviet intelligence community, with extensive foreign networks, reels from its abysmal failure to take reports of impending German aggression seriously, and not only take seriously but interpret correctly, in opposition to the delusions of the Soviet premier. "Imaginary conspiracies [had] blinded [Stalin] to the real conspiracy of Operation Barbarossa."[6] Thus, others had to do what Stalin could not. Foreign Minister Vyacheslav Molotov made the grim announcement on air on June 22, and it was heard as far as London where Soviet Ambassador to the UK Ivan Maisky listened, postponing a meeting with British Secretary of State Anthony Eden just to do so: "Sitting next to the radio, pencil in hand, I listened to what

---

4 Cathy Young, *Growing Up in Moscow: Memories of a Soviet Girlhood* (Boston: Ticknor & Fields, 1989), 216.

5 For just how many warnings Stalin received, see Stephen Kotkin's *Waiting for Hitler* (Harmondsworth: Penguin, 2017) and Richard Overy's *Russia's War* (Harmondsworth: Penguin, 1997). See also Christopher Andrew and Oleg Gordievsky, *KGB: The Inside Story* (New York: Harper Collins, 1990), 262. Churchill had written to Stalin on April 3, 1941 warning of a German plot; and then on April 17 a GRU officer in Prague warned of an attack in June gleaned from senior German officers in Czechoslovakia. But "Stalin tended to see all warnings of a German attack . . . as further evidence of a British conspiracy." Hitlerite Germany encouraged the Soviet leader's paranoia.

6 Andrew and Gordievsky, *KGB*, 269. The NKVD at this point was undergoing reorganization, and it wasn't until 1954 that this bureaucratic shuffling, naming, and renaming of the intelligence branches (from NKVD to NKGB to MGB to KI) finally achieves permanency with the creation of the KGB—just a reincarnation of the Cheka/NKVD.

Comrade Molotov had to say and took down a few notes." Even Churchill addressed the people of Britain and the Soviet Union that fateful day. "At 9 p.m. I listened to Churchill's broadcast with bated breath," wrote Maisky. "A forceful speech! A fine performance! The prime minister had to play it safe, of course, in all that concerned communism—whether for the sake of America or his own party. But these are mere details. On the whole, Churchill's speech was bellicose and resolute: no compromises or agreements! War to the bitter end!"[7]

When Stalin finally emerges from hiding and chooses to speak to the country a full two weeks after the Nazi incursion commenced, his voice alone makes history and touches millions of lives. Stalin frames his Great Patriotic War as the people's fight for freedom. He provides a narrative through which he rouses the people to bravery and charges them with the protection of the Motherland.[8] Surprisingly, Stalin's international broadcast makes no mention of Leninism or socialism or communism. Instead, he shies away from hardline language, focusing on unifying sentiments, even espousing Western terms like "democracy," bringing the struggle of the Soviet people into alignment with the struggle of the British and all other "freedom-loving peoples."

George Orwell comments on this radio event in his wartime diary:

> Stalin's broadcast speech is a direct return to the Popular Front, defense of democracy line, and in effect a complete contradiction of all that he and his followers have been saying for the past two years. It was nevertheless a magnificent fighting speech, just the right counterpart to Churchill's, and made it clear that no compromise is intended. . . . [Both] Britain and the U. S. A. [were] referred to in friendly terms and more or less as allies.[9]

In bending his principles and toning down his bombastic, communist-righteous rhetoric, Stalin signals his willingness to the Soviet, American, and British people alike that he is open to the proposition of military cooperation. And his

---

7 Ivan Maisky, *The Maisky Diaries: Red Ambassador to the Court of St. James's, 1932–1943* (New Haven: Yale University Press, 2015), 366.

8 An iconic recruitment poster featuring a strong mother summoning the sons of Russia to fight, à la "Uncle Sam Wants You," appeared in July 1941, created by Georgian artist Irakli Toidze, with the caption "The Motherland Calls!" (Irakli M. Toidze, *The Motherland Is Calling You*, 1957, Washington, DC, photomechanical print [postcard], halftone, color, Washington, DC, https://www.loc.gov/item/95503600/.

9 George Orwell, *George Orwell Diaries* (New York: Liveright, 2012), 317. Stalin's avoidance of the word "allies" despite the common enemy is "significant," since no treaties exist between the Anglos and Soviets *yet*.

words go far indeed. As the nation listens—some people hearing for the first time the terrifying news—it is broken down in one sense but rebuilt in another, repurposed for the tremendous battle ahead:

> The people of the Soviet Union are now fighting a great patriotic war in defense of our country and extend their ardent greetings to the American people on the occasion of their glorious national Independence Day holiday. It is altogether fitting on this occasion for the American and Russian people to clasp hands more firmly."[10]

This first wartime radio address is crucial to balancing the scales, giving a much-needed advantage, diplomatically and emotionally, to the people of the USSR who are sorely outgunned, unprepared, and outmaneuvered. To keep Soviets listening to the right messages, from the Kremlin primarily, all demoralizing anti-Soviet propaganda must be blocked out. Thus, the unifying technology of radio proves to have a dark side as well—exposed by Goebbels—which creates the need for novel warfare: the blocking or interference of specific radio frequencies, known simply as jamming, which in itself is an obstructing *presence* or force.

Soon after the Nazis cross into Soviet territory, the Kremlin authorizes the military to begin jamming radio signals from Germany to ensure that the people do not hear Goebbels's spirit-sapping drivel—not that jamming is perfect. In fact, as with any physical barrier, the highly resourceful and determined can still get around the costly invisible walls. Knowing jamming's inherent weaknesses, the Soviet government confiscates wireless receivers from all over Russia in addition to blocking Berlin's signals with ferocity.[11] In his diary, Comintern head Georgy Dimitrov confirms the importance Stalin instantly places on radio operations throughout the Soviet Union and in countries bordering the USSR, especially Finland and Poland where anti-Soviet sentiment soars. Furthermore, Dimitrov speaks to Stalin concerning illegal Bulgarian radio transmissions and the possibility of "cutting into broadcasts" from Germany and Austria "on their wavelengths with our announcers delivering polemical apostrophes and brief

---

10 Translated quote from Stalin's speech on July 5, which he rightly noted was July 4 in the US, as appears in a variety of sources, including Nathaniel Lande's *Spinning History* (New York: Skyhorse Publishing, 2017), 190.

11 Orwell, *Diaries*, 316–17. The action is so significant that BBC reports on the wireless usurpation.

statements."[12] It is unclear how much of Dimitrov's musings become reality, but desperation is strong in the highest echelons of Soviet government: anything is worth a try to obstruct the German shortwave blitzkrieg. Redoubling efforts, the Kremlin delivers bullish encouragement and extolls Soviet strength and successes (even when there are none) to sustain morale. Even Western music is permitted—or at least not jammed—out of a desire to dress up the USSR for an alliance with the West.[13]

Cut the Russia Jokes

The pressures of war compose new strains of international cooperation and conciliation over distorted radio waves, generating sightless connections between the USSR and the West. And behind the controls of diplomatic ovation is the BBC, working ceaselessly to orchestrate an alliance where an alliance is not only a contradiction of previous actions but ideologically incompatible. However, with the British flagging in the fight and the rest of Europe in similar dire straits, Russia is exactly what the Allies need. However, are Westerners ready?

In Britain, the BBC's listenership increases exponentially with the turbulence of war, but at the same time, the corporation's programming elitism, which dictates that the people get what they *need* rather than what they *want*, has to change. And change it does, morphing into "an uneasy kind of 'elevated classlessness'" that breaks "new ground" for British broadcasting as it seeks to reach its antennae across oceans in the hopes of building trust and cross-cultural bridges.[14] There is, after all, a singular, clear enemy—an enemy proving hard to crush. Through a variety of cultural programming, fastidious war coverage, and a targeted, diplomatic approach to broadcasting that resist jamming, the BBC brings the battle to the listener, making the global struggle against the Third Reich a personal one for fundamental freedom. In so doing, the BBC, which has been steadily accruing credibility with audiences within and without the UK, is able to take on the

12 Georgi Dimitrov and Ivan Banacs, eds., *The Diary of Georgi Dimitrov* (New Haven: Yale University Press, 2003), 186–87. Judging by Dimitrov's diary entries, the work of the Comintern only increases, such that by 1943 nearly every one of his biweekly entries concerns broadcasting to some foreign country with scrutiny from Stalin or Molotov on content.

13 On the German side, the day after Operation Barbarossa commenced, Berlin radio changed its rhetoric too: instead of the usual "England has declared war! Germany's victory will end this once and for all," the line switched to "German forces will save Europe and the world from Bolshevist clutches." See "Nazis Switch Radio War Slogan," *New York Times*, June 23, 1941.

14 Nicholas, "The People's Radio," 62–63.

challenge of readying the British people for an alliance with Russia, managing to turn the majority of listeners pro-Soviet for the time being—even, purportedly, Churchill's wife. In a private meeting on March 14, 1942, Winston tells Maisky, "My own wife is completely Sovietized. . . . All she ever talks about is the Soviet Red Cross, the Soviet army, and the wife of the Soviet ambassador."[15] As a final confirmation of the BBC's Pied Piper effect, George Orwell soliloquizes on the Red state of things in the UK:

> One could not have a better example of the moral and emotional shallowness of our time, than the fact that we are now all more or less pro-Stalin. . . . It is a case of 'when Father turns we all turn,' and Father presumably turns because the spirit moves him.[16]

Everything, therefore, seems to be moving towards a firm alliance. However, years of antipathy and distrust cannot be completely erased by a handful of warm radio speeches. Ideology remains a sore point. And naturally, as the British are compelled to involve the victimized Soviets in their Allied practices, conflict arises.

The BBC is by now in the habit of airing the national anthems of all Allied countries as a form of solidarity every Sunday prior to the evening news broadcast at nine o'clock. Thus, following the USSR's tail-tucked trudge to the side of the "good guys," the issue of whether to broadcast the Soviet anthem at this time, the "Internationale," surfaces in the FO. Many, including Ambassador Maisky, feel that the answer is obvious: if all other Allies have their national anthem aired, then so should the Soviets. However, the "Internationale" is more than just the national anthem of the Soviet Union. It is also the anthem of the international proletariat and is particularly embraced by the British Communist Party—a conundrum proving the weight of music in both ideology and crises. Maisky learns that Churchill himself is the instigator of the turmoil, blustering about his willingness to perform any deed for Russia's sake *except* provide the communists, particularly British communists, a political win with the BBC airing the anthem:

---

15 Maisky, *Diaries*, 1241. See also Andrew and Gordievsky, *KGB*, 326–31, which highlights the Soviet propaganda efforts aimed at the BBC to encourage pro-Russian sentiment in broadcasts and the positive change in Soviet policy under Stalin.

16 Orwell, *Diaries*, 317. The reference is to a common British nursery rhyme. To what exactly "Father" refers is unclear, as it may reference either Churchill or the BBC, though the latter is less likely since the BBC was personified as "Auntie."

> It came to blows—in the press, in Parliament, in society . . . Duff Cooper [Minister of Information] rang me up on 11 July and asked whether we might be able to find some other Soviet or Russian song to replace it. [. . .] Needless to say, I categorically opposed the idea.[17]

When the day of reckoning dawns, and Big Ben tolls the evening hour, the BBC announces the carousel of official anthems, leading off with the newest victim of German aggression. Maisky, seated in the dining hall of his ambassador's residence, listens to the radio with bated breath, his wife Agnya with him, waiting to hear what the BBC will air at 8:45:

> And? The first item in the programme of national anthems was . . . a very beautiful but little-known Soviet song. There was no "Internationale." After that song, all the other national anthems were played one after another. We were at the dinner table when the BBC demonstrated the British Government's cowardice and foolishness.[18]

Agnya breaks down crying, shouting at her husband that all their years spent in London have been for nothing. It's a mystery how the song was selected since, as Maiksy notes, it is a hardly recognizable tune. Therefore, could it even be interpreted as a sign of solidarity by the Soviet people? Doubtful. Churchill and the FO must have felt that the consequences for boosting the morale of the wrong parties (pro-communist) within the gates would be worse than vexing the communists *outside* the gates.

Fortunately, Maisky smooths over any grievances, and as reward for his diplomatic spirit, he achieves his longtime dream—a British-Soviet alliance. On the same day that Churchill issues his "V for Victory" speech, July 19, Stalin writes to the prime minister:[19] "[T]he Soviet Union and Great Britain have become fighting allies in the struggle against Hitlerite Germany. I have no doubt that in spite of the difficulties, our two states will be strong enough to crush our

---

17 Maisky, *Diaries*, 371.

18 Ibid., 372.

19 The suggestion to use "V" as an inspirational sign did not originate from Churchill but from a former director of the Belgian French Service in January 1941. See n.a., "BBC—History of the BBC," BBC.com, accessed August 25, 2022, https://www.bbc.co.uk/historyofthebbc/buildings/bush-house.

common enemy."[20] In return, Churchill replies to Stalin: "I am very glad to get your message. . . . Anything sensible and effective that we can do to help will be done."[21]

The Voice of the Kremlin[22]

> An announcer is a propagandist, an agitator, as well as an artist. What is important is how you say what you are given to read.
>
> —Yuri Levitan[23]

As soon as the Nazis reach the city of Peter the Great in September of 1941, little Seva and his mother evacuate to the Kurgan region within Siberia, a "God-forsaken place" as Seva recalls—"very cold in winter, very hot in summer." Meanwhile, his father Boris stays behind to work at the front. But Lyudmila recounts the evacuation with thankfulness, for even the ability to stay with her son is a miracle:

> At first, only children, without mothers, were evacuated from Leningrad. . . . My husband, of course, was at the front, and before the war he served in the steamship. And I was alone. But I was lucky not to part with my son, because a new order came out, and by this order young children were to evacuate with their mothers. . . . I remember how I left our Leningrad apartment on Stachek Street—Seva's home. . . .
>
> I remember being put with Seva on some steamer, the wrong boat, and we swam through the floodgates. . . . After the floodgates, we, the young women with children . . . sat on the wagon, and the horse wandered somewhere. And then it turned out that the place where we were going was already in danger and could be occupied by the Fascists, and we turned where there was no road.[24]

---

20 "Soviet Union: Foreign Office Telegram to Moscow, No 855. Stalin to Prime Minister," July 20, 1941. FO 954/24B/346, National Archives, Kew.

21 "Soviet Union: Foreign Office Telegram to Moscow, No 856. Prime Minister to Stalin Reply," July 20, 1941. FO 954/24B/348, National Archives, Kew.

22 George Butchard, "The Soviet Voice That Infuriated Hitler," RBTH.com, October 15, 2013, https://www.rbth.com/arts/2013/10/15/the_soviet_voice_that_infuriated_hitler_30677.html.

23 Craig R. Whitney, "Soviet Star Radio Announcer," *New York Times*, November 1, 1977.

24 N.a., "Kto on takoi?," *Rovesnik* 9 (1982), https://seva.ru/media/?id=1.

Finally, they settle in a collective farm, or *kolkhoz*, which Seva dryly asserts is a "sort of Texas of Siberia" in reference to the immense steppe land used for grain production.[25]

The weeks turn into months and the months turn into an unbelievable year under siege. Then, a second. It's as if the Nazis will never leave and the sun will never shine again. The toll on the people of Leningrad is incalculable. A torturous new norm claims the city, and many artists are squirreled away underground for safety so that the inexpressible may find expression in symphonies, writings, and paintings.

The propaganda machine of Germany continues its diligent labors, doing its best to destroy the people of the USSR. On Sunday night, July 13, 1941, two days after the Anglo-Soviet pact was signed and three weeks into the German invasion, Britain's Political Warfare Executive (PWE) picks up a disturbing broadcast signal from Finland to Russia *in* Russian:

> Proletarians of all countries unite for the war on the Bolsheviks! They have brought Russia to complete disaster. They promised paradise on earth but have not fulfilled their promises. . . . As long as Lenin lived there were some vestiges of equality, but then he died, and his successors did nothing to fulfill his pledges.[26]

The PWE, which fastidiously stays on top of Goebbels's twice-a-day propaganda directives, determines that this message is a rousing call to fight the government and place Stalin's faults in the ears of the Soviet people. Goebbels's basic strategy is to glorify the deceased Lenin, with his German ties, and trample Stalin and Soviet morale mercilessly:

> Stalin is a primitive Caucasian bandit. Stalin must be put in a cage in the zoo like a wild animal. Retreating he ordered all stores to be destroyed. The Germans declared that this will cause famine and that the Russian people will get nothing from the Germans.
>
> It is clear that the war is played out. Citizens, it is impossible to continue the war. The Communists must be wiped out. Citizens, you are the masters of the country! Purify yourselves from the International Filth. Long live free Russia! In three weeks of war Russia lost 1 million men and 400,000 prisoners. Half of her

---

25 Novgorodsev, Museum of London interview.

26 "Intelligence Report on German Propaganda on Stalin," July 13, 1941, BBC Archives.

> tanks were lost, two-thirds of her aeroplanes were destroyed. An enormous amount of territory was lost. . . . Throw your bombs into the water! Down with war! Hail peace![27]

Yet, as loud as Goebbels's hot air machine is, the USSR has its own tactics to combat the incoming German disinformation. Thanks to Lenin, whom Berlin propaganda ironically praises, Comintern radio has the capacity now to shepherd the sprawling nation through this crisis. As the BBC reports, Russia holds her own on air:

> Speaking to their own people the Russians are using all resources of wit, imagination, imagery. They are witty, denouncing racialism, German pompousness, machine-made minds; witty when making terrific fun of Mussolini. Their presentation of war is extremely imaginative—a blend of history, landscape, and eternal human values. And when they ask the workers in factories to speed up production, they do not ask for more guns or munitions, they plead: "Give us more metal," "Forge our swords!"[28]

Since the Soviet government seized many private radio receivers, people typically gather in the streets where mounted loudspeakers amplify and project the Voice of the Kremlin. Who is this broadcasted voice? Neither Stalin nor Molotov, not any official of renown, but a young Russian Jew by the name of Yuri Levitan with a powerful baritone that both soothes and emboldens listeners. "Up and down the country ordinary Russians and military men alike would listen for news of which cities had fallen, which regions had been retaken, and whether there were imminent air raids." According to many listeners, Levitan makes them feel as if they are "part of one big family—with Yuri Levitan at the head."[29]

An aspiring actor from Vladimir, 120 miles east of the capital city, Yuri Borisovich Levitan had moved to Moscow at the age of seventeen in high hopes of gaining admission to the prestigious theatrical institute. However, he failed to impress the committee, and so with his unique voice as his only credential, he auditioned for state radio. The radio committee did not turn him away but stipulated that his Vladimir accent must go. After spending the next few years

---

27 Ibid.

28 "BBC Intelligence Report on Broadcasting Russian Propaganda," July 8, 1941, BBC Archives.

29 Whitney, "Soviet Star Radio Announcer."

perfecting the Muscovite sound, presumably at the expense of the state, is he allowed to speak on air in January 1934. As legend has it, on the night of his first broadcast, wherein he does nothing more than read straight from *Pravda*, Stalin himself from his Kremlin office hears the nineteen-year-old and then rings the chairman of the Radio Committee. The dictator decrees that only Levitan should read Stalin's reports and important news. Thus, Yuri Levitan vaults to a level of renown greater than any he might have experienced as an actor. He becomes the radio news anchor for the USSR, and while Molotov is the first person to make the broadcast announcement of the attack on June 22, Levitan is the second: "Today at four o'clock in the morning, without presenting any claims to the Soviet Union, without declaring war, German forces invaded our country. . . ."[30]

How does Hitler feel about Levitan? According to the presenter himself, Hitler told his soldiers that Levitan must be among the "first to be hanged," only after, of course, he is taken to Berlin from where he will "announce the fall of Moscow."[31] For Hitler, Levitan is "Public Enemy Number One" and places a bounty on this baritone in the amount of 250,000 Reichsmarks.

As the Nazis make their way towards Moscow, Levitan and the rest of the radio station apparatus, anticipating the bombing of radio towers and antennae, secretly evacuate to Sverdlovsk (today's Yekaterinburg, nine hundred miles east of Moscow) from where he safely continues broadcasts. Receiving direct updates from the Soviet Information Bureau in Moscow by phone, Levitan can't possibly know how deeply people appreciate hearing his voice, how vital he is to maintaining the morale of the citizens and Red Army. The attack on the Moscow radio station does come—an explosion in the yard of the Radio Committee building—and the Germans victoriously broadcast the destruction of Moscow Radio and the death of Levitan. However, not twenty minutes later, seemingly from beyond the grave, the Voice speaks, broadcasting from Sverdlovsk something particularly vexing like "one German soldier is killed every seven seconds because of Soviet troops." One Soviet marshal, Rokossovsky, reportedly says that Levitan's voice is "equal to the strength of a single division."[32] And all this power must be protected.

---

30 Olga Belenitskaya, "Moscow Is Speaking: The Voice That Brought Hope to a Nation," RBTH.com, April 16, 2015, https://www.rbth.com/arts/2015/04/16/moscow_is_speaking_the_voice_that_brought_hope_to_a_nation_45303.html.

31 Ibid.

32 Ibid.

In March 1943, the Kremlin announcer is relocated to Kuibyshev (modern-day Samara, southeast of Moscow) where the Radio Committee is based. The dreaded Russian winter helps turn the tide of war, the Soviets gain ground, and the Allies pull into the lead.

At last, thousands of war reports later, after the dropping of not one but two atomic bombs on Japanese targets, on May 8, 1945, the day of reckoning arrives. The voice that so maddens the madman of Europe is called to the Kremlin where late that night he is given a sealed envelope from the commander in chief and told to read this message on air posthaste. Red Square is thronged with people, and Levitan cannot, try as he might, battle his way through the crowds to get to the radio station. The people, not recognizing him by face, shout at him—"We are waiting for Levitan to tell us the news!" And so, desperate, he forces his way back to the Kremlin, which has its own radio station. He tears open the envelope from Stalin as soon as he reaches the microphone, and reads the lines over the air to the people of the USSR in his expansive, commanding voice: "Moscow is speaking. Fascist Germany is destroyed!"

CHAPTER 3

Big Waves

Shortly after the war's end, in June 1945, the Levenstein family reunites in Leningrad, everyone safe and alive if nothing else. Whereas Seva's father Boris has been ravaged by disease and marked for dead (saved from the morgue, in fact, by a friend), Seva's mother Lyudmila returns from Siberia in peak health though Seva himself is pale and thin as a reed. Almost five years old, Seva stands beside his mother on July 8, 1945, in front of Eliseyev Emporium, the Art Nouveau store on the famed Nevsky Prospekt, for a grand military parade intended to welcome home the returning defenders of the Fatherland.[1] After the catastrophic loss of more than twenty-seven million, the demobilization process is bittersweet and fraught with difficulties. The return of over forty-four thousand troops to Leningrad alone forecasts social and economic problems that the Kremlin chooses to conceal from the West through overt demonstrations. While Leningrad has remained largely intact, unlike several other rubbled cities such as Stalingrad, it is nevertheless "amongst the worst affected" by the war. Demobilization for this besieged and demoralized city represents a great challenge.[2]

Seva watches pristine, military-straight columns of Red Army soldiers march down the street to forced fanfare, generated largely by "orchestrated propaganda" efforts.[3] From his perspective, the parade seems more of a funeral march:

---

1 Leningrad citizens continued to call the store Eliseyev Emporium even after the Bolsheviks renamed it to Gastronom No. 1. For more, see Catriona Kelly, "Eliseev and Aprashka," in *St Petersburg: Shadows of the Past* (New Haven: Yale University Press, 2016), 170–209.

2 Robert Dale, "Rats and Resentment: The Demobilization of the Red Army in Postwar Leningrad, 1945–50," *Journal of Contemporary History* 45, no. 1 (2010): 113–33.

3 Ibid., 114–15. "Leningrad's Komsomol cells made frantic preparations to ensure that the city's railway platforms were bedecked with banners, flowers, posters, and portraits of Stalin . . . Propaganda presented demobilization as a smooth process."

> And what impressed me most was that the troops were the color of dust, everything was faded, sort of greenish grey and the faces, those faces you can never forget, they were faces full of power and pride and [an] extreme sort of tiredness. Most men wore moustaches, and they were baked by the sun and frozen through their bones. . . . [T]hat was the taste of what the War must have been like for these people, for those who survived. . . . Because you know Russians got the rough end of the war . . . and they were treated appallingly by their own commanders, because Stalin's philosophy was not to spare people.[4]

Though the Great Patriotic War is officially over, within months of the Allied victory, Stalin proves that he is unable to mentally shift gears to be a peacetime leader. His characteristic paranoia, evident even before the war, intensifies to the country's detriment. He imagines enemies all around him, beginning with his comrades-in-arms and extending across the union. Nobody is safe from his suspicion.[5] He cracks down on culture, commencing a "rigid ideological campaign" in 1946 against jazz and even state-approved classical composers like Dmitry Shostakovich.[6] Stalin's paranoia, a resumption, seemingly, of his prewar spy mania, amplifies his racist sensibilities, thereby channeling his irrational fear toward the Jewish people at large—a demographic that seems to have a higher percentage of educated, highly creative, and cosmopolitan citizens. The *intelligentsia* bristles with notable Russian Jews: among others, Mieczysław Weinberg (prolific composer), Boris Pasternak (famed poet and future author of *Doctor Zhivago*), Solomon Mikhoels (actor), and Faina Ranevskaya (famous Soviet actress).[7] Stalin goes after these cultural intellectuals subtly at first, decrying not Jews directly but the "cosmopolitanism" that his mouthorgans, mainly

---

4 Novgorodsev, Museum of London interview.

5 Stalin's redoubled paranoia (a return of his prewar spy mania) was not entirely unfounded. According to Oleg Gordievsky's accounts from his time in the KGB, there were pockets of resistance to Stalinist rule across the Union, particularly in areas outside Russia where the war was hardest fought, namely Ukraine. See Andrew and Gordievsky, *KGB*, 389–90.

6 Yoshiomi Saito, *The Global Politics of Jazz in the Twentieth Century* (New York: Routledge, 2019), 35.

7 Eugen Neumann (listener) in correspondence with author, March 1, 2019. He wrote: "Intelligentsia, as perceived in Russia, had a broader meaning than just being intellectual. It had a cultural flavor. Intelligentsia [equaled] intellectual people on a high, refined cultural level." He also notes that there is no "genuine intelligentsia in modern Russia. 1990s were its funeral years."

Minister of Culture Andrey Zhdanov, Stalin's longtime protégé, hold to be counterrevolutionary.[8]

In its Soviet definition, *kosmopolitizm* is a "product of Western imperialism, which, in pursuit of its imperialist goals, strives to undermine the value of local patriotism among the peoples of the world, thereby weakening their national sovereignty. The opposite of cosmopolitanism [is] not nationalism . . . but internationalism."[9] But where lies the demarcation between cosmopolitanism and internationalism, and how could the average citizen be expected to understand the distinction? If anyone fails to "speak Bolshevik" in the manner of the apparatchiki, they may be accused of "groveling before the West" or failing to promote international education for enlightenment's sake.[10] It doesn't take long for people to turn on each other, seeking to spare themselves or in many cases acting on their own paranoia. A fresh wave of arrests, mass deportations, conspiracies, extradition of spies, and falsifications causes an unchecked hysteria in Moscow to blossom against Russian Jews.

Leningrad, so far north from the almighty Kremlin, does not register the effects of this "anti-cosmopolitanism" to the extent that Moscow does. Nevertheless, Seva and his family are not exempt from the antisemitic fever. Not long after Seva starts secondary school in 1947, his father Boris runs into serious trouble at the Baltic Shipping Company where he rides high in the chain of command, managing hundreds of ships and thousands of personnel. The perks of Boris's enviable government post are considerable: a capacious apartment, company car, and many additional luxuries. With party members seeking to commend themselves to the Kremlin by proving alignment with the order of the day, an official such as Boris cannot escape malevolent notice. "Everything was a euphemism under Stalin," recalls Seva, "and so my father was an obvious target, being a Jew." Since the end of the war, Boris has observed various employees disappear without notice or clear reason. When he inquires with the higher-ups as to where so-and-so went, he receives an enigmatic, unhelpful response—they "made a mistake." Boris then logically queries, "What if I make a mistake?" The chilling reply: "Make sure it's small."[11]

As it happens, a subordinate of Boris's, second navigator Vladimir Askolonov, makes such a "small" error (i.e., inputting the wrong sign—plus instead of

---

8 Kristin Roth-Ey, *Moscow Prime Time* (Ithaca: Cornell University Press, 2011), 7. For Zhdanov's close relation to Stalin, see also Andrew and Gordievsky, *KGB*, 136, 407.

9 Yurchak, *Everything Was Forever*, 163.

10 For the phrase "groveling before the West," see Roth-Ey's *Moscow Prime Time*, 7.

11 Novgorodsev, Museum of London interview.

minus) while aboard the cargo ship the *Pechenga*. Not only does the vessel travel off course, but a menacing storm also descends, causing the ship to run aground on rocks. The consequences are sizeable—untold damage, destroyed cargo, and the loss of a female passenger swept overboard by a punitive wave. From Leningrad, Boris capably handles the recovery mission, and everything possible is done. But there is no way to recoup the damages.

The incident lands in Soviet courts, which fashions the callous but innocent error into the crime of a fiendish captain (described on the official sentence as "of the nobility," meaning bourgeois) who deliberately conspired with a dissident navigator to set the ship on an ill-fated course. The punishment handed out fits this unholy transgression: the captain, Valerian Dmitriyevich Bushin, dies by firing squad with confiscation of property, and Askolonov, who made the error in the first place, receives fifteen years prison time. As for Boris, he defends himself, proving beyond any doubt that he had made no mistakes and had done "everything humanly possible" to ensure a safe voyage. However, he does make one "small" mistake:

> [W]hen the poor captain was sentenced to a firing squad, my dad who knew him for many years gave him his last embrace publicly. They never forgave him that. . . . So, in the end he was chucked out of the party, dismissed from work, ended with a complete nervous breakdown in hospital for a month.[12]

Through his contacts, Boris obtains a position as an ordinary dispatcher at the Estonian Shipping Company, having to start up the ladder from the bottom all over again. Hence, in May 1949, the Levenstein family moves from their beloved Leningrad, disconsolate and degraded, to Tallinn, Estonia, into a cramped, one-room flat where they learn to survive on a fraction of Boris's former salary.[13] In this way, Seva receives his first taste of immigration.

The West Turns Up

In the same confusing vein as the futile discourse around cosmopolitanism versus internationalism, the state's promotion of certain new technological advances that open the door to Western influence while at the same time

---

12 Ibid.
13 Ibid.

criticizing any undesirable Western influence as bourgeois (when much of it appears to be undesirable) is another puzzling and self-defeating practice. The primary, and really only, technology that grants the full Soviet population access to the outside world is, of course, shortwave radio.[14] What shortwave radio does for Soviets is barely appreciated by the West, which collectively fails to understand that while they (in free societies) have no real use for foreign broadcasts that can travel thousands of miles and be received locally, Soviets in isolated areas with no connection to even the rest of their nation are able, with the turn of a dial, to gain an audible, felt connection to another part of the world. Shortwave brings them information, and it brings *life*.

The fact that the power of shortwave is lost on the West is evident by the collective readiness to hit the off switch following the defeat of the Third Reich. This is particularly the case in the US, where people are unfamiliar with and know next to nothing of shortwave and its benefits, accustomed primarily to MW (medium wave) and LW (long wave) radio—and needing little else. As Alexei Yurchak points out, even the BBC World Service reached Americans via rebroadcasting partnerships in the States.[15] The US media apparatus "rail[s] against any [continuing] foreign information program," which drives Congress to push for termination of the OWI's wartime level radio operations.[16] Shortwave is expensive business, after all, and elected representatives are eager to tighten belts to please constituents.[17]

In the UK, the story is different. As a once-proud empire quite accustomed to reaching its many subjects abroad, Great Britain has a longer history than the other Allies of using radio as a mechanism for connection. Furthermore, during World War II, the BBC proved itself to be the UK's abiding strength, an unrivaled defense against propaganda, and the standout public diplomat and intercessor. Thus, no one considers defunding the BBC's External Services (the eventual World Service) though Parliament contends with an abysmal financial situation.

Still, the unfortunate postwar devaluing of the British sterling forces the Treasury to hit the already strained External Services with a ten percent budget

---

14 Yurchak, *Everything Was Forever*, 175.

15 Ibid., 176.

16 Alan Heil, *Voice of America—A History* (New York: Columbia University Press, 2003), 45. VOA was slated to end in 1945 with the end of the war, as it was under the OWI (Office of War Information), and the OWI was terminated and all responsibilities transferred to newly created successors, such as the USIA and CIA. VOA had no support within the US at the time, and media "railed against" all foreign information programs.

17 Ibid., 46.

reduction and then another subsequent cut of 280,000 pounds.[18] In fact, while Parliament recognizes the value of international broadcasting, the "recurring theme of the fifties, sixties, seventies, and eighties" is "challenge, review, and doubt" as the government forces the BBC into alignment with the UK's "postwar economic situation and changing role in the postcolonial era."[19] Sir Ian Jacob, a member of the FO and eventual director general of the BBC, addresses Parliament in the midst of this financial crisis: "Broadcasting is not something which can be turned on and off like a tap. The audience, and a reputation for truth and quality, is built up slowly and laboriously. Once sacrificed, they are very hard to restore."[20]

Jacob emphasizes that radio is the UK's "only means of injecting anti-communist publicity" into the communist bloc and that "any reduction in the output of the BBC's foreign language services at this juncture would . . . result in a loss of British influence which would take many years to recover."[21] His speech has the desired effect. While the three-year-old VOA develops a hoarse throat in 1945, losing congressional funding, the BBC slogs onward in a quieter postwar ether, managing to expand its language offering despite budgetary adversity. Russian appears to be the first order of business.[22]

Prior to the war, the BBC had been on the verge of commencing Russian-language broadcasts.[23] With the start of Operation Barbarossa, however, fear of offending the Kremlin when the British badly needed its Slavic ally stayed the hand of the BBC and the FO. Now, gauging the autumnal geopolitical climate, the FO asks the BBC to add a Russian service to give "a dispassionate presentation of the facts, both of world events . . . and of British and world opinion about the Soviet Government and its policy, giving the true proportion both of favorable and unfavorable opinion."[24] Thus, on March 26, 1946, the BBC Russian Service (RS) is quietly born, broadcasting to the USSR from Bush House. The

---

18 Alban Webb, *London Calling: Britain, the BBC World Service and the Cold War* (London: Bloomsbury Academic, 2014), 104.

19 Nelson, *War of the Black Heavens*, 86.

20 Webb, *London Calling*, 105.

21 Ibid.

22 Heil, *Voice of America*, 45–46. William Benton, assistant secretary of state for public affairs, saved VOA by transferring it to the State Dept. Despite a significantly slashed budget and going from a "wartime peak of forty language services to twenty-three," VOA Russian Service began in 1947.

23 "BBC History, 1940s," BBC.com, February 8, 2007, http://www.bbc.co.uk/worldservice/history/story/2007/02/070122_html_40s.shtml.

24 Lowell H. Schwartz, *Political Warfare against the Kremlin: US and British Propaganda Policy at the Beginning of the Cold War* (London: Palgrave Macmillan, 2009), 74. From FO memorandum to BBC, March 1946.

intention of the new service is not inimical but diplomatic. Sir Ivone Kirkpatrick, former director of the External Services during the war, outlines the UK's Russia policy guidelines in a letter to the BBC director general. As with all language services, the RS must firstly "project Britain," showcasing British civilization, enterprise, and activity while exuding British sensibility and values.[25] In this way, RS cannot be perceived as unbiased; however, the BBC's own "sensibility and values"—aimed at creating educational, balanced, and, as much as possible, apolitical content—help to maintain its recognized brand of objectivity, if not neutrality. The BBC's careful conduct in launching the RS, foraying into new radio territory, reflects the UK's precarious postwar position in Europe and abroad.[26]

Despite his paranoia, Stalin's reaction to the corporation suddenly speaking in Russian is mostly one of disinterest. Since the BBC's primary goal is purely education, Stalin finds little to worry about, particularly in science broadcasts' discussions of "flower colors" and "mammoth rings"—although it is surprising that he didn't interpret these programs as capitalist subversions. Consequently, the BBC sails under and over the wire without so much as raising the Kremlin's brow.[27] At this point, the aggregate of Western broadcasting to the USSR is still paltry due to both the drastically reduced efforts from the West and the still-limited number of receivers throughout the Soviet Union (less than two million, according to one study).[28] Moreover, few citizens are willing to risk listening to "enemy" voices, regardless of the language.

However, America's fear of communism, enlarged by the threat to Greece and Radio Moscow's output directed at Americans, prompts funds and attention to be channeled to anti-communist operations—particularly to radio.[29] Thanks to President Dwight D. Eisenhower, who had fully appreciated radio's role in aiding the Allies, the budgetary squabbles in Congress are silenced and VOA gets a new assignation within the State Department, receiving renewed support and healthy funding. On February 17, 1947, the primarily European-operating VOA directs its attention to the USSR and *also* begins to speak Russian.[30]

---

25 Ibid., 78.

26 Ibid., 74.

27 See "Summary of Science Broadcasts to the U.S.S.R." Dora Winifred Russell Papers, Internationaal Instituut voor Sociale Geschiedenis, Netherlands.

28 See Maury Lisann, *Broadcasting to the Soviet Union: International Politics and Radio.* Praeger Special Studies in International Politics and Government (New York: Praeger, 1975).

29 Heil, *Voice of America*, 47. Heil suggests that Radio Moscow's "virulent attacks on the West" actually saved VOA and "enhanc[ed]" the BBC.

30 Ibid.

To Stalin, this new programming from America is definitely unacceptable, particularly in light of the creation of the Central Intelligence Agency (CIA) just a few months later.[31] The problem is not cultural entertainment but anti-Soviet information—though ironically, the films and artwork brought back from Nazi Germany and distributed like trophies among Soviets serve as anti-communist propaganda all on their own, revealing the comparatively wealthy lifestyle and culture of other nations.[32] The solution to this Western onslaught? Jamming. A year later, on February 3, 1948, the USSR commences clear anti-West interference against VOA and, shortly thereafter, against the BBC as well.[33] So begins a different kind of war.[34]

---

31 Andrew and Gordievsky, *KGB*, 375.

32 Roth-Ey, *Moscow Prime Time*, 133–35.

33 See the BBC World Service site: http://www.bbc.co.uk/worldservice/history/story/2007/02/070122_html_40s.shtml. See also Higham and Horne, "Bloc-buster Tactics," which states that "the Russian Language service is heavily jammed."

34 Nelson, *War of the Black Heavens*, 20.

CHAPTER 4

Birth of the Cool

Early jazz had debuted in Russia with the Bolsheviks while swing and bebop infiltrated the USSR during World War II due to the alliance with the US.[1] But as the political tide changes post-1945, music and the arts come under fresh scrutiny. Jazz, as an American import, loses all favor and tolerance with the government and is both banned and jammed.[2] Both the creation of the State of Israel and Stalin's fresh campaign against jazz seem to go hand in hand, for no sooner do Jews get a home, than a fiery spotlight shines on the genre, causing the confiscation of saxophones and the arrest of jazz musicians.[3]

While it is certainly not the case that *all* are confiscated, the saxophone is singled out as the instrument of the bourgeois—a weapon even—and exemplifies the "total absurdity" of the political atmosphere.[4] Zhdanov is at the forefront of the musical socialism movement, praising "good internationalism" and condemning "bad" or "rootless" cosmopolitanism: the first is a "product of progressive people's culture" and the second, a "bourgeois product of imperialism." Categorization is left not to subjective opinion but rather "objective scientific laws of the physiology of human musical perception."[5] These laws, obviously, are ambiguous and thus wholly unscientific. The official attitude towards jazz, specifically, is admiration for its roots in the enslaved and working-class coupled with castigation for the "bourgeois pseudo-art" it has become, per Kremlin appraisal.[6]

---

1 Yurchak, *Everything Was Forever*, 166.

2 Starr, *Red and Hot*, 243. "Blaring out of radios across the USSR, the staccato sounds of jazz pierced the shield of Soviet jamming far more successfully than a legato string section could."

3 Dave Laing and Mark Yoffe, "History of Soviet and Russian Rock Music," in *Continuum Encyclopedia of Popular Music of The World: Locations*, ed. John Shepherd (London: Continuum, 2005).

4 Troitsky, *Subkultura*, 103.

5 Yurchak, *Everything Was Forever*, 164.

6 Ibid., 165. See also Troitsky, *Back in the USSR*, 15.

Accompanying this half-baked nonscience of human musicality is the frustrating and contradictory policy on fashion and style—the primary targets being the *stilyagi* ("style hunters" or hipsters) known for their nominally outrageous dress and more worldly or Western identities created through homemade clothing.[7] These *stilyagi* are the "grandfathers of all Western-oriented, music loving subcultures in the Soviet Union" caught up by a certain sense of "independence sweeping the country" following the Great Patriotic War.[8] But the price to pay for even being labeled a *stilyaga* is quite high—social ostracization—which is why such beatniks must necessarily exist in numbers to exist at all. Hence, Moscow, paradoxically to the political persecution, harbors the greatest concentration of *stilyagi* with Leningrad firmly in second place and other cities with a "recent [Western] history."[9] This movement is by no means popular, even though jazz itself is consumed voraciously on a grander scale. But this new cultural subsect is nevertheless a cause for concern at the highest echelons of the state, a sure indication of *stilyagi* influence, disruption, and potential for contagion. "[T]he emergence of a generation of youth alienated from Stalinist society and its search for a mode of expression" are all part of the new jazz which spawns the "major jazzmen and their audiences [in the USSR] between 1935 and 1952."[10]

Moscow resident Alexey Kozlov—an early jazz saxophonist and band leader who remains a legend—is such a *stilyaga*, a *chuvak*,[11] and despises the term, which arose through derogatory means from Soviet humor magazine *Krokodil* in March 1949.[12] But he concedes to music critic Artemy Troitsky that "style" is key for people like him who are jazz lovers, Western radio listeners, jitterbug dancers, so-called "cultural deviants":

> At that time, in the early fifties, there were "recommended" . . . and "not recommended" dances. . . . We had three dance styles. . . . The same thing with clothes. . . . Narrow short pants, big shoes, long checkered jacket, white shirt and tie. Our ties were bright and long, down below the belt and wide at the bottom. . . . Everything, including the ties, was homemade, and it was a real event each time a successful new outfit appeared. Finally, the

---

7 Ibid., 171.
8 Troitsky, *Subkultura*, 102.
9 Troitsky, *Back in the USSR*, 15.
10 Starr, *Red and Hot*, 259–60.
11 On air, Seva fondly calls some of his letter-writers *chuvak* (slang term used between friends). See *Rok-posevy*, July 26, 1987, radio broadcast,
12 Troitsky, *Subkultura*, 103.

> haircut. The model, of course, was Tarzan—long hair combed straight back and smeared generously with briolin. . . . The back was turned up with a curling iron (I remember I constantly had burns on my neck), and definitely a straight parting. . . . the main thing was just to get it to Broadway in place to show your mates.[13]

"Broadway" is a gathering place for *stilyagi* located on Gorky Street, but it's nothing more than a stretch of sidewalk, not even a building itself, signifying the subsocietal strata these youth occupy. Yet, it is not all about style and sound, for certain subgroups of *stilyagi* are well-read and, in keeping with their Komsomol upbringing, actively inform themselves about the world—as Lenin exhorted—and are thereby practitioners of self-education. Even in this intellectual stratum, more concerned with the exchange of ideas than vodka and *vecherinki* (parties), there are hardly any hipster girls, or *chuvikhi,* an important consideration for the coming rock generation. Kozlov attributes this gender disparity to, once again, education:

> All schoolgirls then were brought up in a very strict spirit; they had identical braids . . . identical dark dresses . . . whereas our *chuvikhi* had short hair . . . shoes with heels, checked skirts. . . . It was assumed that if a girl displayed such a free-and-easy manner in the way she dressed then she didn't value her "maiden's honor."[14]

Thus, young women abstain from association with *stilyagi* unless they have the impetus and security to do so since harassment by everyday Soviet society—encouraged by government rhetoric—is prevalent. Plus, there is a darker subsect comprised of thuggish young males, *gopniki,* seeking to enforce communist principles and morals through violence. To be a *stilyaga* means being not only a social outsider, but also a fugitive from Soviet conformity and construct. The choice—and it is a choice when all social currents are moving in the opposite direction—implies a certain desperation for creative expression, a quest for personal identity. The *stilyagi* are the postwar echoes of Western cultural movements, yet developing in independence of such influences for the practical reason of restricted cross-cultural exchange. If seeds of nonconformity can

---

13 Troitsky, *Back in the USSR*, 13–14.
14 Ibid., 14.

sprout in the absence of external influence, how much longer can either the government or official Soviet society suppress such youth dynamism?[15]

Still, the Komsomol believes it is up to this fool's goal. It is now a thriving all-union operation running "Pioneer" camps from Vladivostok to Odessa—around forty thousand summer- and year-long camps are active according to some statistics with about ten million children attending every year. Seva himself is one of these Pioneers, learning to embrace the Soviet way and developing a blind and trusting belief in communism—not that such religious devotion will last.[16] As noted previously, education is the focus of the Komsomol, and it is possible that the Komsomol's contradictory propounding of internationalism, which presumably is achieved through the learning of—but not participation in—other cultures, is responsible for conditioning the youth to see anything presented in an educational format as permissible.[17] Hence, this is why the BBC sits more comfortably with the Soviet psyche than other broadcasters not as concerned with instruction and edification.

The importance of the Russian beatniks, the *stilyagi,* in the fate of the Soviet Union is far greater than it seems. For one, despite not being unique culturally speaking, the *stilyagi* nevertheless are "trailblazers" and have given Russia the black market, which is in its own right a monument to the West.[18] For another, they represent a distinct and measurable attempt, however small, to separate from the official fabric of sanctioned Soviet existence, to hammer out a niche for themselves that they can fill with brazen ties, greased hair, and shocking dance moves. What does this actually signify? The observable and peaceable degradation of the institution in hearts and minds well before the collapse of the USSR; death comes in many different forms and stages, and here is certainly one of the earliest. Nevertheless, though the erosion of the USSR has already begun, Soviet propaganda convinces the world that communist Russia is a very real threat, establishing a bipolar global order based on ideology that will dominate the next several decades. Nascent alliances freeze over and split, birthing NATO to the West and the Warsaw Pact to the East.

---

15 For a visual representation of this subculture in 1955 Moscow, the Russian musical *Stilyagi* (2008) directed by Valery Todorovsky is a fun, if not informative, resource.

16 Novgorodsev in conversation with author, 2019.

17 Shortwave radio was seen as an exploratory "tool" for "the state's project of enabling the development of an educated and internationalist Soviet person." See Yurchak, *Everything Was Forever*, 176. The state's promotion of foreign radio for education's sake while unrealistically expecting listeners to shun the West's influence created a gray area. Listeners could, if they wished, easily justify tuning to voices outside the Soviet Union—though they might prefer to do so privately.

18 Troitsky, *Subkultura*, 110–15.

Coinciding with the shocking death of Stalin in March 1953, America adds Radio Free Europe and the Russian-language sister station Radio Liberty to its anti-Soviet arsenal.[19] The USSR is unprepared, but Washington is even more disorganized and fails to diplomatically engage, giving the Kremlin time to strategize and bring the union back into order.

The Jazz Hour

> So, in the era before Seva, the legendary figure, was this guy Willis Conover who did jazz programs. He was the Seva before there was a Seva, venerated throughout the Soviet space.
>
> —Jeff Trimble, former acting director of RFE/RL[20]

With Stalin's demise, the USSR has much bigger things to worry about than the influence of foreign radio and imported music. The popularity of jazz reaches a zenith in 1955–56 thanks to several factors: governmental changes triggered by the rise of Nikita Khrushchev; "relentless" state promotion of radio technology and new technological developments leading to mass production of more affordable and smaller shortwave radios, which especially impacted citizens in remote areas; and a new baritone, Willis Conover, who becomes the host of the two-hour program *MusicUSA* on VOA.[21]

US ambassador to the USSR, Chip Bohlen, had observed the beginnings of the *stilyagi* movement post-World War II and decided that a popular music program, consisting especially of jazz, would further stimulate the beatniks.[22]

---

19 See Gene Sosin, *Sparks of Liberty: An Insider's Memoir of Radio Liberty* (University Park: Penn State University Press, 1999) for an intimate account of Radio Liberty. Additionally, for the origins of RFE/RL, see Kennan's "Long Telegram."

20 Jeff Trimble (chair of the EurasiaNet board of directors; former acting director of RFE/RL, deputy director of BBG, and Moscow bureau chief for *US News & World Report*) in conversation with author, November 30, 2020.

21 See Ripmaster's *Willis Conover*. For a brief discussion about radio in the USSR in the '50s, see Yurchak, *Everything Was Forever*, 176–77.

22 See Billy Perrigo, "How the U. S. Used Jazz as a Cold War Secret Weapon," *TIME Magazine*, December 22, 2017, https://time.com/5056351/cold-war-jazz-ambassadors/. However, it is worth noting that this is not VOA's first foray into jazz and Conover had produced a few programs for VOA prior to 1955, including a series on Duke Ellington. "Bohlen's proposed jazz program built on existing precursors in American public diplomacy for instrumentalizing jazz as a tool for public diplomacy." See Maristella Feustle, "Liberated from Serfdom," in *Popular Music and Public Diplomacy: Transnational and Transdisciplinary Perspectives*, ed. Mario Dunkel and Sina A. Nitzsche (Bielefeld: Transcript-Verlag, 2019), 119.

Washington took some convincing since, ironically, the genre is viewed just as unfavorably at home by conservatives as by the Kremlin. Nevertheless, in all its subversive, syncopated glory, jazz soon becomes part of the official VOA anti-communist arsenal with Conover contracted to hit the Soviets with the inflections of Louis Armstrong, Dizzy Gillespie, and Charlie Parker.[23]

A well-educated jazz disc jockey, albeit not a musician himself, Conover integrates music history and information into his programs and interviews many of the headliners of the day for the world's consumption. He employs an even manner in his broadcasts, his tone diplomatic and his velvety English, specially written for global audiences, intelligible enough to foreign listeners. There is nothing to pinch the conscience when tuning to Conover, and all the *stilyagi* do so freely—if he can be found on the airwaves.[24] For the *stilyagi*, but not only for them, Conover is an aural idol, a demolition man blowing down the communist's information barricades. Seva is an early listener:

> We listened religiously, like a sermon in a church, every night, to *the* Willis Conover, who announced the performing artist's name with his luxurious deep voice from America. As we now understand, he did not tell us anything in particular, but there was such a magic! He could just say "Count Basie," and we all would go ahhh! Every day the Jazz Hour was broadcast around midnight. When I worked as an interpreter for Intourist [Soviet travel agency] I talked to Americans and they were surprised that we knew much more than they about jazz. It was a way of life for us, a virtual escape from that reality.[25]

Unsurprisingly, many new musical groups form in the USSR, influenced and inspired by Conover. The Kremlin's obstruction of free trade in culture has the opposite effect of helping rather than hindering this "new generation" of radio listeners who go on to create their own homegrown *Sovietsky jazz*.[26] Counterintuitively, the more the state persecutes these cultural deviationists, the more less-extreme practices, such as listening to Western voices, become

---

23 Clifford Groce, "Interview with Willis Conover," Library of Congress, 2010, https://www.loc.gov/item/mfdipbib001532/.

24 Starr, *Red and Hot*, 244.

25 Novgorodsev, interview, Radio Liberty, May 1998, broadcast (as quoted by S. Pantsirev to author).

26 Starr, *Red and Hot*, 260. See also Yurchak, *Everything Was Forever*, 180. "Foreign radio broadcasts had a huge impact on the development of the local Soviet jazz and rock scenes."

normalized and even appear "congruent with the identity of a good Soviet person."[27] Thus, voices like Conover achieve a greater listening audience. With this audience, the demand for physical copies of Western music grows insurmountably.

Supply simply cannot meet demand; records sold in an official, non-black market capacity are scarce and the costs exorbitant for the average Soviet citizen. Not until later in the '60s do people begin to own recorders, which allow them to capture music from their radios. So, what do they do in the '50s? According to Artemy Troitsky, the combination of feverish desire and extreme shortage spawns a "legendary phenomenon": records "on ribs." Also termed "bone records," these do-it-yourself flexidiscs are made from X-ray film obtained from hospitals and clinics either for exceedingly low cost or no cost at all for those willing to dumpster dive for discarded medical X-rays:

> These were actual x-ray plates—chest cavities, spinal cords, broken bones—rounded at the edges with scissors, with a small hole in the centre and grooves that were barely visible on the surface. . . . X-ray plates were the cheapest and most readily available source of necessary plastic. People bought them by the hundreds from hospitals and clinics for kopeks, after which grooves were cut with the help of special machines (made, they say, from old phonographs by skilled conspiratorial hands).[28]

Indeed, necessity is the mother of invention, though the identity of the inventor is debatable—with a huge technical workforce, more than one bright mind undoubtedly arrived at the illicit use of X-ray film as poor man's vinyl.

"Music on the ribs" or "bone records" are themselves symbolic of the healing nature of music, a figurative salve for the broken. Yet, they also represent the further fracturing of the Soviet Union, aided by Western jazz broadcast to the USSR by a personality named Willis Conover who warmed the young and hungry souls of the "cool" generation.

---

27 Yurchak, *Everything Was Forever*, 175.

28 Troitsky, *Back in the USSR*, 19. For a complete history, see Stephen Coates's *X-Ray Audio: The Strange Story of Soviet Audio on the Bone* (London: Strange Attractor Press, 2015) and visit his site x-rayaudio.com for the bone music project.

CHAPTER 5

Rocket Around the Clock

> Everything came together in 1956. In that year . . . the famous Thaw began—a short, colorful period of relaxation in government control. . . . The symbols of the era were Sputnik and Yuri Gagarin. Meanwhile, the Thaw's artistic achievements and subcultural drive came from the children of the pre-war baby boom, known thereafter as the *shestidesyatniki*, the Sixties Generation.
>
> —Artemy Troitsky, *Subkultura*

The year after Stalin's death, in March 1954, Soviet state security evolved yet again, albeit for the last time, into the Committee for State Security (KGB), possibly as part of a post-Stalin political ablution of the USSR to help clean up the communist act and keep the security apparatus under control. Whereas since the end of World War II, the Soviet atomic program has been a crucial focus, the end of Stalin's reign signals a shift from the nuclear chase to the space race. A reset, not with the West but with the communist world, seems to be on the agenda for the leaders of the recovering Union. In fact, in 1956, when Nikita Khrushchev makes his bid for power at the 23rd Communist Party Congress, he boldly denounces Stalin in the presence of not only the full Politburo but also China's Mao Zedong.[1] Khrushchev's so-called "Secret Speech," the text of which is leaked to the CIA and then broadcast by RFE/RL, sparks disillusionment and discord—young Mikhail Gorbachev is in the first category and Hungary in the second.[2]

---

1 Zubok, *Zhivago's Children*, 64.

2 Ibid., 65. See also Andrew and Gordievsky, *KGB*, 428, for the KGB's reaction to the "secret speech."

"The people and the intelligentsia reacted to Khrushchev's speech in different ways. There was a wave of suicides around the country, but young people were filled with optimism and inspiration. And history seemed to justify their optimism. . . ."[3] The previous year, Bill Haley's "Rock Around the Clock" had become the first early rock hit in the USSR (along with "See You Later, Alligator"), and such happy, freeing music captures youth's imaginations and fills them with hope for the future.[4] That is, until the Hungarian Revolution erupts, practically in parallel with the Cuban Revolution, and Khrushchev chooses to employ force to quell the uprising.[5] The invasion is to anti-Stalinists in Leningrad and Moscow's educational centers a "cold shower," but not quite a freezing rain. Students are especially affected and start to feel "alone" in their principles and socialist ideals.[6] This slowing of Soviet liberalization unfortunately precedes the West's publication of Boris Pasternak's semi-autobiographical novel *Doctor Zhivago*, which had expectedly been rejected by presses in Moscow.

The tragic story delineates the postrevolution demise of the Russian intelligentsia, providing a complex portrayal of the loss of life, optimism, and faith as a result of the mired events of early twentieth-century Russia, from tsarist rule to World War I to revolution. Zhivago, the title character, is a member of the intelligentsia whose life is mottled by darkness but sprinkled with happy moments—a representative allegory of all intelligentsia who are patriots of culture, knowledge, and intellect, rather than of politics, power, or the pursuit of either. The CIA, even, realizes this book represents a threat to Soviet authority and uses it to full advantage.[7] Furious, Khrushchev launches a vicious campaign against Pasternak for his betrayal and the humiliation he has caused the USSR. Stalinist's black-and-white logic returns, and anyone who isn't found to be "with" the Soviet Union is clearly "against" it.[8] In this way, the Soviet leadership botches de-Stalinization and squanders the opportunity to win the hearts and minds of the youth and intelligentsia; they instead end up "alienating the cultural, intellectual, and scientific elites" who had exhibited the greatest optimism and patriotism at the start of the Long Sixties.[9]

---

3 Troitksy, *Subkultura*, 116.

4 Troitsky, *Back in the USSR*, 19.

5 Lovell, *Russia in the Microphone Age*, 190. The Hungarian uprising was believed to have been a radio-assisted revolution (RFE-assisted, specifically). This taught the Soviet authorities "the importance of effective broadcasting."

6 Zubok, *Zhivago's Children*, 170–71.

7 Peter Finn and Petra Couvée, "During Cold War, CIA Used Doctor Zhivago," *Washington Post*, April 5, 2014.

8 Zubok, *Zhivago's Children*, 171.

9 Ibid., 191.

Diminuendo and Crescendo in Blue

An important program of Willis Conover's during this turbid climate features performances by Hungarian jazz musicians who remain nameless for their safety. Jazz experts on Conover's show describe the Hungarians' music as "spiritual" and not an imitation like "typical European" jazzers with a "much stronger mainstream influence."[10] How many young Soviet listeners, both those disillusioned by Khrushchev's Thaw and those who remain pro-Soviet, hear this program and empathize with the greater Hungarian population, with their moral rather than political fight, and subconsciously retreat from their Komsomol education principles? Such are the seeds of dissent, measured in spiritual—not physical—change.[11]

Sixteen-year-old Seva continues to be one of Conover's devoted listeners. He dreams of escaping his family's hole-in-the-wall flat in Estonia and tunes in to VOA, to his mother's displeasure, for the freedom it provides him from his restrictive environs. Through Conover, he hears rock 'n' roll and jazz, and is drawn to both. In the Baltics, away from Soviet ideological centers, he no doubt feels safe enough listening to foreign radio and doesn't believe he is betraying his communist upbringing in any way. After all, the confusing attitude that the Soviet establishment exhibited towards not only shortwave radio, but also imported popular cultural leaves much room for interpretation. The youth may easily conclude for themselves that consuming foreign influences is acceptable, even encouraged in certain contexts, and edge closer to the West without fear of falling into the category of anti-Soviet.[12] Moreover, it is the case that even by the end of the decade, it is an easier thing to catch one of many foreign broadcasts aimed at the Soviet ether than any of the existing five channels of state radio, especially so in the Baltics and other peripheral regions where not even Channel One, broadcasting to the full breadth of the USSR, is guaranteed to be received.[13]

---

10 Willis Conover, "Music USA #695-B, Hungarian Jazz Guests, Audio Recording," November 21, 1956, University of North Texas Libraries, UNT Digital Library, accessed December 14, 2021, https://digital.library.unt.edu/ark:/67531/metadc790677/m1/.

11 Troitsky, *Subkultura*, 125.

12 As Yurchak writes, the "open-endedness of meaning" of cultural forms generated an "ambiguous dynamic," wherein from the '50s to the '80s "foreign cultural forms . . . were simultaneously critiqued and promoted, attacked and allowed to develop by the Soviet state." This is seen in many of the Soviet press articles that came out between the '50s and '80s, which attempted to both castigate Western culture as decadent and immoral while acknowledging the need to adjust official policies. Yurchak, *Everything Was Forever*, 165.

13 Lovell, *Russia in the Microphone Age*, 150–51.

In January 1957, Washington announces the Eisenhower Doctrine, which grants the US unilateral authority to employ force in the Middle East to protect the rights and integrity of those states if said states feel threatened by neighboring powers.[14] Under these discouraging auspices, Seva finishes grade school, and, having received many acting awards in Estonia, including at the national level in 1954, he now aspires to be an actor. Since all the best drama schools are in Moscow, Seva, with expectations soaring higher than Sputnik, ventures to the capital city with dreams of being a star and banking on admission to the premiere Moscow acting academy.[15] However, whereas Sputnik succeeds in becoming the first satellite to orbit Earth in October 1957, Seva's rising rocket dies unceremoniously:

> The way that entry exams are organized, acting schools test their students before the actual . . . curriculum exams. So, I went to Moscow and did one school and then the other. I remember that the chances were very slim, they were taking seventeen students that year and there were five thousand applicants. And many applicants came from the republics under the auspices of very powerful people. So it was, you know, just no go from the start.[16]

Seva, exceedingly forlorn, returns to Estonia. Now, regardless of his lack of Soviet convictions, he must follow his father's edict—and footsteps—and take the naval route. "You tried it your way," his father says. "Now, you do it mine."[17]

The one bright spot in this decision is that Seva is able to go back to Leningrad, his childhood home. There, he passes the entry exams to the Marine Academy, officially the Leningrad Higher Marine Engineering School named after Admiral S. O. Makarov (LVIMU), and spends the next five years in grueling, labor-intensive study:

---

14 The doctrine was a direct result of the complex Suez Crisis of the previous year, involving a war in Egypt. Eisenhower's administration did not create the doctrine because of the USSR's threat directly, but it was clearly a preventative measure to keep the USSR from filling the power vacuum created in the aftermath of the crisis. For an overview, see Peter Hahn, "Suez Crisis," OSU.edu, October 2021, https://origins.osu.edu/milestones/suez-crisis-1956?language_content_entity=en. See also Andrei Gromyko, *Memoirs* (New York: Doubleday, 1990), 168–69, for Soviet position.

15 Novgorodsev, Museum of London interview.

16 Ibid.

17 Ibid.

> The first thing they do to you, they did to me anyway, they cut your hair off completely, they give you some awful sort of cotton clothes and we were sent to dig potatoes. Which was the custom in Russia in those days, that all students, especially all new students, had to do their bit for agriculture. We were put on a ship and in 1967 it was interesting to see that this ship still had two wheels on the sides just like a Mississippi passenger liner of a hundred years before that. And we sailed across Ladoga and Onezhskoye Lakes, sort of towards north-east into the depths of Leningrad area.[18]

Seva entering Leningrad Naval Academy (credit: seva.ru)

The ancient passenger liner loftily bears the name of a seventeenth-century Russian national hero and martyr, Ivan Susanin. By Seva's judgment it is "a floating mess." The sailors receive only enough rations for five days and are tightly crammed into the boat, three to a bunk. In such deplorable conditions, "so was forged the union of the intelligentsia with the people!"[19]

---

18 Ibid.

19 Ibid. Masha Gessen confirms this apparent purpose that drove the pro-enlightenment class: "Everything the intelligentsia did, it did in the name of the People. Indeed, all great internal

In his first year, the village to which Seva is sent contains a small Finnish tribe of gypsies. It had a total of only eleven houses and no electricity, running water, or method of communication:

> The local farmer didn't have any chimney, so they were doing still sort of sixteenth-, seventeenth-century stuff, whereby you burn your wood, make your stones hot, but the smoke comes out of the door. So, if you want to get in you have to crawl on the floor where the smoke hasn't reached yet because it tends to stay higher. And they were black almost, because there were no chimneys, so everything was covered in soot inside. It was an eye opener for me, you know, after forty years of Soviet Regime to find a village with no electricity like that.[20]

The isolation and primitiveness of this community remove whatever lingering notions about Soviet advancement and modernization state propaganda might have instilled in Seva. Does Soviet communism truly have an interest in the fate of *all* peoples, or is it no better than any other political system, caring mainly about proving the rightness of the ideology? Moreover, do these villagers feel like twentieth-century Soviet citizens, much less communists?

In his second year, Seva winds up on an old sailing ship to train as a sailor. After enduring a monotonous twelve months of seafaring life, he realizes he must do something—anything—stimulating and creative. Within the academy, there is a brass band, and Seva, artistically inclined as he is, wonders if music might not be the ticket out of boredom. "So, I joined them and took some lessons and played this small sort of tuba thing very soon." But then, Seva learns that within the naval band there is a smaller group meant for entertainment and dances, and they flirt with jazz. The bandleader gives Seva a Soviet-approved clarinet before he heads for his next sailing practice trip and says, "You better learn to play this, boy, because you're going to play clarinet next year."

Equipped with his new instrument, Seva, for his third year of rigorous education, embarks on a hell ride as a stoker, not a sailor, on what he deems the "last coal-powered steamship in Russia" in 1959. He stays in the belly of the beast by the furnaces, which are a kind of horrific symphony unto themselves:

---

struggles raged over the fate of a mythical People as a whole." Masha Gessen, *Dead Again: The Russian Intelligentsia after Communism* (London: Verso, 1997), 7.

20 Ibid.

> I can tell you this is pure unadulterated hell because you go down and there are these furnaces that go "whoo," they are burning coal violently and then the main stoker where the coal burned actually grabs it and there is a special sort of tool, he breaks it up first and he pulls it straight on the steel floor. And you have a pile probably four or five-foot high, maybe a ton or maybe more, absolutely burning bright red coal.

Seva assists the main stoker, pouring water over an accumulated pile of burnt red coal, which hisses steam and belches black smoke. At the end of his four-hour shifts, his arms are completely useless, his nerves too frayed to function. Nevertheless, he takes his clarinet, hands unresponsive, and struggles to play his first squawking notes. Weeks pass in this maritime inferno. His tenacity wins out, and as typically results with those who practice, he shows improvement. Maybe he's no Ornette Coleman or Benny Goodman; but still, he's inching closer to being a real jazzman.

Sovietsky Jazz

By the early '60s, the Komsomol realizes that they are losing the battle for the attention of the youth, specifically to this esoteric Western genre. Heeding a proposal from a defender of Stalin-era jazz, the Komsomol opens a number of "jazz cafes," which are meant to "lure the young elite back into the fold and to curb the anarchistic tendencies of jazz music and its followers."[21] The first two cafes open in Moscow in 1961 and they turn out to be a success as far as the government is concerned, meaning that they are able to somewhat control traffic and incorporate Soviet maxims, leading to more such clubs throughout the USSR. The essential goal is accomplished: instead of Soviet hipsters "huddling furtively around shortwave radio to hear Willis Conover, the cafes brought in clean-cut young communists to hear jazz by Soviet musicians."[22] However, the *stilyagi* aren't hoodwinked or pacified with the very Western-style clubs and the after-hours jam sessions, particularly with the increased presence of the KGB at every establishment as foreigners multiply at these joints. To make matters worse, the musicians are barely compensated, if at all. It's unsurprising that most of these jazz clubs only last a short while—albeit long enough for the KGB to gather intelligence on foreign patrons.

---

21 Starr, *Red and Hot*, 268–69.
22 Ibid., 270.

Nevertheless, the ostensible overtures the Komsomol makes towards jazz and the youth are superficial at best. One of the earliest jazz musicologists in Russia, Leonid Pereverzev,[23] holds public lectures in Moscow, using slides and recordings, beginning in the late ’50s and continuing into the ’60s. Instead of praising his wholesome methods of youth education, the Komsomol reproaches him through one of its youth magazines, *Smena*, calling him the “ideology god of Moscow jazzomaniacs” who “translate[s] the delirium of Willis Conover.” Pereverzev influences even those who are not overly enthusiastic about the genre but have ears to hear, such as future jazz trumpeter and educator Andrei Solovyov[24] who is a mere boy living in the village of Novogireyevo.

Andrei is, unsurprisingly, an avid, attentive listener to Western broadcasts: “On the radio, I listened to the daily programs of Willis Conover, Peter Clayton’s program on the BBC World Service, and especially loved the program of Alexei Leonidov [also on the BBC].”[25] Many people, Andrei says, have their first tape recorders by now, and they record state radio and television broadcasts of Russian jazz musicians like the Leonid Utyosov Orchestra or the Oleg Lundstrem Orchestra—the latter being one of the earliest Soviet-sponsored jazz bands, inspired by Duke Ellington before Ellington even achieved international stardom.[26] Hearing these programs doesn’t automatically make Andrei a “jazzomaniac,” but his father’s interest nurtures his own:

> The first “flexidiscs” and vinyl records of jazz music appeared at our home in 1965, when my father bought a large radio set with an integrated record player. We had the Glenn Miller Big Band, Louis Armstrong’s Hot Five / Hot seven, and Soviet vocal ensembles like the Accord Quartet that used jazz elements in their arrangements and intonations. . . . [But] I listened with greater

---

23 Cyril Moshkow, “Jazz Writer Leonid Pereverzev,” Jazz.ru, 2007, https://www.jazz.ru/eng/pages/pereverzev.htm.

24 Preferred transliteration.

25 Leonidov was the pseudonym of Leo Feigin, British producer and founder of the highly successful Leo Records. Born in 1938 in Leningrad, Feigin emigrated from the USSR in 1973 and ended up working for the BBC as a Russian translator, eventually working on jazz broadcasts. He left the BBC and went on to New York in 1979, recording for his own label. He is the author of several books on music, including *Russian Jazz: New Identity* (London: Quartet Books, 1985). Solovyov correspondence with author, December 2020.

26 Oleg Lundstrem Jazz Orchestra website, lundstrem-jazz.ru, accessed January 3, 2021, http://www.lundstrem-jazz.ru/eng/history_bio.php.

> pleasure to the collections from the "Musical Kaleidoscope" series dedicated to pop music from different countries.[27]

This program showcases the Beatles, which Andrei, like millions of other Russians, particularly loves. However, it is nearly impossible to get copies of their records:

> On central Gorky Street (now Tverskaya) there was a service called "Sound Letter"—*zvukovoe pis'mo*—where you could read a message in front of a microphone or record a song for one ruble. The sleeve was a paper photo with a view of Moscow, covered with a thin layer of plastic. Right in the presence of the customer, a "sound letter" would be cut. Its length was no longer than four minutes. From these handmade discs The Beatles, Creedence Clearwater Revival, Shocking Blue, and some other bands that were popular at the junction of the 60s and 70s, first sounded for me.[28]

And for those who can't make these "sound letters," radio fills the gaps. The unchallenged king of Beatles fans in Russia, Nikolay Vasin, owes his lifelong passion to one poor quality, homemade recording of the group aired on BBC radio in Riga, jamming and all.[29] Even Boris Grebenshchikov, a very young man in the '60s, hears and records a part of the British group from the radio—a life-changing moment for him:

> I thirsted outright, in the end, to listen to that music that travelled around, but came to me in a most distorted way. . . . I switched on the radio, placed the tape recorder in front of it. . . . And there and then everything became clear to me: who I was, what I wanted to do and why I wanted to do it.[30]

---

27 Andrei Solovyov (Soviet jazz expert, trumpeter, and educator), email to author, December 2020.

28 Ibid. According to Solovyov, the first appearance of the Beatles was with the song "Girl," released in the USSR, though the album cover is ambiguously marked as performed by a VIA. Thus, Andrei didn't know it was by the Beatles until much later, in 1972, when the Beatles no longer existed as a band (and Beatlemania in Russia had already reached its zenith).

29 Yngvar Bordewich Steinholt, *Rock in the Reservation: Songs from the Leningrad Rock Club 1981–1986* (New York; Bergen: Mass Media Music Scholars' Press, 2004), 38.

30 Ibid., 62. Translated from Smirnov, *Prekrasnyi diletant: Boris Grebenshchikov v noveishei istorii Rossii* (Moscow: LEAN, 1999).

How many artists and millions of fans are likewise born—just one song on the radio, one fragment even? That's all it takes to transform a life, potentially permanently, and, in Grebenshchikov's case, to make a future Russian rock star.

Don't Get Around Much Anymore

In 1961, astronomical highs are weighed down by political lows. Even as the Soviets appear to be winning the space race, the divided and unstable Berlin straddling two Germanys is evolving into a real problem.[31] East Germany, the German Democratic Republic, has been clocking an egregious outflow of "refugees" running to the Federal Republic of Germany, or West Germany, through Berlin ever since it closed its border in 1952. In fact, this brain drain has levied such a high cost on the political and economic health of East Germany that the ruling faction of the government has, for years, been weighing "the erection of a barrier" as a crude method to stop illegal immigration.[32] The problem climaxes in 1961. After Kennedy fails to reach a peaceful and agreeable compromise with Khrushchev on the "German question," the GDR deploys the National People's Army on August 13 to physically cleave Berlin and mark the eastern part as GDR-controlled territory. Some accounts hold that construction on a fence made out of barbed wire and cinder blocks begins that very night, while Berliners aren't awake to protest; other accounts say that it takes a week before construction begins. Regardless, within roughly two weeks, the Berlin Wall, the physical manifestation of what Churchill in 1946 had termed the Iron Curtain, is complete.[33]

As observers note, not only is this dangerous, it is a direct challenge to the other occupying powers, namely Great Britain, the US, and France. Tensions rise to the point of near-military clashes between American and East German

---

31 For the space race, see Paul Rincon and Katia Moskvitch, "Profile: Yuri Gagarin," BBC.com, April 4, 2011, https://www.bbc.com/news/science-environment-12460720. See also Jamie Doran and Piers Bizony, *Starman: The Truth Behind the Legend of Yuri Gagarin* (London: Bloomsbury Publishing, 2011), 2. For how the Potsdam Agreement, following World War II, divided Berlin among the Allies, see Stalin, Truman, and Attlee, "The Big Three Report on The Potsdam Conference," *Current History* 9, no. 49 (1945): 240–50.

32 James A. McAdams, "An Obituary for the Berlin Wall," *World Policy Journal* 7, no. 2 (1990): 358, http://www.jstor.org/stable/40209151.

33 Heil, *Voice of America*, 47. While the term "Iron Curtain" has been famously ascribed to Winston Churchill from a speech given in Missouri in 1946, Churchill is not the originator of the phrase. See Patrick Wright's *Iron Curtain: From Stage to Cold War* (Oxford: Oxford University Press, 2007).

forces. Khrushchev writes a long letter to Kennedy in September pushing for American agreement to a border control solution: "The main thing is that events are unfortunately continuing to develop in the same unfavorable direction. . . . Far from bringing the possibility of agreement between us on disarmament closer, we are, on the contrary, worsening the situation still further."[34] Kennedy does not immediately concede, and so Khrushchev orders Soviet forces to the border with West Berlin and constructs the Berlin Wall proper, which he euphemistically refers to as "border control."[35] Wanting to avoid further conflict, JFK does not object, though many Berliners (on both sides) do. Neither has the foresight to predict the trouble that such a barrier will bring.

Rocket Games in B-Flat

At last, Seva completes his duties aboard the coal-powered ship and returns to the naval academy in Leningrad with clarinet in hand. He demonstrates to the band director that, despite the impossibility of learning an instrument while surrounded by smoke and red-hot coals, he can actually "play a little." Therefore, seeing *obvious* talent, the director orders Seva's conscription into service as a musician in the pseudo-jazz band where he must play not only clarinet, but also saxophone—no longer banned after Stalin's death.[36] Surprisingly, this academy possesses a rare tenor saxophone: an 1871 French model that simply can't be bought, even if one has money. It is one note shy of the modern version of the instrument, but it is this irreplaceable horn that ends up in Seva's hands. How exciting it is to play a saxophone made just thirty-one years after Adolf Sax invented the S-shaped instrument.[37] Improving rather rapidly with his nineteenth-century horn, Seva becomes increasingly engaged in musical pursuits, eventually landing on a state-sponsored television program performing with another band outside of the academy.

Then, things go south—or north, in this case. Seva is on track to graduate, finally, after several intense years, but before he can receive his diploma, he needs one final mark on his transcript to fulfill his military training component as a submarine navigator. He is sent on a four-month stint to one of the harshest of

---

34 "Letter from Khrushchev to Kennedy," Sept 29, 1961, Department of State, Presidential Correspondence: Lot 77 D 163.

35 Nikita Khrushchev, *Khrushchev Remembers* (New York: Little Brown & Company, 1970), 504–5.

36 Starr, *Red and Hot*, 235, 248, 259.

37 Novgorodsev, interview with author, September 2015.

Russian military bases in the Arctic—Severomorsk, on the northern (*sever*) sea (*more*) coast. The population of this closed town stands at just over fifty thousand today, but in 1962 it was about half that number. Since 1933, Severomorsk has served as the headquarters and housed the main base for the Northern Fleet (Severny flot or Red Banner Northern Fleet prior to 1991), which explains why Seva and his class from the academy were sent to this important submarine location:

> Now, you have to remember what was happening in the autumn, and from October onwards, end of September, we have no daylight. I remember in November and early December the dawn comes at half an hour before lunch, at lunch it's evening again, so you have a greyish sort of sky in the east for half an hour and that's your daylight. . . .[38]

Considering the extreme conditions, those stationed there might prefer life under water. But not Seva. He and a few of his musician friends are desperate to wriggle out of submersion:

> We made sure that we stood at the end of the queue and did not get assigned to any submarine. As a result, we were free all day, went to the Officers Club there, swam in the pool, but we had nowhere to sleep. In the end, we came to the music platoon, said that we are jazz musicians, demonstrated our skill there, and after a week and a half, I was sitting in this jazz orchestra of the city of Severomorsk, playing the first alto. . . . We wrote them some orchestrations. In short, we became part of the dance orchestra and the officers played three times a week.[39]

They became part of the entertainment for the local officer's club, which had been in sore need of assistance with event organization. "Because it is a big base, you know . . . about 15 to 20,000 people or maybe more, so [the] Officer's Club was a pretty important place and the quality of music on weekends or sometimes on Wednesdays was pretty important too."[40] As officers, Seva and his friends are

38 Novgorodsev, *Integral pokhozh na saksofon*, 130.

39 Novgorodsev, "My protivostoiali vlasti po mere sil, chast' 1," Spetsial'noe Radio, August 7, 2017, broadcast, https://specialradio.ru/art/654/.

40 Novgorodsev, Museum of London interview.

able to move about the base freely. Food is no problem as all officers are fed, regardless of station or assignment. However, since they deliberately situate themselves "between the cogs," they have no assigned place to lay their heads:

> To be homeless, without a place to sleep, is difficult and unpleasant even in the tropical summer, and here there was a polar autumn outside, turning into winter. Frost, darkness, blizzard. Immediately after dinner, we went around all the crews where our cadets were listed, found out who was going to the night outfit, and asked the bed owners to let us sleep at least for the hours of their duty. We told the guys from the orchestra about our torment, and they slowly let us into the empty bunks of the musical platoon. We made a mouse nest in a far dark corner. . . .[41]

It is during this polar autumn that the Cold War dips into subzero temperatures. In October 1962, Khrushchev and Kennedy engage in a nuclear standoff, and the former goes so far as to make a seemingly impulsive maneuver, playing with Cuban alliances and medium-range ballistics. By Khrushchev's own rationale, he is defending the sovereignty and rights of communist Cuba, despite having had qualms about Fidel Castro's unorthodox rule, against a looming and threatening America.[42] Although reckless, his action is not without provocations. First, in 1960, the US Information Agency (USIA, which funded VOA) had determined to begin expanding shortwave broadcasting into Cuba and launched, essentially, a concerted anti-Castro campaign; if the role that Radio Free Europe played in the Hungarian Revolution has taught Khrushchev anything it is that more Western-funded radio could lead to disastrous consequences for the Soviets' primary communist ally in America's sphere of influence.[43] Second, the US had started to send U-2 spy aircraft into Soviet territory to conduct aerial reconnaissance not long after Eisenhower had requested (and been denied) mutual "open skies" for surveillance of military capabilities in 1955.[44] On May 1, 1960, one of these planes is shot down by Soviet missiles in the Sverdlovsk region. Pilot Gary Powers is captured, having survived the resulting crash, and admits to having been sent to sweep Soviet territory in hopes of verifying Kremlin claims about

---

41 Novgorodsev, *Integral pokhozh na saksofon*, 129.

42 Andrew and Gordievsky, *KGB*, 467. See also Khrushchev, *Khrushchev Remembers*, 512.

43 Heil, *Voice of America*, 69.

44 Andrew and Gordievsky, *KGB*, 469.

its nuclear arsenal.[45] Third, the unsuccessful CIA-supported Bay of Pigs invasion in April 1961, which had attempted to bring Castro down, led to both an increased fear of US military action against the USSR and also smug satisfaction that the US couldn't squelch communism in its own backyard.[46] Undoubtedly, none of these events justifies the placement of medium-range missiles in Cuba. Even if such a move were strategically sound—and it is not—the end result cannot achieve the amelioration of tensions. But Khrushchev, acting not at the behest of Castro, doesn't see that he's doing anything but playing defense since the US has already positioned intercontinental ballistics in Turkey—just at the USSR's southern doorstep.

The Kennedy-Khrushchev rocket games spread fear across the USSR until things come to a climax. One night, at about 3:00 a.m., a deafening alarm rings out across the entire military base, putting all units and services on combat alert No. 1. "Vitya and I woke up, stuck our heads out from under the warm blanket and began to think: what should we do, where do we go on alert?" In the end, they decide not to go anywhere at all, as it occurs to them that they are not assigned officially to any platoon, unit, or otherwise; and so, living in the cracks as they have been, they remain right where they are. It turns out to be a regrettable error in judgment, for not fifteen minutes later the lights come on in the bunk room and heavy boots troop in. "Who didn't respond to the alert?" booms a formidable voice. Seva and Vitya peep out of their burrows with clear chagrin and find to their horror a cadre of military officials standing before them menacingly with "sparkling shoulder straps"; and at the tip of the spear formation is the rear admiral himself, the head of the base. But Seva and Vitya are not full-time employees, not military proper: they are simply kicked out of their unofficial quarters.

> For several days we slept in the cold dressing rooms of the Officers Club, and then I ended up in a hospital bed. Many years later, comparing dates and facts, I realized that we were raised by military alert for a reason, and the whole army and navy of the Union of Soviet Socialist Republics were preparing for possible hostilities.[47]

---

45 Gromyko, *Memoirs*, 171. See also Andrew and Gordievsky, *KGB*, 468–69. Perhaps it is because of this U-2 incident that Moscow publicly gave the Cuban regime full diplomatic recognition and support in May 1960.

46 Ibid., 468–69.

47 Novgorodsev, *Integral pokhozh na saksofon*, 130.

In retrospect, it was the Cuban Missile Crisis that had triggered the alarm and inadvertently robbed Seva and Vitya of their beds and, shortly after, Seva of his health.[48] Indeed, after the intense stress of the winter conditions, Seva becomes gravely ill and lands in the base hospital:

> [T]hey were treating me for something they couldn't treat so they were giving me huge doses of antibiotics. . . . Something cracked in me and my digestive system has never been the same.[49]

After weeks of intense suffering, the sun finally emerges for Seva, and his health improves enough for him to return to Leningrad, graduate, and receive his diploma. But he is irrevocably changed, and not just physically.

One year after the crisis, which ends with both nuclear powers agreeing to withdraw their respective missiles, President Kennedy is assassinated in Dallas, Texas. Khrushchev remains alive and well, although not as secure in his position as he once was, especially after the Cuban madness. In 1964, while vacationing in the Black Sea, Khrushchev receives an unexpected summons to the Kremlin and finds himself confronted with a figurative firing squad of his comrades in arms. It is a trying moment for the advocate of "Peaceful Coexistence" who supported de-Stalinization and earned a place in history for attempting to thaw the ice between the US and the USSR. On October 15, Khrushchev announces his "resignation" and steps down as Soviet premier.

Leonid Brezhnev takes his place, and if, as a leader, Nikita Khrushchev might be characterized as overly experimental and extemporaneous, Leonid is ultra-conservative and decidedly ineloquent. Thus, instead of the "colors of socialism being painted in yet brighter tones," they begin to fade, and the optimism of the Long Sixties fades as well.[50] Khrushchev lives out the rest of his days in internal exile, recording his memoirs on tape, which escape capture by the KGB to eventually be published in English translation.[51] The KGB-assisted coup represents a devastating end for his reign, but unlike his predecessors in the position of Communist Party's general secretary, Khrushchev, at the very least, comes away with his life.[52]

---

48 Novgorodsev, "My protivostoiali vlasti po mere sil, chast' 1."

49 Novgorodsev, Museum of London interview.

50 Troitsky, *Subkultura*, 122.

51 *Khrushchev Remembers* was published in 1970. After he died, in September 1971, Little, Brown and Company issued a second set of memoirs in 1974, and a third volume came out in 1990.

52 Andrew and Gordievsky, *KGB*, 477.

CHAPTER 6

Between Jazz and a Hard Rock Place

> Somewhere in the mid-60s in one of the TV shows there was a plot showing how vilely depraved young people in the West are. And the main element of "corruption" according to the program's authors was rock music. I don't remember if The Beatles were shown, but I do remember the shots of people breaking chairs in the hall with a commentary: "you see what these Beatles are driving people to do?" And all this went to the instrumental "Can't Buy Me Love." I was still a rather naïve Pioneer at that time.[1]

The change in atmosphere in the Soviet space, from Khrushchev to Brezhnev, is felt by all, but especially by the intelligentsia. Artemy Troitsky notes the new cynical mood in the arts, the state's treatment of the slightest indiscretion by artists, and the increase in alcoholism.[2] Unlike much of the USSR, Seva is able to escape and all but ignore the new premier Leonid Brezhnev. He starts his first job is at the Estonian Shipping Company where he has the opportunity to see some of the world beyond the boundaries of the Soviet Union:

> I began as a fourth officer and then became a third. . . . We were on a line from Riga, Riga to Bremen in Germany, going through Kiel Canal and all that. I was amazed to see how neat nature was in Germany, you know, grass . . . mowed and it looked something out of a fairy tale. . . . Everything was so small and neat. And we

1 User D. Vasya (forum response), Beatles.ru, February 24, 2010, https://www.beatles.ru/postman/forum_messages.asp?cfrom=1&msg_id=9617&cpage=816&forum_id=3#1221423.

2 Troitsky, *Subkultura*, 123.

> come from these vast spaces of nature, which is hostile to you, you know, if you are not careful it will kill you.[3]

The contrast in landscape diminishes the USSR in his esteem.

After eighteen months of working as a navigator, he returns for a visit to Leningrad—he'd accumulated about eight weeks' worth of leave having taken no days off for more than a year. There he reunites with jazz musician friends and spends a week or so performing in random venues. With the nation's politics in flux and no one keen on talking about the changes, people are increasingly drawn to live music and Westernized entertainment. Seva and his friends, who also have no interest in politics, reap the benefits.[4] They get an offer from one of the official concert agencies after a wildly successful gig to go on the road; all that is necessary is an audition with the artistic committee—a ritual performed before cultural officials—and then registration with the personnel department. Sounds simple enough, but Seva is still employed as a navigator, and what's more he is obligated to remain employed for three years minimum by law. To get out of the obligation, he falsifies documents and invents a duodenal ulcer. Ten days or so later, he appears at the Personnel Department, and so dawns his career as an official Soviet (jazz) musician.

Seva's real break comes when he receives an invitation to join the Leningrad Jazz Orchestra, a well-known group directed by the venerable Joseph Weinstein. For years, Seva, while employed in Leningrad, had frequented the Palace of Culture (*Dvorets kultury*) to listen to this group, never in his wildest fantasies dreaming that he himself would someday become a member.

Bandleader Weinstein, a person of "atomic energy" and one of those who survived Stalin, the Nazis, the KGB—everything—had launched his first jazz band in 1938 as a young man of only eighteen. A military officer and music student, he'd been caught up in the siege of Leningrad and then appointed bandmaster of the Krondstadt defensive zone in early 1942. Weinstein's orchestra had performed concerts often under artillery fire. For his exemplary service during the siege, he'd been one of the earliest to be awarded the Order of the Red Star by Stalin. His Leningrad Jazz Orchestra did not come into being until many years

---

3 Novgorodsev, Museum of London interview.

4 When asked in a 2019 interview if he felt that his radio programs played a role in changing the mindset of the Soviet people, Seva replied: "[F]rom the time when I lived in the Soviet Union and used to be a musician . . . I was never interested in politics. In our circles, it seemed to be a kind of tasteless thing to take part in dissident movements as we felt that it was sleazy. When I started to work at the BBC, I didn't change this principle and did not turn into a political creature." Tolkunov, "Seva Novgorodsev."

later, after the war had ended and the KGB had come after him for reasons that amounted to ideological insubordination. But Weinstein's dynamism and Red Star kept him well above water, and his orchestra gained regional fame in the '50s. In fact, "of the dozens of nominal swing bands functioning in the USSR in the fifties, only two stood out in terms of the modernity of their repertoire, the competence of their musicians, and their overall orientation towards jazz: those of Oleg Lundstrem and Yosif Weinstein."[5]

"Weinstein had all the stars," confirms a former member of the group.[6] The band had achieved a reputation as a dance group that played "proper stuff"—meaning American luminaries. Stan Kenton, Count Basie, Duke Ellington. *Real* jazz. And they weren't obstructed by the Soviet censors, partly because the orchestra avoided staged concerts in favor of big dance halls and partly due to the communist spirit exemplified through these sorts of large, collective ensembles.[7] Thus, Seva's membership in this orchestra represents a crucial opportunity for him and his musical development. "Joseph W." educates Seva on the difference between the "hip" and the "passé" under the nose of their isolationist anti-West regime. These are his happiest years and the time in which he begins to develop a genuine connection to an audience—the bored, disenfranchised Soviet youth—as a jazz musician.

Seva (middle top row) with members of the Leningrad Jazz Orchestra (credit: seva.ru)

---

5 Starr, *Red and Hot*, 257.

6 Vladimir Marochkin, "Interview with Late Soviet Rock Artist Vladislav Petrovsky," *Spetsial'noe Radio*, March 24, 2006, broadcast, https://specialradio.ru/art/id212/.

7 Novgorodsev, *Integral pokhozh na saksofon*, 181.

The Stagnant Years

From the US to China to West Berlin, the '60s are usually characterized by protest, cultural revolution, and political turmoil.[8] In the USSR, however, the relative stability of the Brezhnev administration, which seems to have no other agenda than to keep firm control on the nation, has brought about what will later be termed a period of "stagnation."[9] However, Eastern Europe has been undergoing massive structural changes, which "radically" alter the bloc's geopolitical positioning.[10] This worrisome movement prompts a split response from the Soviet establishment: increased discipline with technological modernization *or* gentle reforms to better match up with the capitalists, otherwise termed "socialism with a human face." It is this contradictory response that triggers the Prague Spring in Czechoslovakia, which cleaves the nation, ousting one leader in favor of another—Alexander Dubček—and ushering in a series of democratizing reforms. Such dramatic change rattles Moscow, but the intelligentsia views this movement as a welcome burst of hope:

> The year 1968 seemed to offer a light at the end of the tunnel—the Prague Spring. But, as the joke, goes, this light turned out to be the headlights of an oncoming express train. The events in Czechoslovakia, as local leaders attempted to reform Communism from the inside, terrified the Soviet Party elite, seemingly proving to them the deplorable consequences of excessive liberalism. . . . The Sixties Generation had, on the whole, rapidly welcomed the Czechoslovak slogan . . . so the clank of the tank tracks on Prague's cobblestones sounded like the tolling of a funeral bell to them.[11]

---

8 Zubok, *Zhivago's Children*, 282. "In the East, the 'cultural revolution' in China [is] entering its third year. In the West, 'New Left' radicalism rage[s] on and around university campuses from West Berlin . . . to Berkeley, California. The rapid growth of the anti-Vietnam protest movement, the assassination first of Martin Luther King in April, then of Robert Kennedy in June [1968] . . . plunge[s] the United States into radical politics."

9 Yurchak, *Everything Was Forever*, 7. "The term stagnation (*zastoi*) . . . emerged . . . only later, during the time of Gorbachev's reforms."

10 Stephen Kotkin, *Uncivil Society: 1989 and the Implosion of the Communist Establishment* (New York: Random House Publishing Group, 2010), 30.

11 Troitsky, *Subkultura*, 123.

Moscow reacts swiftly to crush the Czechoslovak spirit by mobilizing the Warsaw Pact. The sights and sounds of Soviet tanks in the streets of beautiful and Westernized Prague are broadcast around the world, and the West is reminded that the USSR is an enemy with serious military capabilities.[12]

The Czechoslovakia invasion of 1968 impacts the Russian intelligentsia and the Soviet people more generally. It dispels lingering "illusions about Socialism and the Soviet system" on the one hand and triggers a period of "great faith"—faith in the permanence and enduring stability of Soviet life.[13]

> Time stood still in the Soviet Union of the 1970s and early 1980s. . . . People would hold the same jobs for decades, probably for their entire lives. We would grow up and grow old, not only in the same country ruled by the same leaders but, in all likelihood, in the same neighborhood and even the same apartment, seeing the same people, reading the same books, and thinking the same thoughts.[14]

This assurance of an eternal USSR expresses itself as a deep, shared cynicism that spreads like ink, inspiring *anekdoty*, jokes where people can "comment on the world they observe" without directly criticizing, that appear everywhere from unknown sources. Brezhnev is the brunt of most *anekdoty* due to his drunken behavior and increasing ineloquence.[15] As scholars note, such pessimistic witticisms are most pervasive in repressive environments, wherein government hypocrisy, mendacity, and cruelty are a set condition of life. But while jokes are a normal part of any given society, cynical humor in particular is a form of truth signaling, cleverly exposing the hypocrisies and "intentional disinformation" configured into state media without technically violating any conventions.[16] Furthermore, as Paul Sheeran has argued, "the ability to undermine the rigors of social programming through various acts that range from open defiance to the nuances of a lyric, a joke, or the exchange of a grumble (circulated and *amplified*) is explicitly the idea of cultural politics—the politics of unreason."[17]

---

12 Kotkin, *Uncivil Society*, xv.

13 Ibid.

14 Gessen, *Dead Again*, 23.

15 Yurchak, *Everything Was Forever*, 107, 248.

16 Leon Aron, "Russian Jokes Tell the Brutal Truth," *The Atlantic*, November 29, 2019, https://www.theatlantic.com/ideas/archive/2019/11/russian-jokes-tell-deeper-truths-about-putin-and-trump/602713/.

17 Sheeran, *Cultural Politics in International Relations*, 173.

Conspiracy culture arises, likely due to both the influx of external sources of information and the absence of information within the USSR. The Soviet establishment inadvertently teaches the public how to be conspiracy theorists by hiding truths and providing improbable explanations for reality, blaming an undesirable something or someone for an unrelated problem. The public catches on to the formula, even if subconsciously, and people begin to generate conspiracy theories. Seva explains it best with (appropriately) an *anekdot*:

> On a late autumn evening of one of those stagnant years, when grain purchases from abroad were disrupted in the Soviet Union . . . I was returning from work from the Gorky Palace of Culture, where I played in the orchestra at dances. A dead drunk man stood in the semi-dark front door. In general, in Russia it is believed that if a person stands and does not fall, then he is not drunk yet. But this one was definitely drunk. His eyes glazed over, with an unseeing gaze he was looking somewhere into the distance, and when I passed by, with his last strength, with his blackened lips, he barely audibly said: "The Jews ate the whole loaf." In other words, he wanted to say, that the representatives of the Jewish nationality bought up all the bakery products and ate them so that indigenous hares, like my friend here, got nothing. This is conspiracy theory.[18]

This is the environment of the '60s and '70s, then: carefully creative and exploratory, yet deeply cynical and suspicious. Soviet society, particularly the intelligentsia, increasingly turns to foreign broadcasts and entertainment, looking for escape in the Imagined West. Everyone expects nothing, and this is its own kind of comfort.

Downbeat Détente

If the violent crackdown employed in Czechoslovakia seems antithetical to the policy of détente, which had only begun the previous year in 1967, it nevertheless makes sense in the context of the unadvertised "Brezhnev Doctrine," all

---

18 Seva Novgorodsev, *Rok-posevy*, July 22, 2000, radio broadcast.

but authored by KGB chief Yuri Andropov.[19] This suggests that the KGB may be the true originator of Soviet foreign policy and the true ruling power domestically, controlling everything down to cultural confluences. Nevertheless, despite Andropov's practically omnipresent and omniscient KGB, jazz and rock continue to spread in different, sometimes overlapping circles of society. Rock is the genre that exerts a heady, alarming influence over the youth. Because of this, the KGB adopts a new tactic by which it hopes to isolate, observe, and treat this growing infection. Symptomatic of this "quarantine method," the KGB creates, or sanctions the creation of, a *beat club* at Melody and Rhythm Cafe in Moscow in 1969 (comparable to the earlier attempts at jazz clubs). "The Komsomol . . . [is] the ostensible sponsor of the club, but despite extravagant promises, the club actually produce[s] very little."[20] In conjunction with the club, the Soviet authorities decide to promote their version of a boy band with a group called (politically correctly) Happy Guys:

> The basic message of the group was that the world, or at least the USSR, was fine. This occurred at a time when American youth were listening to protest songs by Joan Baez, hearing Bob Dylan advise "Everybody must get stoned," and turning on to the "heavier" sounds of Cream and Led Zeppelin.

As one might imagine, the group isn't wildly popular. Likewise, after only a year of existence, the beat club disbands once the KGB has "obtained hefty dossiers on club members."[21]

The government isn't the only camp resistant to rock. Soviet jazzmen are as well, but for artistic reasons and musicality considerations. According to Vladislav Petrovsky, a late Soviet-era rock singer, "Every jazz musician is *stilyagi*. . . . They were all in their thirties, and they didn't take to the rock at first. 'Why should I listen to the Beatles?! It's three chords! It's not interesting when Charlie Parker plays fifteen chords!'"[22] And so, for a time, jazz and rock exist alongside each other but in somewhat separate worlds.

---

19 Kotkin, *Uncivil Society*, xv. "Yuri Andropov . . . had long undergirded the Soviet resolve . . . [and] manipulated the more cautious Brezhnev [into] using force in Czechoslovakia in 1968." Andropov was KGB chief from 1967 to 1982.

20 Pedro Ramet and Sergei Zamascikov, "The Soviet Rock Scene" (Washington, D.C.: Kennan Institute for Advanced Russian Studies, 1987), https://www.wilsoncenter.org/sites/default/files/media/documents/publication/op223_the_soviet_rock_scene_ramet_1988.pdf.

21 Ibid.

22 Marochkin, "Interview with Late Soviet Rock Artist Vladislav Petrovsky."

The Beatles in front of a bust of Lenin (courtesy of A. Troitsky)

In Leningrad, jazz still thrives in the musician community, while in Moscow underground rock sessions begin to emerge during the early 1970s.[23] One of the first rock bands to achieve popularity in Moscow is Mashina vremeni, or Time Machine, led by singer/songwriter Andrey Vadimovich Makarevich, in whose development radio played a substantial role.[24] In 1968, the very same year that the Warsaw Pact rolled into Prague, a fourteen-year-old Makarevich, born to highly educated intelligentsia parents, hears the Beatles on the radio, purportedly for the first time.[25] While he may well have heard such imports before, Western music now carries greater meaning for Makarevich. He embraces such foreign influences even as the government begins to vilify the West more openly. In that same year, the young Muscovite founds the cover band Deti (the Kids). Soon after, he launches Time Machine, which makes its debut with songs and lyrics in Russian written by Makarevich.[26] Artemy Troitsky, actively operating for various state-run publications and media, but as always guided by his own developed tastes, calls Time Machine the "unquestioned number one group

23 Troitsky, *Back in the USSR*, 38.

24 Time Machine is considered to be Russia's oldest active rock band, although Akvarium is also very active.

25 The age of fourteen seems to be a commonality among most of these listeners, a defining year in which maturity, political sensibility, and taste come together and turn passive listening into an active deliberate practice.

26 Steinholt, *Rock in the Reservation*, 26.

of the period" and not just in Moscow or Leningrad.[27] Others corroborate that from 1976 until the next decade, Makarevich's group dominates the genre, giving rise to the term *mashinomaniya*.[28]

Yet another forerunner of Russian rock, emerging from the underground music scene in Leningrad, is Akvarium (Aquarium), famously associated with guitarist and lead singer Boris Grebenshchikov—favorably christened the "Bob Dylan of Russia" by Western media.[29] But Akvarium does not bill itself as a rock band, and in this way it is able to exist in the undefined space between rock and jazz, escaping much of the official state criticism.[30] Even so, the decade of the '70s is hostile to all musicians who attempt to exist outside of officialdom. Musical growth happens, if at all, at underground concerts, organized and held in whatever apartment, room, hall, or space possible.

The Sound Hunter

> I played in a big band conducted by Joseph Weinstein, and 90 percent of our repertoire were arrangements transcribed from recordings. This is a very complicated process, and we had only a few musicians with perfect hearing who could transcribe an orchestration from tapes recorded from the radio—with all its rattles and noises and so on—so that it sounded like the original when we played them. Basically, we played all your big band material. You name it, we did it, because we were under American influence. It started long before I got into the band (we were all listening to Willis Conover). I followed Weinstein's band, and I remember all these [media] campaigns against us. So, the origin was perceived clearly as American.[31]

In Leningrad, Joseph Weinstein's Orchestra is doing quite well, and Seva benefits both personally and creatively. During a gig at a big dance hall, a Tatar beauty, Gala Burkhanova, approaches Seva at the backstage door. Elegant, tanned, a young Gina Lollobrigida, she says with euphemistic cheekiness, "Young man, can I

---

27 Troitsky, *Back in the USSR*, 40.

28 Steinholt, *Rock in the Reservation*, 27.

29 Sally McGrane, "Meet the Bob Dylan of Russia," BBC.com, October 21, 2014, https://www.bbc.com/culture/article/20141013-meet-the-bob-dylan-of-russia.

30 Troitsky, *Back in the USSR*, 40–42.

31 Novgorodsev, interview by Matthew Orr, March 28, 2019, in *The Slavic Connexion*, podcast, https://www.slavxradio.com/seva-in-russian

carry some instrument of yours? You can tell them I am your sister, after all we look similar." She slays him. In short order (November 1965), wedding bells ring, launching Seva into a new chapter of his life. But it is also in this incubation period with Weinstein's orchestra that Seva works to develop his own sound—a matter of infinite importance for a saxophonist—and is able to immerse himself in an English-language environment, tuning in to American and British radio only. A self-proclaimed Americanophile in his youth, he somewhat innocently embraces everything connected to the Stars and Stripes, revering this Imagined West.

Then, in the summer of 1967, he sees a documentary featuring the now-revered jazz drummer Art Blakey performing in Japan with tenor saxophonist Wayne Shorter. Shorter's deep, bluesy sound leaves an "indelible, magical impression" on Seva and becomes his obsession. For him, the sound corresponds to the hopeless outlook of the Russian people who have been driven into the cultural underground.[32] He wonders how he can achieve such a tone and concludes, logically, that there may be some aspect of his instrument that is different or inferior to that of his American idols. He checks the iconic Blue Note albums and observes on the cover artwork, the same engravings, the same general outlines on the mouthpieces of their saxophones. It turns out John Coltrane, Ben Webster, Coleman Hawkins, and Lester Young, just to name a few, all played on an Otto Link No. 6. Now, this is hardly a secret amongst the jazz cats in America, but in the USSR, such information is only for the underground. The magic of the mouthpiece is in the metal. Seva feels convicted that this is the key to the sound he seeks; he *must* obtain one.

According to the instrument catalog he consults, his aspiration costs sixty American dollars, an exorbitant sum. Moreover, American dollars are forbidden to Soviet citizens under penalty of jail or even death. So, what to do? Though tempted, Seva shuns the possibility of an easy illegal route, no doubt thinking of his wife who works for Aeroflot, and searches for another moneymaking avenue, which will still allow him to continue playing with Joseph W.

"In those years," Seva notes, "a trip to the USSR was considered exotic in the West, and more than a million tourists came to Leningrad in a year." Seeing an ad looking for additional help at Intourist, the Soviet travel agency founded by Stalin and primarily staffed by officers of the KGB, he enrolls in coursework to become a guide-translator in January of 1967 as he has already taught himself the English language.

> They had such an influx of tourists in the summer that they took in translators, even such unreliable people as me. I studied for three months. Eight hours a day. But I passed thirteen exams on

32 Novgorodsev, *Integral pokhozh na saksofon*, 214.

> the main objects of Leningrad . . . and was called to work as soon as the season began. And I worked with luxury Americans, who were supposed to have a personal translator and a car. Morning and evening.

The KGB monitor him as he mingles with tourists, mainly the rich Americans. At the end of every day, he is required, as are all employees, to make an entry in a journal and provide a profile of those foreigners with whom he interacts.

> A modest door led into the building of the European Hotel from the side of the Arts Square (where there is a monument to Pushkin). Climbing one flight of stairs and entering another inconspicuous door, the guide-translator goes into a quiet room, where they speak in a whisper. He's given a laced and sealed thick, battered book, where it is necessary to write down impressions of tourists. I understood who would read all this and why and therefore I wrote the same thing every day: "He treats the USSR positively and sympathizes with the cause of socialism."

Seva is careful to avoid any political tangles.

In pursuit of his precious Otto Link, when tourists who are pleased with his service ask what they might do or purchase for him upon their return to America, Seva invariably gives the details of the particular mouthpiece he needs from the States and why. Many reply affirmatively—sixty dollars is not so much for them. Unfortunately, several are frivolous, rich American students who likely forget all about him and his earnest request by the time they return home, even though he gives some of them money to cover shipping costs. His hope dwindles as American after American fails him, or even if they don't fail him, he still receives nothing—such an item would likely be confiscated before reaching his hands. Still, he persists in his job for the tour season and continues playing with the orchestra.

One particular couple, elderly, wealthy, and jazz afficionados, are in Seva's charge for longer than the others and the three of them form a special, familial bond. He invites them, in fact, to attend a concert of his in a romantic, storied garden in Leningrad. They are so impressed with the talent of their tour guide that, like many others before, they ask what they might do for him. Seva gives his usual spiel:

> I admitted about the mouthpiece. I said that for a musician, sound is his reputation, this is the voice with which he speaks on his instrument. They nodded their heads understandingly. But so

> many times I was deceived by promises that this time I was afraid to hope. I tried to forget, I tossed it all out of my head, especially since the work of a guide became intolerable for me—I lasted only forty-five days.[33]

One fine day, when he has all but forgotten about his dream, he receives a small parcel, covered in customs stamps. Inside, swaddled in fitted foam, is a golden, new Otto Link No. 6 mouthpiece. He is overwhelmed with gratitude. Though it takes Seva some work and time to achieve his own magical sound, the voice that will evoke pathos and capture the hopelessness and passion of his lot in the cultural underground. But when he finds it, at long last, he can only say, "Thank you, America."[34]

The Fine Young Men

Having achieved a regional reputation and cut records with the orchestra for Melodiya, the premiere Soviet international record label, Seva is more or less content remaining where he is in Leningrad. However, Weinstein seeks to take his show on the road, to move from informal dance halls to sanctioned performance stages in the hopes of achieving legitimacy in Soviet society. In order to do this, to be legitimized, a group must satisfy one or more artistic councils, whose task it is to judge artistic worth according to those "scientific principles" of human musicality.[35] This aim for fame is something Seva disagrees with, but he goes along with Joseph W., to the inevitable detriment of his marriage.

Spending months on the road touring without returning to Leningrad, Seva is unable to maintain any real connection with his wife. Gala sends him papers for a divorce while he's on an extended engagement in Moscow at the invitation of the Union of Composers. It's no doubt this personal conflict that plays into his anger over a particularly grim clash with the Ministry of Cultural Affairs. This invitation represents to the jazzers a chance to break through the barriers of communism and become a lawfully recognized genre, accepted by the orchestral crowd and thereby the Soviet public. But all sorts of "evil people," like the composer

---

33 Ibid., 216.

34 Novgorodsev, "The DJ Who 'Brought Down the USSR'" (talk at the University of Texas at Austin, March 27, 2019).

35 Yurchak, *Everything Was Forever*, 154.

Kobalevsky and pro-Soviet orchestras, smash any such hope.[36] They decry Weinstein's crew as a weak imitation of American jazz. Seva, in his indignant misery, both personal and creative, writes a letter in defense of the jazz orchestra.

Of course, his letter, wittily and scathingly composed, makes its way into the wrong hands, and there are promised consequences. Nothing happens, though. Brezhnev's incursion into Czechoslovakia occupies the authorities' attention:

> All year we rehearsed in the Palace of Sailors at the port and passed eleven art councils. Nothing happened. We played the same jazz compositions. We sat in the same jackets, with the same light, lowered and raised the curtains. Party functionaries who hated their work and had to listen to what we play came there. And we improve, add-on, polish.[37]

After many failed attempts and auditions in front of art council after art council, the Leningrad Jazz Orchestra finally makes it to a major stage through an "incredible number of compromises."

> There it was necessary to convert jazz into Shostakovich, while in front of us walked three dancers portraying fascists. Some singers sang stupid Soviet songs. But in general, once we had reached an acceptable level, little remained from the initial idea of taking jazz to the stage. . . .[38]

All the compromises grind the band down and diminish the spirit of the players—Seva, in particular. He feels like quitting, finding that the idea of jazz on the Soviet stage is just not fully justifiable because jazz is far too "esoteric" a genre for the vast majority of the population. Many musicians, including Andrei Solovyov, begin to realize there is a fundamental disconnect baked into the culture itself:

> Jazz is a rather complicated music, and it requires some work to understand it. . . . [T]here were not enough direct emotions, sexuality, and sharp blues-rock intonations. In addition, jazz is not so much connected with the processes of social life. And rock music, transferred to Russian soil, made it possible to tell the truth, sing about something important in their own language.[39]

---

36 Novgorodsev, Museum of London interview.

37 Ibid.

38 Ibid.

39 Andrei Solovyov, email to author, December 2020.

Seva shares similar realizations and experiences:

> People in the big cities understood [jazz], but if you drove outside, there I saw glassy eyes in the first three–four rows where usually sat party workers and local leaders. And well, they understood almost nothing. . . . Rock conquered the people more, because there is pathos. You can stand up with a guitar in your hand, make like a drunk, and you are at this moment a folk hero. You're the sound of strings conquering the whole hall. The bass rumbles so that in the seventh row the man's heart stops. That's the kind of power.[40]

Creative suffocation is ultimately why Seva decides to leave Joseph W. to join another band, a vocal and instrumental Russian folk group named Dobry molodtsy (Fine Young Men). Here he hopes to musically "fight the power." He is hardly alone in wanting to develop some sort of creative protest, which results in his turning to coded performances.[41] Expectedly, coded performance does not call for revolution but, rather, through a wink and nod—as with *anekdoty* and humor—suggests that there is something wrong with the Soviet way of life.

Both Time Machine's and Akvarium's songs are very much part of this coded performance; the lyrics are not explicitly political but take on a potent meaning in the setting of state censorship, nonetheless. And likewise, Seva's music is a deceptive artform, using the guise of traditionalist folk songs to veil borrowed Western musical styles. In this way, there is some comparison to be made to Akvarium. Musically speaking, Akvarium and Dobry molodtsy strive to blend and borrow and broker the old with the new, or newer, introducing unacceptable ideas in unassuming packages. In Akvarium's case, these packages entail high poetry. Such camouflaged truth is both dangerous and unquestionably important as a precursor to change in a totalitarian regime, particularly when delivered in a musical form that appeals to a large and important swath of the population: the youth.

---

40 Novgorodsev, Museum of London interview. See also Sergei I. Zhuk, *Rock and Roll in the Rocket City* (Baltimore: Johns Hopkins University Press, 2010). See also Sheeran, *Cultural Politics in International Relations*, 74–75, 78.

41 Sheeran, Cultural Politics, x. "In the context of preserving spiritual faith in an environment of repression, music had been a tool through which [spiritual faith] could be maintained in public through coded performance."

CHAPTER 7

After 'While, *Krokodil*

By 1972, Dobry molodtsy's managing agency Roskontsert appoints Seva as bandleader—*rukovoditel'*—for a variety of reasons, not the least of which is his experience maneuvering through political barriers and dealing with cultural authorities.[1] It is in the beginning of this new chapter that Seva decides the Russification of his surname may be useful now that he is not in an explicitly jazz group. Levenstein is incompatible with old Russian folklore. When his name is announced on stage, he feels a strange and uncomfortable reaction:

> [T]he need to change the name arose in 1970, when I became the head of the ensemble. Imagine: from the stage they announced—vocal and instrumental ensemble "Dobry molodtsy," artistic director Vsevolod Levenstein. And then, there is rustling in the hall. After this happened several more times, I realized that in the USSR it is necessary to either leave the job or change the name. So, I took a creative pseudonym—the name of the *pompolit* from my sailing days, a very good man. Then, when we became famous and were often invited to the radio and television, I could not go to any TV studio: the pass was given with one name, and the passport with another. So, I officially got a passport on which was written: Vsevolod Novgorodsev. . . . I thought it would help me live to retire. . . .[2]

---

1 Novgorodsev, interview with author, 2015.

2 D. Tockman, "Interview with Seva Novgorodsev," *Rossiskaya Gazeta,* April 2018. Seva jokes ruefully about the name change as a ticket to help him live longer, but he mentioned something similar to the author in an email, saying that he had to be careful and that the "guarding angels" must have been keeping watch over him all these years.

Dobry molodtsy typically performs two sets, the first consisting of Russian folk songs arranged in the style of Blood, Sweat, and Tears, and the second comprised of pop songs complete with a costume change—something largely alien to jazz concerts but a regular performative aspect of rock. The group plays selections from Chicago's first album and others but foregoes the English words, singing instead in Russian in fashionable high voices.[3] Because they are careful, the group's choice of music appeases the cultural authorities and the KGB for a time. Though they gain much initial success, jealous musicians of an era gone by stir trouble. Telegrams come into Roskontsert complaining about the group disgracing Russian folk music. Consequently, for six months or so, Seva and his group cannot get a single gig, finding themselves "smashed to smithereens," in his words, by eleven artistic committees.

Seva with *Dobry molodtsy*, circa 1972 (credit: seva.ru)

Paradoxically, Seva and his Fine Young Men live in the lap of luxury in the most glamorous hotel on the Moskva River, the Rossiya Hotel, which is covered by the agency, but there is barely a kopek in their pockets. If they don't perform, they don't eat. Such is the Soviet system. One of the other bandmates, the trombonist, manages to get along on barely a bread roll and a packet of dry soup per day. What cruel irony being so richly accommodated and yet "hungry as

3 Marochkin, "Interview with Late Soviet rock Artist Vladislav Petrovsky."

wolves," watching rich foreign hotel guests dine on delicacies. Despite these hardships, the band does not waste time and records its first album. However, even here international politics and strict censorship interfere in frustrating ways. Keyboardist Vladislav Petrovsky recounts the story:

> An incident happened with the song "I'm going to sea." One morning, the editor of Melodiya, Ryzhikov, telephoned Seva: "This is sedition! What a nightmare! It's horrible! Rewrite everything immediately!" We rushed to Melodiya. It turned out that at that same time the meeting between Leonid Ilyich Brezhnev and US president Richard Nixon was being prepared, and the line from our song "There is no happier meeting on the whole Earth" was taken by the Arts Council as a hint and also a mockery of Pariah politics. Fine! We rewrote. So then, it sounded like this: "There is no happier meeting. Trust me." But what is the difference?[4]

The meeting Petrovsky references is the second US-Soviet summit of the Nixon presidency, but it is particularly significant because Brezhnev travels to Andrews Air Force base. This is the second negotiation on the Strategic Arms Limitation Treaty (SALT II) and is therefore a matter of international import and a great milestone in the détente period. Clearly, political tensions remain high, and even music groups must be attuned to global relations.

Realizing the band will probably starve to death, Roskontsert organizes a semi-official tour for them to Stavropol. There, Dobry molodtsy performs for several officials including the first secretary of the Stavropol Regional Committee of the Communist Party, Mikhail Sergeyevich Gorbachev. In Stavropol, the ensemble is well-received, much to the relief of the concert agency and the Fine Young (Starving) Men. The tour turns out to be just the ticket. Soon after, their record gains radio play and the group gradually achieves fame.

The Montarbo Scandal

Dobry molodtsy tours far and wide across the Motherland, playing four or sometimes five concerts a day, enjoying some national success and popular acclaim.

---

4 Ibid.

They travel all the way east to the Sakhalin Island, a mere ninety miles from increasingly Westernized, Hollywood-influenced Japan. But as Seva explains, "The further east you go [in Russia] the more backwards the local authorities are, and they still saw this kind of music as the utmost stress to their control and power."[5] It is here, ironically the farthest he has ever been from Moscow, that Seva's career as bandleader comes to a poignant finale.

The group uses an Italian PA system (Montarbo) because there aren't any good Russian ones to be had, according to Seva. And this minor choice, albeit major for musicians with any sort of ear for decent sound, is all it takes to enrage the locals who cling to their traditions and repel anything that errs on the side of different. Dobry molodtsy might play Russian folk, but their style and jazz-rock flavor threaten societal norms. As a result, the critics tear Dobry molodtsy to shreds in the papers—"These people insult the essence of Russian music, performing on the Montarbo rubbish." As with the Joseph W. incident, Seva responds with indignation, employing more of his delightful wit and a sprinkling of spirited rage. He writes his critics a letter saying, "everyday thousands of piano players insult the memory of Tchaikovsky, Rachmaninov, Rubinstein and such by performing [their compositions] on Blutner, Beckstein, and Somme pianos." Naturally, the humor is received even more poorly than the Italian technology and the dubious reinvention of folk songs. The offended Russians send their own letter to the Moscow Ministry of Culture, lodging a formal complaint against Dobry molodtsy, and despite the usual sluggishness of state operations, for this one issue authorities are amazingly expeditious:

> I was summoned to the head of my department [at Roskontsert]. He said, "Look I have nothing against you. . . . Please don't leave the band because we need you there, but we have to do something, we have to show that we have reacted, so you are no longer bandleader."[6]

Seva graciously remains with the group for one more year, but takes the opportunity to reassess his role. At this time, fasting and meditation are fashionable and popular practices amongst musicians to address diseases of the body and mind. Seva embraces these new trends, incrementally augmenting his periods of fasting from three days to a week and then finally, towards the end of the year,

---

5 Novgorodsev, Museum of London interview.
6 Ibid.

a twenty-one-day fast in isolation, which he credits with giving him the clarity to reevaluate his life:

> Now on the sixteenth day . . . I had a spiritual experience, you know. You're half dead so your flesh is no longer there to hold the spirit and you kind of fly free of it. And I saw myself. I asked myself, you know, "what am I doing? Entertaining people . . . playing silly songs," and so I just left the whole thing there and then and went home.[7]

Making an irrevocable decision, he quits the band and the agency and returns to Leningrad in an attempt to reconnect with his family. Just as alcoholic Brezhnev suffers his first heart attack, Seva unites with ex-wife Gala and their son Renat. He's made enough money touring that he's able to stay at home for the most part, wooing Gala daily, taking his son for walks in the park per her instructions, and playing the occasional gig. Still, he feels his life is in "absolute disarray." Weeks pass, and he succeeds in persuading Gala to remarry him, although they are unable to completely heal the painful rift developed through their long separation.

Flight from Socialism

Even though Seva is all but divorced from the Soviet concert scene and remains out of the limelight, the KGB still encroaches upon his life. His wife Gala Burkhanova is a Tatar, a Turkic ethnic group mainly associated with the predominantly Muslim Tatarstan republic. Her education and exotic appearance make her an ideal employee of Aeroflot—the premier airline of the Soviet Union, which by 1975 has amassed a terrible record: a total of 721 plane crashes over forty-four years resulting in 8,231 passenger fatalities.[8] Despite the heinous statistics, Aeroflot remains the largest in terms of passengers transported of any airline in the world.

Gala works at the ticket office of Aeroflot. A fluent French speaker, she converses with foreigners passing through Leningrad en route to another country. She does her job well and does not seek to alter society in any great way. Like

---

7 Ibid.

8 Oliver Smith, "Aeroflot: From World's Deadliest Airline to One of the Safest in the Sky," *Daily Telegraph*, February 9, 2016, https://www.telegraph.co.uk/travel/news/Aeroflot-from-worlds-deadliest-airline-to-one-of-the-safest-in-the-sky/.

her husband who is a "cultural patriot," according to his self-identification, she doesn't imagine herself leaving the Soviet Union—that is, until an incident occurs.[9]

The KGB *rezident* officer where Gala works finds reason to dislike her and imagines her conspiring with Western spies. And so, he sabotages her, stealing a book of new tickets from her desk. There follows an investigation, and Gala is accused of negligence. Craftily, the KGB officer goes to her and says that he will smooth things over for her if she resigns. Mortified, Gala wants nothing more than to leave the country. However, Seva argues that the oppression of being a foreigner will outweigh the benefits: "You are going to be the same Russian speaking people in a foreign speaking land, you are never going to be on par with the local population, you are going to be second grade for as long as you live with your funny accents and your manners and being totally different." After six months of pleading, Gala and their son wear Seva down. They carefully make plans for emigration. Through a contact of Gala's, they find out if the KGB will allow them to leave the country. The answer comes unexpectedly one day: yes.

Filing their applications, they exchange their Soviet passports for exit visas and purchase many suitcases, loading them up with personal belongings and also things that can be sold for cash, like cameras. Only the equivalent of ninety dollars per person is allowed by the Soviet emigration authorities, and so other things must be brought to make ends meet in the unknown future that awaits them. The small family of three goes to the Leningrad Airport in November 1975.

Behind the barrier, friends and family members wave teary goodbyes, knowing very well they may never meet again. Gala is also in tears while their son Renat looks on in mute shock and disbelief, clinging to his mother. In Seva's hand he carries his saxophone, which he decided to take with him at the last minute.

The family of three leaves everything behind, proceeding into the unknown beyond the Iron Curtain. Ironically, they fly Aeroflot.

When in Rome

After quite a bit of unexpected traveling—first to Austria where the Jewish Agency rejects their application to enter Israel because Seva simply isn't Jewish enough and Gala "being Muslim Tartar" isn't kosher—Seva and his family

9 Novgorodsev, interview by A. Gorodetskaya, jewish.ru, January 10, 2020, https://seva.ru/media/?id=258.

finally end up in Italy by way of the International Rescue Committee. And since the agency is based in Rome, the country-less and homeless trio ends up in the beautiful city, in the tiny resort town of Lido di Ostia.[10] They settle temporarily in the so-called communist district while they wait for their emigration papers to be processed. Where they will be sent is anyone's guess, but Seva cites his marine diplomas and such in the hopes that he will look like a desirable immigrant; he doubts that his musicianship and noteworthy recordings will have a similar effect.

Living in a flat by the beach, he watches with amusement as the Partito Communista Italiano holds meetings just under his window. Seva spends his days acquainting himself with the beauty of the Italian countryside, learning Italian cooking, and making a little money.

Since the Soviet authorities took their passports, rendering them essentially refugees, Seva has to go to La Questura di Roma—the police station (part of the Ministry of the Interior)—where he applies for an Italian travel document (*titolo di viaggio*), which will allow his family to cross the border. He sits down with one of a hundred clerks in the giant building and the clerk asks for Seva's address. Seva says, "Via Umberto Cagni *ventuno*." The clerk looks surprised and says, "Oh! I also live in Umberto Cagni *ventuno*. Do you have any children?" To which Seva replies, "*Mio figlio Renat*—" And the clerk exclaims in Italian, "Oh, my name is Renato as well!" They share a pleasant giggle, and the clerk tells Seva, "*Settimana prossima*." Come back next week. So Seva does. And every week he hears the same phrase, albeit each time from a different clerk: *settimana prossima*.

Having brought suitcases full of saleable items as permitted according to the customs lists, Seva and other émigrés participate in the Sunday "trade" at a market called Americana on Porta Poese, located in a bombed-out part of Rome:

> [T]here was a slum area which was transformed into a, just an ordinary sort of . . . Portobello Market type, you know, all sorts of things were sold there and there was a Russian section. . . . And Italians tended to like it because pension owners could buy good quality sheets for cheap and camera shop owners could buy new Russian cameras for next to nothing. The trade was brisk, and we would start at four in the morning, arrive while it was still dark, bonfires burning you know. And in this dilapidated shack there was this tiny little Neapolitan prostitute who was old by then,

---

10 Novgorodsev, Museum of London interview.

> with the most powerful voice you could ever hear, and she would rent the food boxes for us, a pound a piece for a day, so you had something to put your stuff on. . . .

Seva and fellow Russian traders observe KGB operatives watching over a stall selling records of Western music. Seva jokes, "Maybe they want a camera, too." This is how they spend their day, every Sunday, trading in the Porta Poese:

> Obviously, we were not used to trade, and it was pretty degrading, I mean we felt degraded anyway. So, by 10:30 when the bars were open the three of us—me, the musician and navigator; the dentist next to me; and there was some sort of designer, technical designer—used to get sloshed on a bottle of vodka and spend the rest of the day being quite merry and irresponsible. But it gave me my first taste of trade, you're never out of pocket, something is always sold, there is . . . a little money always to be made.[11]

During these days he haggles with some passing Dutch students and buys his first car: a VW Beetle for a whopping $180. The license plate is Dutch and features the letters DJ, although this means nothing to Seva at the time.

The building in which Seva and his family live teems with émigrés, and so visitors are always coming and going. One day, a former classmate of Gala's from Leningrad University appears at the doorstep of their building—Leo Feigin.[12] He recognizes Gala and exuberates over encountering her here of all places. But when he sees Seva, he fairly explodes. A former jazz fan of Seva's from the Joseph W. days, Feigin cannot understand what such a talent is doing in a shabby little flat outside of Rome. Feigin explains that he's now working with the BBC World Service, living in London, and is only in Rome to visit his mother who is en route to America. He urges Seva to join the BBC Russian Service. At his wife's eager prodding, Seva agrees to take the necessary exams and translator qualifications. Having already immersed himself in English and worked as a tour guide for the Soviet travel agency Intourist, he passes the exams easily. The BBC is ready for him to come aboard, but the proper papers have yet to come through.

During one of his fruitless visits to Questura, Seva finds himself seated next to an American man, also about thirty-seven years old. Blonde, blue-eyed, this man sees that Seva is reading a volume in English. He strikes up a conversation with

---

11 Ibid.

12 Preferred transliteration.

Seva, introducing himself as Joel. Apparently, this Joel works with the Vatican as part of the American Baptist mission in the film commission and is seeking an interpreter for film screenings. Thus, Seva begins to work with Joel, going to meetings where they show popular scientific films with underlying religious themes. As the months go by, the audiences grow larger:

> So, this Joel started taking me around, meeting other people from other missions, giving me literature to read. Meanwhile, I slowly realize that I probably will never leave Italy, because they can't find my file, it's been lost in the depths of Italian bureaucracy. And while reading all this literature that Joel gave me, I gradually came to a logical conclusion about the, you know, the structure of the universe, the reasons for its existence, etc.[13]

Frustrated with his limbo status, Seva approaches Joel and asks to be baptized, the final anti-Soviet, pro-Western sacrament. "I said, 'Okay, Joel, I accept' and [told him] just organize things as you see fit." Joel takes him to a four-hundred-year-old church in Rome in Piazzo di Popolo and there in the heated marble *font* he baptizes Seva, and the musician is reborn.

A few days later, on a Wednesday, Seva again goes to Questura and somehow ends up seeing the exact same clerk as the very first time—Renato. He looks at Seva without recognition at first but then something clicks in his head. *Umberto Cagni ventuno . . . Figlio Renat . . . Porque madona!* Renato opens the drawer in his desk, and there, inside, lies Seva's file—and *only* Seva's file. The clerk hastens to scribble on it in bold: "*URGENTA*." Within ten days, Seva and his family leave Rome behind and fly to London, to a new land, where an entirely different adventure begins.[14]

---

13 Novgorodsev, interview with author, September 2015.

14 Ibid.

Part Two

1976–91

CHAPTER 8

Smoke on the Water

> Of course, DJs must have some technical knowhow, but in my opinion, what is much more important is that they should have had some musical education. Music is one of the most powerful means of education, of forming a world view. . . . Just as medicine should be in the hands of specialists, so too, should music.[1]

London is a far cry from Moscow or Leningrad in 1976—not just in the narrow winding roads or the double-decker buses or the sound of English with its many vernaculars, but in the city's very atmosphere. This is the Imagined West, and it is not quite as any Soviet citizen *imagined* it to be. Seva, however, appreciates the culture, which he perceives to be noncompetitive, and the quiet speech of the English, remembering with distaste the sheer volume and overbearing nature of the American tourists he had guided around Leningrad.[2] "I felt comfortable in England from the very beginning," he recalls, "because it was my kind of theoretical motherland in a way."[3] Additionally, he finds that he fits right in at the World Service; and not only fits, but is able to easily interact with virtually any employee:

> Now, in Russia, I had problems of finding friends because my criteria were: he must have some sort of higher education, be interested in Western culture, be a decent person, not be connected with the KGB, you know, and . . . how do you find them? Now the first day I entered the BBC meeting room, there they all have

---

1 Vitaly Kiselev, *Molodyozh' Moldavy*, November 1984, As featured in Lorna Bourdeaux's *Valeri Barinov: The Trumpet Call* (London: Marshall Morgan & Scott, Ltd., 1985), 42.

2 "Seva Novgorodsev," *Vremenno dostupen*, May 24, 2009, TV Center, television broadcast.

3 Novgorodsev, Museum of London interview.

> higher education, they all speak English, they definitely are *not* connected with the KGB, they're interested in Western culture. So, the BBC Personnel have sort of seized them for me. . . . All of them became my friends to various degrees. So that was wonderful, coming to work and not feeling a foreigner. . . .[4]

Despite his diminished status as an immigrant in this new land, Seva has unseen forces working in his favor when he arrives in the thrumming capital of this faded colonial power. In fact, the timing of his career change simply could not be better. Thanks to détente, a host of cultural products from the West have flooded the Eastern Bloc and the main urban centers of Russia. In Soviet Ukraine, as well, Western films and British hard rock bands have become (since roughly 1975) the most popular commodities among youth, spreading to and infecting even the most provincial cities and towns.[5] The admiration for British rock is largely due to geographical factors, as LPs from American rock bands are harder to come by. Moreover, unlike jazz, which is "still elitist," the hard rock that invaded the USSR during the '70s, in the words of Sergei Zhuk, "led to mass pop music consumption which affected millions of Soviet young people by the end of the Brezhnev era."[6]

Thus, not only is rock music unimaginably popular across multiple sectors of the Soviet population from young industrial workers and peasant migrants to city dwellers,[7] but also physical copies of the music, the original LPs, are hard to come by, leading to an increased valuation of imported cultural products—*and* of information. For example, in Ukraine, only periodicals such as *Rovesnik* and *Komsomol'skaia pravda*[8] and Russian broadcasts from Moscow give the youth any information about the music and the artists themselves. Such resources are limited, although as the '80s approach, the Soviet authorities attempt to engage the youth in dialogue through a flurry of articles that start to appear in all the

---

4 Ibid.

5 Sergei I. Zhuk, "Paradoxes of Identity Construction during Détente," in *Youth and Rock in the Soviet Bloc* (Lanham: Lexington Books, 2017), 138.

6 Ibid.

7 Ibid. Though Zhuk is referring mainly to Soviet Ukraine, the same applies to other parts of the Eastern Bloc and Soviet Russia, though to a lesser extent as Western cultural imports have further to go to reach Moscow versus Kyiv.

8 A newspaper founded in 1925 in the USSR as an official all-union publication and an official arm of the Central Committee of the Komsomol. According to BBC Monitoring, the paper reached peak distribution in Russia in 1990 with twenty-two million copies.

typical publications on the subject of rock music.[9] All this official information is expectedly laden with political messaging, conspiratorial exaggeration, and anti-Western refrains with desperate choruses: *the CIA is the malignant root of all rock* OR *according to physicians, rock music is exceedingly harmful.*

Consequently, by forbidding and depriving the youth of the products and information they so greatly desire, the Soviet government inadvertently contributes to the "intense idealization" of Western culture. "Cultural fixation" arises, causing young people to actively seek out Western sources of information.[10] Here, foreign broadcasting plays a significant role and makes a marked, widespread difference, especially in Russia, where youth have far less access to physical imports than in republics located on the fringe of the West. Thus, for the soon-to-be DJ, the culturally embedded dependence on Western radio and extreme "cultural fixation" on Western products open up tremendous opportunities—and promote deeper psychological erosion in the USSR.

Seva in his BBC studio, circa 1977 (credit: seva.ru)

9 Bourdeaux, *Valeri Barinov*, 41. Roth-Ey also writes: "By the 1970s, listeners in the Soviet Union had access to an unprecedented range of programming, from sports to radio theater to pop music to documentaries and youth-oriented talk shows to news. Yet late Soviet radio, for all its diversity and sophistication, retained fundamental vocal parameters." This meant that most Soviet presenters sounded staid, as listeners attest, since the "barriers" to personalization were great and there was little to no "emotional latitude." See Roth-Ey, "Listening out," 571.

10 Zhuk, "Paradoxes of Identity Construction during Détente," 138–39.

The First Broadcast

In the new country, Seva and his family must forge a new identity and sense of place. The problem of where to permanently settle is foremost on his mind as he learns quickly to abhor public transportation, which has all the reliability of an old mule. Early in his probationary period, the busses have already made him late to work several times. "Bus number fifteen—just forget it—from Kensington; they used to play dominoes on the terminal stations so the buses would either not come at all or come five—you know, zoom-zoom-zoom—one after another." Thus, London turns him into a dedicated cyclist, and out of necessity, his residence has to be within a five-mile radius of Bush House. As it happens, he finds a Camden address that fits the bill, though the structure is dilapidated and in desperate need of renovations.[11] Furthermore, this "ruin of a house," as Seva calls it, has a sitting tenant protected by English labor laws who is a confirmed constituent of the Communist Party:

> The tenant, Mr. Stanley Pitt, moved into this house in the 1930s when he was a boy of nine. Completely asexual, a loner with no family, a trade union activist, and a member of the Communist Party! [. . .] I could not afford a builder and was slaving away every night after work, moving around London on an old bicycle to save money. Tired, dirty, smeared in plaster. . . .
>
> Mr. Pitt, always on the dot at 7:30, used to go to his pub around the corner where he spent all his adult life. Always whistling, merrily and in tune. Always saying to me the same sentence (with a dose of sarcasm): "Enjoying yourself?" And I thought: "I ran away from communism only to find it downstairs in my house!"[12]

Despite such proximal aggravations, Seva diligently goes about his new line of work. Every day for six months, he puts in his eight hours at the Bush House, cycles to Camden where he repairs the ramshackle building, then returns to his flat and his family late at night, only to do it all over again the next day. He works himself to complete exhaustion:

---

11 Novgorodsev, Museum of London interview.

12 Novgorodsev, correspondence with author, September 17, 2015.

> Six months later when just one floor, the kitchen, and the living room were ready, I was covered with some unsightly sort of red pimples all over. It was nervous stress plus over-work plus probably bad diet or whatever, but I did succeed, I did manage to get this house right and we moved in, and I was just gaining more and more space in it as the years went by.[13]

In his cycling to and from Bush House, he makes note of unsubtle men watching him. "There were a lot of KGB intrigues around us," he says, and also around his parents in Leningrad. He hears that his father, as a result, has become seriously sick. This is proving "a dangerous game," but Seva doesn't stop playing, or rather he doesn't have much choice. He has to earn a living, he has responsibilities, and there is no turning back now. "I risked my freedom and even life just to earn a few hundred pounds."[14]

As a novice broadcaster, he begins with reading news and simple translations over the air, converting English to Russian:

> Now to earn a little more money I was involved in technical translations. Because being trained as some sort of engineer you have some technical know-how. And technical translations were plentiful at the time because Russians were buying lots of equipment and all the documentation had to come with it. . . . But a few months later when I managed to get the technique together it was getting faster. I could just read off the page, reading English, saying Russian into my microphone. My wife was spitting brass tacks at me whenever I was missing a comma or a full stop or my diction wasn't good enough, so under pressure from her I was more and more meticulous in my dictation. So out of need a technique was born.[15]

He starts to painstakingly pre-record each script, then type it out and edit it for on-air reading. After a short time, because of his music background, the management suggests he should co-host the Russian language show *The Program of Pop Music from London*. Seva does not immediately jump at the notion, no doubt because the sort of music being aired—modern rock and pop—does not match his tastes.

---

13 Ibid.
14 Tolkunov, "Seva Novgorodsev."
15 Novgorodsev, Museum of London interview.

Then, the current DJ of the program, Sam Jones (Sam Yossman), a man with Lithuanian roots who had fought in the Israeli military, suddenly leaves for America to try his hand at business (although his departure is hardly permanent).[16] The responsibility unquestionably falls on Seva—who else is there with not only deep Russian and Soviet understanding but also musical experience and a time-developed stage personality?

Still, Seva hesitates, "not filled with any personal ambition." He is, after all, a jaded musician who has spent years adroitly slipping between the cracks of official society and the cultural underground, avoiding KGB attention. How could deejaying a pop music program from London keep him out of trouble? However, Gala's intense prodding wins out, and Seva accepts the position and the risk, launching headlong into new and unfamiliar territory:

> There was no DJ genre in Russia when I started, so I learned from my English colleagues, the stars of BBC Radio 1 and Radio 2—I had my heroes there to whom I listened every day, trying to translate their technique into Russian language. It was quite difficult at times, because no one, myself included, had that art of speaking for a given number of seconds. If you look at my old scripts, you see markings that say you have thirty-two seconds to introduce the next music, and you should start from the third second and finish by the thirtieth, to allow some time for mixing. So, I wrote scripts first, measuring with a stopwatch how many words I should utter, at what speed, etc.[17]

Overlaying Stevie Wonder's "Sir Duke," Seva's mellow, distinctively Russian voice, passing through a BBC compressor, makes its first solo on-air introduction on June 10, 1977, a very different experience for him than his performance career.[18] On stage, one can see and hear and feel those who are listening and watching, but behind a microphone in a soundproof studio, there's no way to know who, where, when, or how an audience might be listening. Nevertheless, as a past listener, he doesn't have to operate entirely on blind faith. He has heard this program:

---

16 "I'm a BBC Patriot," Lithuanian Jewish Community, February 25, 2016, https://www.lzb.lt/en/2016/02/25/im-a-bbc-patriot/.

17 Novgorodsev, interview by Matthew Orr, March 28, 2019, in *The Slavic Connexion*, podcast.

18 Roth-Ey notes that Seva "had a loose-limbed vocal style, a lightly ironic, conversational approach. . . . Seva was at once more and less fathomable than either Conover or Goldberg. His voice, audibly made-in-the-USSR . . . was a radically individual and un-Soviet one." Roth-Ey, "Listening out," 573.

> I had been touring Russia with a band for twelve years before the emigration, so I understood the audience: to what they react to, and to what [they] don't. It was very important for me not to leave people indifferent. Then, during the tour, I saw enough of the hardships of young people in faraway towns, who felt absolutely miserable. So, I was very sympathetic towards young people. Therefore, I tried to entertain them, I tried to show them that there is some other way of life. . . . In general, I treated them like friends, and it was important for me that the program was captivating and funny—I don't know why, but I felt it was important. . . .[19]

Сева Новгородцев

ПРОГРАММА ПОПУЛЯРНОЙ МУЗЫКИ   сост. 9 июня 77 г.

ГРАМС : SIR DUKE on 52 5" - V.O.(10")
Добрый вечер и привет из Лондона.Сегодня речь пойдёт о самых популярных пластинках недели - как здесь,в Англии,так и в Соединённых Штатах. SIR DUKE on 2'57" V.O. (33") on 3'47" CR.F

ГРАМС : Популярность пластинки определяется не жюри и не критиками - она решается за прилавками магазинов. Чем больше покупают какую-нибудь пластинку,тем больше у ней шансов оказаться на верху списка.
И если песня опустилась на двадцатое место,как,например,эта, это вовсе не значит,что она стала менее популярной - её просто меньше покупают,она уже у всех есть. Американский певец и композитор СТИВИ УАНДЕР и песня СЭР ДЬЮК - на двадцатом месте в Англии ,на третьем - в Соединённых Штатах.

ГРАМС : HOTEL CALIFORNIA on 31" V.O. (25") on 5'40" Cross fade
Это - песня "ОТЕЛЬ КАЛИФОРНИЯ" в исполнении группы ИГЛЗ - ОРЛЫ, которая стоит на девятом месте в Британском списке и на 25 -м в американском. Однако долгоиграющая пластинка,откуда взята эта песня в течение уже нескольких недель находится в числе наиболее популярных - как в Англии,так и в Америке. Расправьте крылья,ОРЛЫ !

ГРАМС : GOOD MORNING JUDGE on 4" V.C. (14") on 2'48" CR.F.
На пятом месте - песня "ГУД МОНИН ДЖАДЖ" - С ДОБРЫМ УТРОМ,СУДЬЯ и группа 10 СС,название которой обозначается на бумаге цифрой 10 и двумя русскими буквами "С". С ДОБРЫМ УТРОМ,СУДЬЯ ..

Seva's first broadcast script (credit: seva.ru)

---

19 Novgorodsev, in *The Slavic Connexion*, podcast, https://www.slavxradio.com/seva-in-russian. See also Sheeran, *Cultural Politics in International Relations*, 85.

Indeed, he has, through his travels, toured the country, seen some of the remotest regions, and learnt of the many unfortunate situations in the USSR, particularly those of young women and Muslim communities under the thumb of the KGB. He thinks now that he has the chance to provide the people, those audiences he can still visualize, some "spiritual support."[20] Striving to be as entertaining as possible from the start, he naturally employs the humor he knows, and has known from youth, to enliven his listeners' situations. He works to write jokes that are short and funny. He stays until two or three in the morning in the office, testing these jokes on colleagues who work the night shift. If they don't laugh, he rewrites them. Gradually, he develops a style that defines the genre and makes him an aural sensation.[21] Even in a pop music program from London, he covers history and in doing so makes history himself in an early episode:

> Good evening, friends. In today's issue of *Melody Maker*, on page six in "News from the United States," is an article called "Beach Boys and Santana Go to Russia." A message from San Francisco journalist Joel Salton reports that on July 4, the Americans' Independence Day, in Leningrad on Palace Square, will be a free concert featuring the Beach Boys, Santana, and Joan Baez. According to estimates, there could be roughly 250,000 in attendance. . . . The concert is funded by the famous denim company Levi Strauss. . . .
>
> In San Francisco on this occasion, a press conference gathered, where they all talked about the development of cultural exchange, about the friendship of youth. A representative from the Soviet consulate also spoke, saying everything that is supposed to be said in such cases: about the strengthening of friendship between the Soviet and American peoples, about the exchange of cultural values. I read the article—I was happy, it's a good message printed in *Melody Maker*. But what's this? In small type under the article is the following: "When the newspaper went to print, on Tuesday, we were informed the concert was canceled. . . ."
>
> So, how to explain such an incident? The *Daily Mail* writes: "Political observers believe that the concert was the victim of a sharp cold snap between the Soviet Union and the United States. In addition," the newspaper writes, "Brezhnev always feared that free access to pop music for Soviet youth will lead to increased

20 "Seva Novgorodsev," *Vremenno dostupen*, May 24, 2009, TV Center, television broadcast.

21 Novgorodsev, Museum of London interview.

> influence of Western ideology." For Soviet leaders, this concert was supposed to be a kind of showcase, an ostentatious event, refuting the view that behind the Iron Curtain are persecuted rock bands.
>
> The article says that about two million dollars were spent on the preparation of the concert, a huge amount of equipment and radio equipment was already on the way to Leningrad. . . . British cinematographer Dmitri De Grunwald spent about two years organizing the event and invested about a million dollars in it, according to the newspaper. Last week, he was summoned to Moscow by phone. Over dinner, for vodka and caviar, he was told no. "But why?" asked Grunwald incessantly. "Unfortunately, it is impossible, impossible," was the unvarying answer. It was useless to address the top, the newspaper says, for apparently, the decision was made at a high government level, perhaps even in the Kremlin, and how can you fight invisible giants?
>
> From Russia, a newspaper writes, nothing is heard about the youth's reaction, and in time the authorities will, of course, find an excuse for the canceled concert. "We have nothing against popular music," they will say. . . . But they hardly mention how young people in many Russian towns fashion guitar pickups from handsets and include them in amplifiers from movie mobile installations. They don't mention the prices of the latest records of famous rock bands. "Perhaps, even the workers who take apart the huge iron pipes and boards in Palace Square understand that they're breaking something more than the usual concert stage."[22]

This broadcast excerpt represents one of the earliest examples of how Seva begins to develop his brand of international rock journalism; he incorporates multiple sources from California to London to St. Petersburg, delivering a story pieced together from verified facts, government intentions, *and* political tensions, all filtered through the cultural lens he shares with his massive target audience. As proof that even Seva's broadcasts have a listenership, a future secretary of the Leningrad Rock Club recalls with clarity hearing Seva announce the Beach Boys and Santana concert and then the subsequent cancellation as well:

> The organization of the concert was in full swing, the announcement given by Seva Novgorodsev in his broadcast on the BBC;

22 *Rok-posevy*, June 30, 1978, radio broadcast, https://seva.ru/rock/?id=29&y=1978.

> there was even a note in the party city newspaper *Leningradskaia pravda,* but almost at the last moment everything was canceled, of course. Thousands of people had come. They were dispersed [by police], including by water cannons. In general, nothing happened except the crackdown.[23]

At a time when music and politics are indivisible, such on-air rock journalism is undoubtedly even more important for reaching and informing the general public than broadcast news and political commentary. Seva's approach is digestible for both the adamantly apolitical and the pro-Soviet rock lover.[24] Indeed, Seva's program represents the start of a critical component of the international education of the USSR youth—and their liberation as well.

The Poison Umbrella

Among the many émigré recruits at the BBC's External Services is Georgi Markov, a Bulgarian writer who defected from his country in 1969 despite a close relationship with the president Todor Zhivkov and his daughter, head of culture for Bulgaria, Ludmila Zhivkova. Georgi works in a studio right next to Seva's on the fifth floor, in the southeast wing of Bush House. Since defection, Markov has been and continues to be a freelance contributor to RFE, the scripts for which, according to his English wife Annabel who also works for the BBC, are "highly critical of the Bulgarian government" and particularly "vitriolic" following the death of Markov's father in 1977.[25] Seva is acquainted with Markov and his wife but is careful to maintain social distance when outside the safety of Bush House, knowing the nature of Georgi's emigration. Zhivkov's continued favor keeps Markov out of trouble; nearly a decade after leaving Bulgaria, Markov is yet untouched. While his work for RFE is obviously controversial, there is nothing political about his work at the BBC, a credit to the strict broadcast guidelines all but forbidding personal commentary on government matters.[26]

After years of incendiary RFE broadcasts, in early 1978 the final straw for the Bulgarian government comes when Markov reads on RFE straight from his

---

23 Olga Slobodskaya (former secretary of the Leningrad Rock Club) in correspondence with author, January 2021.

24 According to several TV, radio, and print interviews, Seva was mainly interested in the spiritual and intellectual state of his listeners, in providing them "spiritual support" and alleviating their suffering, which is why humor became his tool.

25 "Bulgarian Dissident Killed by Poisoned Umbrella at London Bus Stop," *Guardian,* September 14, 2012.

26 Ibid.

memoirs, which contain, amongst other things, particularly harsh criticism of Zhivkov. Markov begins to receive death threats and, as a result, grows paranoid. Then, on September 7, on his way to Bush House, while crossing Waterloo Bridge over the Thames, he feels a sharp sting in his leg. He looks behind him in time to see a man in bowler hat and striped trousers—codename Piccadilly, as it is later revealed—pick up an umbrella that he presumably dropped and jump into a taxi. Arriving at Bush House, Markov tells a few colleagues, including Seva, about the incident, but most think the tale farfetched and symptomatic of his paranoia. By evening, however, the pain hasn't subsided, and he's taken to the hospital with a high fever. Four days later, he dies. The cause of death is determined to be a ricin-filled pellet embedded in his leg.[27]

Investigators find several bystanders, who'd been at the same bus stop on the Strand, one of London's busiest streets, who testify, in curiously accurate detail, that Markov had been stabbed with an umbrella by a "Communist agent 'with a thick foreign accent.'" The press descend on the BBC's head of Europe Region for a comment: "I just visited Bulgaria and had a wonderfully warm welcome. So, I say that the possibility of foul play is very remote indeed." Seva and his colleagues mount on a wall of Bush House a five-by-ten-foot poster, which he'd instigated, called "Self-Delusion." The poster features an old photograph of black plantation hands playing poker, two of them passing a card under the table with their feet. The caption reads, mocking the BBC's head of Europe: "The possibility of foul play is very remote indeed."[28]

The Markov case is never fully resolved, though by January of the following year, a London court rules that he was murdered and according to a forensic scientist the ricin pellet in his thigh matched that which had been injected into another Bulgarian defector in Paris.[29] KGB involvement is not directly confirmed at this time, but it is at least publicly suggested, and Seva, like many of his colleagues, is now more on edge.

Seva can hear the ticking on the phone whenever he calls his mother in Leningrad, indicating that the KGB is listening. Nothing can be said either verbally or in writing. His mother asks him tearfully, "When will you stop this? When you die?" But he's just barely started, and he feels pressed now to make the most of his position. Like the founders of the BBC, he understands that the microphone is a sacred thing—a powerful tool. So, what will he say?

---

27 Jack Anderson, "Assassination in London," *Washington Post*, September 8, 1991. See also Andrew and Gordievsky, *KGB*, 644–45, for KGB insider account.

28 Novgorodsev, *"Markov I Zhivkov,"* BBC.com, September 2, 2016, https://www.bbc.com/russian/blog-seva-37236233.

29 "World News Briefs," *New York Times*, January 3, 1979.

Featured Listener: Andrey

I lived for five years in Czechoslovakia when I was school age. My parents were working there. I started listening to Seva when I was thirteen or fourteen years old. I had the best radio in the Soviet Union—my father gave it to me—and it was very expensive for that time. 280 rubles. The monthly salary of the average person was 130 rubles. So, it was more than double. My father just earned a very good salary. For that reason, I always heard the BBC, some of Voice of America. But Radio Svoboda—no. Because I didn't like their programming. On the BBC it was mainly intelligent, educated people giving cultural programs, such as about books, new and interesting books. So, I listened to Seva always, and I listened to Sam Jones. I even called in to Sam Jones. And to call someone you had to go to the post office, you had to write your name and number on a paper and give it to the operator. And at one post office I was told this number does not exist because it was in London. The second post office, I succeeded, and they connected me with Sam Jones. But it was too late by then, they had moved on to another topic. I never wrote any letters to Seva. I preferred to just listen to the broadcasts and to later travel to the UK...

Seva for me is always the sole interaction between Russia and the West. I listened to Seva in the first place because he was an intellectual—intelligent—person. Seva helped me to establish myself as a man of culture. Since it was when I was young. It was very interesting for me to know if Seva smoked. Because I wanted to be like him. Whether he was drinking or not, didn't matter. But smoking! That was very important for me to know.

Now what do I listen to? I listen to jazz, Swiss jazz. And I started to listen to Radio Svoboda because there are no more broadcasts about culture for us on the BBC Russian Service. On Radio Liberty, I am listening to Artemy Troitsky and before that Dmitry Savitsky.[30]

---

30 Dmitri Savitsky was a Soviet-born, Russian French writer and poet who hosted the program *Vremya dzhaza* at Radio Liberty from 1989–2004. Interview conducted by author and S. Pantsirev in St. Petersburg, May 2019.

CHAPTER 9

Round Midnight

> This is your program, *Moscow Mailbag*. . . . The first letter today comes from Dan Gendren of West Warwick, Rhode Island: "What will happen if the Salt II is rejected here in the United States?" Well, very unpleasant things will happen . . . There will be the loss of the most elementary trust between [our countries], and I'm afraid we will go back to the dark days of the Cold War. There will be the continuation of an unbridled arms race that will cost billions. Incidentally, did you know that the world spends one billion dollars per day on arms, as if inflation isn't enough in the West, or that you haven't had enough of it. Then, what will happen? New monstrous weapons and weapon systems will be developed, and certainly the danger of a nuclear holocaust will be much greater than it is now. Not to mention the fact that there will be a general worsening of the international situation. So, I think it is absolutely in the interest of your people, no less than it is of ours, to see that Salt II is ratified.
>
> —Joe Adamov, host of Radio Moscow's *Moscow Mailbag*, from a 1979 broadcast to North America[1]

While the Soviet establishment concerns itself mainly with the continual nuclear threat presented by the American West, which bleeds into Radio Moscow's international broadcasts, Seva carries on with his new work as a broadcaster, continually honing his craft and developing technical as well as oratory skills to improve his performance. Though he broadcasts Deep Purple, Queen, and Black Sabbath, he personally continues listening to and practicing jazz, albeit in greater freedom than ever before, proving he is a musician in word and deed.

---

1 For more on Radio Moscow's English-language program *Moscow Mailbag*, see the WNYC archive: https://www.wnyc.org/series/radio-moscow/about. This program was aired prior to the signing of the Salt II treaty by President Jimmy Carter and Leonid Brezhnev on June 18, 1979, in Vienna. See Lawrence Freedman, "Salt II and the Strategic Balance," *The World Today* 35, no. 8 (1979): 315–23.

Playing the saxophone and also the flute keeps him mentally sane despite the "mad speed of work and permanent brain tension." While he doesn't actively seek gigs or opportunities to perform, a few chances do come his way. Mainly, however, it is to and from Bush House he goes, meticulously preparing and recording program after program after program. His impressive rock knowledge is built painstakingly, and he approaches the genre from an intellectual standpoint—it's not his tempo, but he can clinically appreciate the genre if he must.[2] He is thirty-seven years old when he begins his career, broadcasting a popular music program, which, although not explicitly for youth, earns mainly youth attention. Thus, he must play what is current:

> I had to move like a surfer on his board, catching the latest waves of changing musical styles. I got through punk, grunge, new wave, and other subcultures. And I think that any mentally healthy and balanced person struggles against new things in life, especially against new music. . . . I had to step over myself all the time and it was not a pleasant experience. . . . I listened to at least ten–fifteen albums a week. At one point, I learned how to listen with my musical ear to ten–fifteen seconds of each song just to understand if it consisted of some melodically interesting ideas or good vocals.[3]

Over these first few years, unbeknownst to him, the popularity of his thirty-minute weekly pop broadcast grows exponentially. In Russia and Ukraine and regions where the BBC's Russkaya sluzhba is received, Friday nights with Seva become a ritual, sometimes for the entire household, though many of the older generation remain wary of listening for fear of either the repercussions or concern about the mental corruption the Kremlin has warned them of.[4] Despite jamming, many listeners across the USSR are able, with a little (or a lot of) work, to tune in to the BBC's shortwaves, though some within range of major jamming stations aren't so lucky and remain amazed that anyone can hear Seva at all.

Dmitry Tolkunov, barely a teenager living in Moscow, cannot get a clear signal for the BBC; it's all distortion and crunchy noise with fragments of Seva's compressed voice and jarring snippets of music. As he says: "Trying to catch BBC radio waves turned into a kind of risky national sport which improved the

2 Roth-Ey, "Listening out," 569.
3 Tolkunov, "Seva Novgorodsev."
4 From correspondence with former Soviet listeners carried out between 2018 and 2020.

technical skills of many young Soviets who invented special antennas and even customized their radios by soldering extra diapasons in order to catch the voices from the other side."[5]

Just as Seva had in his youth tried to circumvent the Soviet jamming of Willis Conover, young people now work to tune into Seva's broadcast, an endeavor that Seva labels a game of "catch me if you can."[6] The KGB keeps judicious tabs on his every broadcast, transcribing them to send to the Central Committee of the Communist Party. But logically, in order to do so, they have to be able to hear the rock presenter, and so they leave a frequency unjammed. Even in the city, people are inventive enough to amplify this KGB-designated narrow bandwidth.

The need for such technical know-how and willpower does create a barrier to entry for many, but not everyone has to become a tech guru to listen, and often moving the radio set from one side of the room to the other can achieve the desired results.[7] Furthermore, outside the city the chance of hearing foreign broadcasters markedly increases. The military and countryside dachas are at the greatest advantage and get the best reception. Given that the Kremlin undertakes "selective jamming" at this time, prioritizing certain broadcasters and certain broadcasts in an effort to obstruct political commentary and news, the culture programs sometimes get through.[8] As the '80s begin, Seva's program becomes an exception to the culture rule. However, in the end, jamming may be of little consequence overall:

> In distant rural areas, jamming wasn't efficient, but villagers had almost no interest for such broadcasts. Nevertheless, in the small towns there were young people who liked rock music, and for them Seva was the main and sometimes the only source of information. Scarce jamming there enabled them not only to

---

5 Tolkunov, "Seva Novgorodsev." Tolkunov further writes that one of the main reasons for the KGB's extreme jamming efforts was that Seva's music programs "became one of the main sources of knowledge about what was going on at that moment in Western music, . . . [which] made Seva . . . a hero . . . and helped a lot of generations . . . expand their mind and understand that there was a bright and interesting world on the other side of the border."

6 Ibid. The use of the word "catch" by so many listeners, and Seva himself, indicates the sense of gain or achievement associated with receiving desired voices and, conversely, a sense of loss or losing out when the voices can't be heard.

7 Vassily Aksyonov, interview by Brian Lamb, C-SPAN, November 1, 1989, television broadcast, https://www.c-span.org/video/?9801-1/say-cheese.

8 Mark Pomar (former director of VOA Russian Service) in discussion with author, December 2020. See also Sheeran, *Cultural Politics in International Relations*, 94.

> listen to him regularly but to record the music on tape. (Due to multiple subsequent copying, the music records which villagers owned were often of such low quality that the sound of a shortwave transmission was even better.) It should be noted that Soviet receivers were of rather good quality. My classmate had a Panasonic radio, but he sometimes had to come to me to listen as mine [Soviet make] was better. The jamming station was within two km of my house and interfered even with tape recorders and LP players.[9]

Realizing that a significant audience is developing for the BBC's "Cinderella hour" DJ—so-called because of the midnight time his broadcast airs in Moscow—the Soviet government forces state TV networks to schedule their programs for the same slot as Seva's half-hour show.[10] "In the 70s and 80s [the government view of Seva] was definitely negative. Even during *perestroika*. The popular TV show *Vzglyad* (View or Look) . . . which many regard as a sign of new times, was most probably launched to counteract Seva, as the time of its broadcast coincided with that of Seva's transmission, and the father of one of its journalists was a KGB man."[11]

This deliberate scheduling seems to begin in 1981, when in fact Russian rock is gaining status and traction with the Komsomol. The cultural authorities undoubtedly prefer to generate their own rock informational content at home than allow an "anti-Soviet" traitor to fill the ears of millions of citizens.[12] The overlap in programming is so noticeable that letter writers cannot resist mentioning all the competition:

> As you know, Seva, at 23:00, the Yankees also transmit pop music from the enemy voice—but you have some enterprising competitors from Moscow television, which are now broadcasting

---

9 K. Zaitzev (listener), correspondence with author, March 2019.

10 William Kremer, "The DJ Who 'Brought down the USSR,'" BBC.com, September 5, 2015, https://www.bbc.com/news/magazine-34157596.

11 K. Zaitzev, correspondence with author, March 2019. Seva states in his interview with Tolkunov in *All Andorra* that *Vzglyad*, which in his opinion was "really revolutionary for its time," was started on order of the Central Committee to draw young people away from his programs. "One of *Vzglyad*'s presenters told me about it and he was the son of a KGB general . . . As you see, everything was really challenging."

12 Seva is repeatedly referred to as "anti-Soviet" and a "traitor" in a number of state-run publications during the '80s. This remains the "official" view until *perestroika* and then, after 1990, the narrative completely flips.

> foreign stage melodies at 23:00. At first, they show all kinds of renegades like Karel Gott, after which come soreness and itchy allergies, followed by a couple of sketches on the same television program from the Warsaw Block, and at the conclusion, even Gloria Gainer or [Whitney] Houston may appear.[13]

Another listener attests that perhaps this tactic is even more effective than jamming: "No doubt, jamming affected the number of listeners very strongly. It is just human psychology: the majority prefers easy ways, even if they are rotten (in this case 'the easy way' was Soviet television and Soviet radio)."[14] But even these state-level machinations—so-called soft power combatting soft power—do not deter Seva's rise to fame: "From the 1970s onwards, the show drew vast audiences. . . . His unique radio voice, its intonation and character, was a revelation in comparison with the usual wooden style of Soviet broadcasters."[15]

Democratizing rock music and information throughout the USSR, Seva's programs begin to influence Soviet counterculture. They are not anti-Soviet, but they can hardly qualify as pro-Soviet either, which makes him seem like an agent of MI-5 to the KGB. Of course, he is no such thing. Yet, he encourages without directly encouraging his fellow countrymen and women to shrug their shoulders at the beast of Bolshevism, which contributes to the development of his voice—much like with his saxophone. He, as a presenter, must cultivate a certain personality:

> The next point I think is the clandestine nature of my first attempts to be what I became. . . . You can imagine the BBC, it's a former imperial radio, a sort of world service. . . . Initially all the presenters in the studio had to wear bowties. It was a very stuffy thing, and only people from a certain background were

---

13 Novgorodsev reading a letter from Yevgeny of Kyiv, *Rok-posevy*, October 16, 1981, radio broadcast.

14 Eugen Neumann (listener), correspondence with author, Feb 26, 2019. Corroborating Eugen's sentiments, Roth-Ey writes in her 2020 article, "To listen through jamming required application, yet Novgorodsev's correspondents tended to describe all 'listening out' as a purposeful act, subject to discipline and reflection, even when their audition was not hindered. And jamming as a presence—again, even in its material absence—also contributed a sense of drama to listening." See Roth-Ey, "Listening out," 563.

15 Sheeran, *Cultural Politics in International Relations*, 93. Not all Soviet broadcasters are in fact "wooden," and someone who should be noted for his subtle acts of defiance on air starting in 1983 while working for Radio Moscow is Alexander Danchev. Also on Radio Moscow, Joe Adamov, host of American programs, presented an interesting, if not successful, attempt to make scripted responses sound improvised and natural.

> accepted. . . . Their guidelines and rules were very, very strict. They wouldn't allow any ad-libbing or free speech on the air, because BBC was very proud that their sources were double- or triple-checked, that they are absolutely balanced, and that they're purer than distilled water.[16]

So, what is a *chuvak* to do when he doesn't like the rules by which he must play and is not a fan of meticulousness in general? He finds a way to circumvent the stuffy and the proper, and adds in some color, maybe even some polka dots to those bowties. Gradually, a culturally specific style emerges that requires, ironically, nothing less than meticulousness to deliver:

> I started cracking all those little jokes, and they were sort of minute to start with—flecks of intonation or maybe a word substituted, etc. But I didn't want to attract any attention to it, so I resorted to the old and trusted Russian technique: 'playing a fool.' You write this script, you record a program, and with absolutely innocent face you put it on a shelf. Because what can you say in a pop program that can have political repercussions or bring the BBC into disrepute?[17]

Left: Jamming tower 1984, Moscow; Right: Listener holding Panasonic radio (credit: K. Zaitzev)

16 Seva Novgorodsev, conversation with author, September 2015.
17 Ibid.

With the editors focused on ensuring scripts are free of politicisms, Seva's texts slide under the radar. The power of humor against the Soviet system is immeasurable and profound, allowing joke-tellers to keep their souls and "spiritual faith" while objecting to the state.[18]

Sounds and Letters

Then, letters start to arrive. The amount of mail Seva receives from every corner of the USSR (and even beyond) is extraordinary. The initial waves of epistles err on the side of furtive and formal, but closeted sentiments do appear—things that cannot be said aloud nor thought of except through the act of writing. The letters are not all praise, nor are they full of censure. In fact, the majority are a combination: laudatory and thankful, but offering specific criticism or frank commentary as if talking to a close friend. Seva personally appreciates the critical ones and reads them on air:

> I have always loved letters where they criticized me—because if you scold yourself in public, there will be those who will want to stand up for you. . . . In all these letters there is a hint, in a very Russian way, between the lines, that only those who know can understand. Therefore, I often did not even read out the letters of praise: it is not interesting to listen to someone praising himself. But those letters with a critical hint, they created, firstly, trust—even if you scold the presenter, he will still read it on the air—and secondly, they created some kind of dramatic tension. So yes, I took the criticism with pleasure. . . .[19]

Whether all instances of criticism are in fact genuine or just a way to ensure a letter will pass the KGB smell test can only be speculated on. After all, the KGB monitors all outgoing correspondence to the point that the gum Arabica practically oozes off resealed letters that were steamed open before finally arriving in Seva's hands.[20] Several of his approving writers even end up imprisoned or at the least monitored and harassed by KGB for contacting him.[21] Others mail

18 Sheeran, *Cultural Politics in International Relations*, 105–6.

19 Novgorodsev, interview by Matthew Orr, March 28, 2019, in *The Slavic Connexion*, podcast, https://www.slavxradio.com/seva-in-russian.

20 Kremer, "The DJ."

21 Ibid. See in this volume "Featured Listener: Yevgeny," who details his persecution by the KGB for writing to Seva.

dozens and dozens of letters before even *one* finally makes its way through the Iron Curtain to London.

A writer from Moscow opens his umpteenth epistle, the one that "makes it" to Seva:

> Huge greetings from our radiant Moscow to your foggy London. Your faithful listener Slava has written this a great number of times. What's happening? Every month I write a letter in a certain number of copies, and you have not received a single one—it upsets me very much. But I do not despair, I will write again.[22]

Yet another listener from Kalinin, in southwest Russia, Evgeny, expresses similar difficulties: "I am writing you my forty-ninth letter in two years, and as you can see, I am not losing hope." This missive reaches London, finally, together with letter number fifty by way of Evgeny's older brother who is stationed on a ship near Singapore from where the letter is actually mailed. Thus, Seva fondly calls Evgeny "*nash dorogoi piatidesiatnik*," meaning "our dear fiftieth" (a clear play on the word *shestidesiatnik*, child of the '60s). Evgeny and Slava are rewarded for their faithfulness and tenacity, but others are hardly so lucky. What difficult fates letters—and their writers—from the USSR have! With so much trouble and interference commonplace, it stands to reason that if Seva normally receives hundreds of letters, how many thousands (or more) don't make it to London at all?[23]

Not long after the mail starts coming, Seva decides that in his Friday time slot, once a month (or very nearly that), he should have a dedicated program to listener letters and fulfill their song requests.[24] This segment first airs on March 30, 1979, and swiftly becomes an ever-growing attraction, not only for the listeners but also perversely for the Soviet apparatchiki who brand this new program as a seductive ploy of the West—even more so because the reward for having a letter read on-air is a brand-new LP from the UK.[25] This is a true prize for anyone of any

---

22 *Rok-posevy*, January 22, 1982, radio broadcast, https://seva.ru/rock/index.php?y=1982.

23 Roth-Ey writes that postal censorship was indeed a problem and that Seva himself would write to listeners and share tips on how to increase the odds of their letters making it to him, such as sending via a traveler. See Roth-Ey, "Listening out," 565. However, as listeners have related in their personal stories, the KGB could still intercept these letters and writers could still get in serious trouble.

24 This is an example of how Seva adapted the techniques of his DJ role models, such as John Peel on BBC Radio 1, and applied them to the Russian radio space.

25 As shown on the list of broadcasts of *Rok-posevy*: https://seva.ru/rock/index.php?y=1979.

station in life in the USSR. The motivation to write to Seva, though, is not just about the physical reward. There is a much greater, unarticulated spiritual reward:

> This idea of reading letters from people . . . as part of the program is something that has been a staple throughout the history of US Cold War broadcasting. Because it makes a huge impression on the audience on shortwave when some garbage collector in Chelyabinsk hears his letter read by people like Seva Novgorodsev or like the people who did these kinds of programs at Radio Liberty. . . . These kinds of things made [radio] very personal and intimate for people. . . . Seva was absolutely a master of that.[26]

As it turns out, letter-reading is not only a practice or tactic of the West, but also is a "central" strategy of Soviet radio as well, with both domestic and international programs "actively" soliciting letters from the audience: "In the late 70s, the main Soviet youth program, 'Youth' ('*Yunost*'), claimed to base about 70 percent of its programming on listener letters; and teenage soul-searching . . . was a familiar genre on the Soviet airwaves."[27] The Radio Moscow program *Moscow Mailbag*, which reaches Americans and Canadians on the North American shortwaves has been reading letters from listeners for years. However, in this case, only short questions from letters are read on air and then answered in length by host Joe Adamov; this approach is almost the opposite of Seva's, which grants even long letters the courtesy of a full read with minimal commentary from Seva in many cases. Even if there were no difference in approach, the difference in sound is marked. Even the affable and American-sounding Joe Adamov, who admirably throws in um's to colloquialize a Comintern-approved script, holds up poorly when compared to Seva's sincerity, inimitable warmth, and comfortable but well-spoken—also scripted—Russian.

It should be noted that the sort of intimacy that features prominently in Seva's programs is deliberately absent from Soviet programming that is a "one-way street by design." In essence, there is no give and take; listeners are the only ones doing any sharing while the program hosts do little more than read the scripts given to them and, in most cases, never indulge the listeners with anything of a personal nature. Seva, in contrast, gives the impression that he is speaking to his audience like friends, despite the script, despite the rehearsals required by the BBC before going live. Moreover, when reading letters, he starts to adopt

---

26 Jeff Trimble in discussion with author, November 30, 2020.
27 Roth-Ey, "Listening out," 575.

the practice of treating his listener like he or she is in a shared experience with him, using plural pronouns. "*Our* next letter is from . . ." Or "Nikolay writes to *us* from . . ." To further heighten this relational familiarity, Seva starts using a writer's name's diminutive—or pet name—on air. Sergey from Moscow, for example, instantly becomes Seryozha, which not only presumes a certain closeness but dramatically shrinks the physical space between DJ and listener. His program and style gradually create a separate safe space that all are invited to join regardless of views and experiences.

On-Air Moral Decay

The Soviet authorities understand the significance of Seva's letter-reading segment and note its alarming popularity, and pretty soon the act of engaging with Seva in this manner comes under attack in one of the state papers—*Penzenskaia pravda*. Disguised as a true crime story, the article is about the decline of three young characters, whose attempt to escape to Turkey is just the pinnacle of their journey to the abyss, brought about by the trifecta of Western influence—jeans, radio, and film. These Soviet boys are led astray by a very "dark character" from Penza who enters the scene. He—Sergey Evin—comes to these impressionable youth, bearing the forbidden fruit of the West: glistening ink-black Western rock records and tapes with Seva's recorded voice, purportedly seducing the boys into a life of drugs and debauchery. The article's author, A. Kislov, proceeds to dramatically outline Evin's degeneration, which had begun unsurprisingly on the radio:

> [I]t all started . . . at the age of fourteen, with a passion for rock music.[28] He began collecting information about rock ensembles, including foreign radio voices . . . and in particular Seva Novgorodsev. . . . One day Evin decided to write to Novgorodsev . . . to request a song performed by a band that he liked. . . . After some time, the BBC broadcast that a song was being performed at the request of Sergey Evin from Penza. . . . The exoticism of such attention swelled his chest, and Evin, who was imbued with sympathy for Novgorodsev, enters into correspondence with him.

---

28 The age of fourteen seems the typical age at which a young person becomes active in their listening or develops a real interest in music.

> Seva bought Evin carefully and methodically. First, a song on request with the mention of the youngster's name, then, letters of greetings. Then, Novgorodsev recommended Evin to take part in the contest of guessing the names of Western artists. Of course, Evin soon became one of his winners. This was also preplanned.... Then Evin began to receive parcels from abroad with discs of trendy ensembles. He showed considerable commercial acumen; he arranged for them to be copied and sold for large sums of money....
>
> Similarly, [these young men] were also imbued with sympathies for the Western way of life, and they were united by this "musical interest" multiplied by an interest in... jeans. They met regularly, strummed guitars, drank, listened to the latest records that Evin supplied, and received information from Western radio. Each tried to outdo the other in boldness of judgment. In the course of such verbal competitions, the most unimaginable plans were born. Snezhkin wanted to be a dictator. Barchenkov did not crave leadership but wanted drugs. . . . Evin made no plans but gave out information and secretly grinned.
>
> Once they made up some poems and sent them to their idol on the BBC. And even surprised themselves when they heard them read aloud in one of the programs.[29]

One poem is about the wonders of the hydrogen bomb, and in it the young men advocate for the use of the explosive and praise the power felt in its detonation. The obvious message, then, is that Seva is making youth terror organizations through the devilry of rock music. Kislov closes with an apt statement: "It is not enough to talk about the need for class consciousness... they must be educated. It's difficult, but it's more reliable than talking and then finding out with bitterness that all the conversations were in vain."

Unfortunately for *Penzenskaia pravda*, the Soviet people, not only the youth, have discovered the joy of holding conversations with Seva and with each other through letters. To prove that Evin is not quite the villain the article makes him out to be, the following is an excerpt of one of his letters to Seva in 1982, which offers some criticism, and, thus, makes it onto the air:

---

29 A. Kislov, "Otkuda eto v nikh?," *Penzenskaia pravda*, September 26, 27, 1985, https://seva.ru/media/?id=3.

> Hello Vsevolod. First of all, many thanks for the record. It would be nice if you played something out of the ordinary from time to time. I have been listening to you for four years. Along with your program, I am equally addicted to literary broadcasts. Sometimes people say that your programs have become worse. In my opinion, this is not so; they all maintain the same high standard. Sometimes there are highs . . . sometimes lows. For example, the old program about Presley did not seem to me to be successful. . . .[30]

Evin is one of many who offer candid, constructive criticism, as if Seva were a close family member they don't need to flatter or compliment. Most critical writers still believe that Seva is at the top of the pyramid of radio hosts, saying he supersedes the likes of Tamara Dombrovskaya from VOA, Pavel Sergeev from RL, or Radio Canada's music hosts. Evin also makes mention of a key issue that bothers many Soviet listeners: "Sometimes in the letters you read, you can hear the doubts of writers; people say, 'do you really send records?'"[31] This concern and wavering faith in Seva's commitment to the people points to the fact that undoubtedly far fewer records actually make it to the prizewinners than are sent, especially when so many letters sent to Seva never reach him and therefore never earn a reply. Undoubtedly, this is all part of the KGB's grand strategy: to demoralize and discourage letter writers by preventing the majority from reaching the addressee. However, listeners remain undeterred and continue to write despite the obstacles and risks.

Something very special develops from this substantial mail traffic between Seva and his people. Seva's style improves, at least partially due to criticism received from his *zemliachki* (countryfolk). Moreover, a cautiously optimistic stratum of society develops in which communication that can't be carried out freely on the ground, or within the physical borders of the USSR, takes place with Seva as their unofficial spiritual guide (and in fact, more than one writer calls him this very thing).

This long-distance correspondence is a precursor to certain kinds of modern social media, wherein no voices are heard, nor faces seen, and yet written words

---

30 "Letters and Requests," *Rok-posevy*, April 2, 1982, radio broadcast, https://seva.ru/rock/?id=203.

31 It is difficult to know how many records actually got through, but it is a safe assumption that, since many letters themselves didn't even reach Seva, and the level of doubt Evin conveys in his letter, the records were probably in large part confiscated by authorities and only relatively few could have made it into listeners' hands.

are able to convey meaning and emotion. The people are hungry for more than just information about the outside world. They want a connection. Connection implies that they themselves have worth. Their voices count. Through these letters, they express their thoughts, convey news, and also speak to other writers, to neighbors near and far whom they are unlikely to ever meet in person and with whom they cannot easily discuss what truly interests them. Of course, this is still not really free, unfettered communication. The universal understanding is that KGB reads the letters, decides which go through and which don't—like some intermediary, omnipresent god network. Most listeners are smart enough not to mail correspondence from their own personal addresses, but there is always the chance of reprisal, always the chance that a letter will be traced back to its writer by KGB.[32]

Word Play

By 1980, the BBC World Service realizes that "something is happening"—otherwise why the devil is P. O. Box 76 overflowing with airmail all the time—and they decide to investigate. Editors who are knowledgeable in Russian listen to tapes of the pop program and check Seva's scripts, which he has faithfully filed away. What do they find? Nothing political. But by Seva's own account, "they were horrified, because this chap was allowing himself a freedom that was never [permitted] in his contract."[33]

Letters of complaint regarding Seva's dubious humor reach the head of Russian Service:

> She was a lady from an aristocratic family—Mary Seton-Watson. Her husband [Hugh Seton-Watson] was a famous historian,[34] a professor in Oxford, and he was a fan of Joseph Stalin, so they were left of center. And she became a spinster in her middle, maybe late fifties and was very much a horse woman. She kept a stable of horses. Obviously, in a million years, she would

32 Many listeners reported that they would mail their letters through friends, from a post office and specifying no return address, or would secure a P. O. box (as mentioned previously) to include as their return address.

33 Novgorodsev in conversation with author, September 2015.

34 Dr. Hugh Seton-Watson (1916–1984) was a famed British historian and political scientist who focused on Russia and Eastern Europe. He died in America while visiting for a lecture. See *New York Times*, December 22, 1984, obituary section.

> never understand the kind of jokes addressed to the disaffected working-class youth of Russia, from her position of class superiority. . . . You know, she would cross out my jokes and I would write the kind of jokes she wouldn't understand. In a way, she did a good service both to me and to the style because it wasn't obvious from then on. And it became a subculture whereby [Soviet] people understood what I was saying but not necessarily their superiors or censors or whatever. And so, this is how it all developed. . . .[35]

To circumvent restrictions and further tussles with Mary Seton-Watson, who begins to literally watch the broadcasters in her service,[36] Seva pushes himself to craft even more clever witticisms that only Russians raised in the USSR would understand. In this way, he avoids further controversy—in the UK at least. In Russia, it is an entirely different story. With their esoteric agricultural information constantly blitzkrieging the population through radio and TV—"All this 'yields' and, you know, all this kind of 'crop rotations' and what-not"—it is easy for him to twist the "silly stupefied language" of the officials and make a joke out of it all:

> They were getting nervous—the Soviet system, you understand, has highly trained psychologists and KGB Officers and Information Officers at their disposal. They could overlook any so-called facts that were broadcast in their direction from the West, but they couldn't cope with a joke, because a joke goes around all their carefully constructed defense systems. A joke goes straight to a person, and he laughs and that's it, because in a joke, like in a nutshell, you get everything. Like there were food problems, obviously everybody knew about them, but the radio was blasting about the achievements of Soviet agriculture, so people would say, then, "If you want your fridge to be full of foodstuff just plug it into [state] radio."[37]

---

35 Novgorodsev in conversation with author, September 2015.

36 This habit earns her the nickname "Mary Sitting Watching." "Novgorodsev," *Vremenno dostupen*, May 24, 2009, TV Centre, television broadcast.

37 Seva Novgorodsev, Museum of London interview.

An additional source of joke material stems from state media's constant news about heavy metal production, a convenient thing for a rock 'n' roll DJ. Nobody, unless cut from the fabric of Soviet society, can appreciate such jokes, as is the case with most *anekdoty*:

> I kind of created a language built up of their converters and stainless-steel additives and all this kind of stuff that I cannot translate into English because it's a specific technical language that exists within the realm of Russian [language] and which is incredibly funny if taken out of context. So, people were splitting their sides open.[38]

It's these jokes, wry, seemingly off-the-cuff, and nearly impossible to intelligibly translate, that spread his name across the whole country. As scholar Paul Sheeran writes, "His jokes were even more famous than he himself—often people recited them without mentioning their origin. It would not be overestimating to say that Seva was known to virtually everyone—even for those who never heard his broadcasts."[39]

The heavy use of Russian vernacular is where VOA's Willis Conover and Seva Novgorodsev necessarily diverge. Seva quite simply enjoys a greater audience impact because he is a creature of the same language and culture as his listeners. Musical skill and knowledge are important, and both DJs are beloved, but only one is truly understood on a spiritual level, despite Conover's "special English"—that is, understandable, simple phraseology designed for international audiences.[40] Moreover, Western jazz proper is still a thing of cultural elites in the USSR, while rock music is bringing this radical sound of "anti-revolution"—that is, anti-communist revolution—to the masses on a sea of authentic Russian vernacular and humor. As such, Seva nurtures and cultivates "political consciousness" in listeners without explicitly trying.

Consciously or not, Seva draws from Conover, whose style and formula of "music plus information" and reading letters over the air carry into Seva's broadcast toolbox to potent effect. The people are already familiar with this format, and now it's coupled with the music they want to hear *and* coming from someone who is a music practitioner and Russian himself. Before long, though the name Vsevolod and its diminutive Seva are common in Russia, only one Seva

38 Ibid.

39 Sheeran, *Cultural Politics in International Relations*, 94.

40 Yurchak, *Everything Was Forever*, 180.

is known to everyone.[41] Undermined by Soviet media, Seva still gathers hungry listeners by the droves, and the Soviet Union rocks with the belly laughs of an estimated twenty-five million souls.[42]

Kto on takoi? (Who Is He Really?)

In addition to the letters he receives, Seva gains an idea of his impact and the composition of his audience through the particular Soviet papers in which his name with increasing frequency appears—and by which he understands he has earned the Politburo's attention. Printed slander about him finds its way to his mailbox, either through friends or listeners or BBC Monitoring itself. Fascinated that he's becoming more famous in his absence than when he was a performing artist in the USSR, Seva begins to accumulate these articles and mentions and files them into boxes sardonically marked "PERSONAL FAME."[43]

Which state newspapers report on him and what do they say? One of the earliest is *Rovesnik*, the most popular Russian youth journal at this time, controlled by the Komsomol.[44] In publishing anything at all about Seva, the Komsomol indirectly indicates that it has noticed that youth are listening (and writing) to Seva, and they are eager to interrupt this trend posthaste. A *Rovesnik* piece titled "Kto on takoi?" published in 1982 makes its way to London, to Seva.[45] Unlike other pieces of "Personal Fame," this one cuts him rather deeply for it features an interview with his own mother in Leningrad.

The article begins innocently enough with a letter from a female reader and listener of Seva's in Belarus:

---

41 Even Roth-Ey notes that Seva is known simply by the diminutive of his first name, a feat in and of itself. Even Stalin and Lenin, who are only surname famous, can't claim such a level of familial popularity.

42 The estimate of twenty-five million is listed in several sources. See, for example, Leo Hornak, "The DJ Who Brought Led Zeppelin to Soviet Audiences Retires," *The World*, September 4, 2015, https://www.pri.org/stories/2015-09-04/dj-who-brought-led-zeppelin-soviet-audiences-retires.

43 William Kramer, "Seva Novgorodsev," BBC.com, September 5, 2015, https://www.bbc.com/news/magazine-34157596.

44 William Risch, ed., *Youth and Rock in the Soviet Bloc: Youth Cultures, Music, and the State in Russia and Eastern Europe* (Lanham: Lexington Books, 2014), 129, 138.

45 The same year, 1982, veteran BBC Russian Service presenter Anatol Goldberg dies at his post in Bush House.

Dear Editors!

A month ago, I heard on KV the pop music broadcast of Seva Novgorodsev on the radio station BBC. . . . He talks very interestingly about music, rock music I mean. He carries himself and speaks like an old acquaintance, unofficially, and I liked that too. But that was the first time. Now I'm cooling off a little bit. Not to the program, but to him. . . . He, whether or not you understand, is "my friend," generally speaking, but he uses phrases like "prosperous capitalist reality" or something like that, and so, now I'm starting to get frustrated with him.

I'd really like to know something about him: who he is, where he comes from, etc. If you can't tell me about him in the magazine itself, then please do so in a letter.

Thank you in advance,
L. Makovsky, BSSR, Gomelskaya oblast, Rechitsa-8[46]

Whether this is a real letter and whether this young woman wrote these exact words cannot be proved; however, *Rovesnik*, with apparent alacrity, dispatches one of its staff writers to knock on Lyudmila Mikhailovna's door to get the full scoop on her treacherous son. Subtitled "Rasskaz materi," meaning simply "Mother's Story," the article purportedly includes Lyudmila's words without any redaction or revision. However, like the letter, the faithfulness of the printed transcript is unknown. None of the interviewer's questions are included, either, and so it's impossible to know how much her answers and resulting "story" have been invisibly navigated. Moreover, the editor sneaks in a neat Soviet-red summary, which ascribes maximal pathos to her touching narrative and casts blame upon the heartless son of this *staraia matushka*—old mother—of the Motherland.

"My son was born in 1940," Lyudmila says, according to the journalist. "And all children who were born during the war are weak." She doesn't only mean weak of character, but also physically, due to the stress of war and the scarcity of food

46 N.a., "Kto on takoi?" Roth-Ey says that in response to the piece, listeners reacted overwhelmingly: "The *Rovesnik* smear spread widely, to judge by the BBC mail bag: one correspondent wrote that it was harder to get your hands on the magazine than Solzhenitsyn's *Gulag Archipelago*" ("Listening out," 569). Quite the statement considering *Gulag Archipelago* was circulating in *samizdat* or via illegal foreign editions at the time.

when they were young. A wartime mother, she holds, lives in fear of losing her child—her happiness—to the grave. She covers the wartime period most extensively, both no doubt a result of state propaganda preferences and because the impression of that time remains dominant in her mind. But she leaves out all mention of the circumstances that ultimately forced them to migrate from Leningrad to Tallinn, where she claims Seva's father had to "re-create" the Estonian Shipping Company in 1949. "After all, the ships belonging to the bourgeois private individuals in Estonia were taken away, destroyed; there was only one pathetic boat left, as my husband told me. The new Estonian fleet began with this one vessel."

It's clear that the desired story is that Lyudmila and Boris are hardworking Soviet citizens who had fought bravely in the Great Patriotic War, survived to help rebuild the USSR, and slaved to give everything to their son who ultimately grew up to disappoint and betray them—as Soviet youth now disappoint and betray the sacrifices of their forefathers by listening to this voice of sedition on the BBC.

Lyudmila says Seva had exhibited talent and developed a passion for music at an early age. Neither she nor her husband, she readily confesses, had any musical inclination whatsoever, and so it was a mystery to all where Seva's good ear for melody and rhythm had come from. "Seva rushed to the stage . . . joined youth gatherings with a guitar. I didn't think it was bad or that it could ruin my son. However, now it is difficult for me to evaluate anything objectively. I don't know who to blame or what is the cause for what later happened."

What "later happened" is this: Boris and Lyudmila finally relocated to Leningrad after twenty-two years in Tallinn, and by this time (approximately 1971), Seva had already achieved a certain level of fame and married Gala Burkhanova. According to the article, Lyudmila really loved Gala's "beauty, Soviet manners, and strong character," but found something amiss in the familial connection. "They had their own life," Lyudmila says of Seva and Gala. Then, her son suddenly decides to leave the USSR. "It was a terrible, unexpected, unforeseen blow. . . . I had lost my son forever and could not help him. I could not save him." She goes on to explain that this news had caused Seva's father to fall seriously ill due to "nervous shock." The article, however, fails to mention Boris's more serious hospitalization after being stripped of his position in the Baltic Shipping Company and kicked out of the Communist Party. Following this heartrending part of the story is the somewhat out-of-place statement: "My husband received the Order of Lenin in peacetime for his work." In other words, Boris and Lyudmila are patriots, valued by their homeland, and should not have to be tarnished by their son's heinous choices.

It is hard not to be pulled in by her emotive statements about how in this year, 1982, she gets by on a meager salary in close quarters with her husband, working in a clinic that hired her despite her age and from which she is able to get the medications they now need. "You don't know how you're going to die," she tells *Rovesnik*. Apparently now Boris is silent, won't say hello to his son, and Lyudmila blames her husband's fragile state on her son whom she nevertheless loves. As the interview draws to a close, Lyudmila reminisces about a time, three decades ago during the Great Patriotic War, when soldiers had given *kasha* to little Seva in order to keep him alive. Lyudmila's final line echoes strangely: "Yes, I know. I've been told by many that he is a wonderful musician!" An ambiguous conclusion.[47]

The rollercoaster tale judges the wayward Soviet son, but it is the afterword from the editorial office directed to the initial writer, which makes plain that the article is indeed an attack on Seva and the youth who listen to him:

> Of course, you understood, Comrade Makovsky, that his mother answers your question about Seva Novgorodsev. Our correspondent met her in Leningrad and word for word recorded her terrible and sad story about the boy saved during the hard years of the war by the kindness and sensitivity of hundreds of people, who then grew up to betray those who saved him, who loved him. Betrayed those young soldiers who went to their deaths, betrayed those peasants who shared with him the last piece of bread, betrayed those honest and ordinary people who "had nothing accumulated, no wealth, except their youth and a son"—his father and mother. He betrayed the Motherland. . . . Who is he, really?! Jew? Russian? Or Englishman? Judge for yourself. For us he is a nobody. No family, no tribe. Garbage.[48]

Strong words for a youth magazine. Seva is wounded by this very personal attack, but he understands the reason for the article. He's making an impact at home, though he can't fully see or understand it.[49] The blind medium is, after all, not only blind for the listener, but also for the broadcaster. A certain degree of blind *trust* must also follow—again, for both the presenter and the audience. Blind, indeed, but never deaf.

47 Seva's mother digresses and leaps from topic to topic in such a way as to suggest major redaction of the original interview. However, it is possible that she is actually under a great deal of duress during this interview and says the words she thinks the state wants to hear. The mention of "guitar" seems out of place, as Seva's instrument was the saxophone.

48 N.a., "Kto on takoi?"

49 Sheeran, *Cultural Politics in International Relations*, 94. "'Seva's influence on Soviet counterculture . . . was VERY significant during the pre-perestroika years.'"

Featured Listener: Alex

I can remember I was seven [in Moscow]. My parents are making dinner, and I'm just back from school . . . On the radio, some of the Western broadcasters are playing. Sometimes my parents didn't have time to listen, but I was always listening and would tell them afterwards what I had learned. At the time it was not possible to learn any news on the TV (because of all the propaganda). All the news started with agriculture; it was the most important thing to have such reports every day.[50] But my parents were interested in what really happens, what Soviet propaganda was not telling them . . . e.g. plane hijacking, dissidents and dissident movements in general, literal readings of banned books, etc. Sometimes they would go into the kitchen and ask me, "So what are the Voices saying?"[51]

I started to understand that they [VOA, RFE/RL, BBC, DW, etc.] were different from each other. I wasn't sure why, but my parents thought that Radio Liberty was the most anti-Soviet. My parents were Soviet people (born and raised) and so their opinion was that the BBC and Voice of America were okay to listen to, but Radio Liberty was not, somehow. When I was fifteen, my cousin gave me a tape cassette and there was a recording from the air on that cassette (from the German station) of a music program—it was not very good quality. But on it was a very interesting DJ with a very interesting style, and he played music that was banned at the time like Akvarium. It was about 1985. I found him on my radio and started to listen to him weekly. I learned his name was Seva Novgorodsev.

So, I became a regular listener, and I told all my friends about him. I was in secondary school at the time. From those broadcasts of Seva's, I learned about Western music, which was totally unknown to me before, and I started to understand it was not uniform: there were bands I liked and bands I didn't like at all. Seva included a lot of jokes about Soviet life at the time, which were always interesting. At first, I didn't like those jokes because I was still a Soviet kid despite listening to Radio Liberty and such. But in time I started to love and started to understand the meaning of those jokes . . .

---

50 Additional input from another listener during the same conversation: "It was interesting later on when everyone started to listen to Seva because he knew about the agriculture emphasis . . . —food was always scarce, people were always starving—and deliberately used a lot of the specific style of language in his programs. Turning the Soviet jargon on its head is how the West termed it" (Conversation with author, May 24, 2020, Moscow, Russia).

51 Soviets during the Cold War called foreign radio broadcasts *golosa*, meaning "voices," purportedly because of VOA.

Then I learned there were many such people as myself, and every Friday night we gathered throughout the country, around our radios, to listen, to laugh together at Seva's jokes. Moreover, Seva started to have the program's "Letters from Listeners," and he would send out records for those who wrote or called in with the correct song names. Everyone wanted to get those records because it was the real England, the real British LP, because it was not possible to buy them except on the black market. I remember getting my very first letter from the BBC, and I just displayed the envelope in my room with all the British stamps of the Queen. It was beautiful . . .

CHAPTER 10

It's a Hard Rock Life

> *Dobryi vecher, druz'ia.* The other day a curious book fell into my hands: Methodical Recommendations of the Organizer of Disco Clubs and Discos—issued by a serious organization with a very long name. . . . Let's read: "Recently, a new form of youth leisure, a disco club and discotheque, has become widespread and very popular; according to the most conservative estimates, their audience numbers over a million boys and girls." Okay. "In the Ukrainian SSR during 1978–79 the number of discos has tripled, and now there are more than 800." Good. "In the Tatar ASSR, in just one year, 1979, their number increased from 50 to 330. Programs of the best disco clubs are characterized by clear political orientation." It is obvious, comrades, an indisputable fact—there is a mixing of music with politics, and that is something for which we are sometimes criticized. It's a theme of our programs as you know. . . . But let's get down to business: today's program is dedicated to your letters and requests. . . .
>
> —Seva, *Rok-posevy*, August 21, 1981

If the Long '60s had been colorful and creative and promising for improved Soviet relations with the West,[1] the '70s under Brezhnev seem intent on crushing all hope and optimism. In Leningrad, for instance, life for ordinary citizens is "very bleak," according to rock bassist Sasha Titov:

---

1 See Donald Raleigh's *Soviet Baby Boomers* (Oxford: Oxford University Press, 2012) and Yurchak's *Everything Was Forever, until It Was No More,* both of which relate the cultural history and the generation known as the *shestidecyatniki.* For radio listening, see Raleigh, *Soviet Baby Boomers,* 146.

> Our city had a Tier 2 distribution level which meant we had fewer products and lower quality of life than Moscow. However, the rest of the country lived even worse. The only way to settle in Moscow and Leningrad was to get registered which required a very strong reason. . . . Getting married would do it. My first wife was a music teacher from Kabardino Balkaria who wanted to move to Leningrad. She paid me 600 rubles to marry her, which I spent on gear.[2]

Despite significant hardship, soon-to-be seminal rock bands are performing critical work, developing their artistry, finding their sound, learning to differentiate between serious rock and meaningless tripe. Seva's counterpart on the other side of the Iron Curtain is journalist and music critic Artemy Troitsky who seems to operate in some strange intermediary bubble between the official apparatchiki and the artistic underground. Troitsky warrants recognition for elevating and invigorating the Russian rock scene during a decade of political, economic, and social stagnancy. His tastes, which are anything but soporific, safe, or Soviet, appear to be a determiner in the success and failure of bands in the developing Russian rock scene.

Much like Seva, though one could never say they are similar in character, Troitsky is difficult to drop into a neat category. While Troitsky's reach cannot be as large as Seva's, his impact on the ground is decidedly complementary and vital for the development of Russian rock as a genre and a movement. Possessing an indefatigable spirit coupled to a stubbornly nonconformist palate, Troitsky plays many roles in the Soviet cultural underground: entrepreneur, social engineer, music critic, journalist, networker, artist manager, educator, talent scout, media personality, influencer, and promoter. He enters the rock scene with passion and vision, and simply by virtue of these qualities and an obvious devil-may-care attitude, he becomes the focal point of a still-forming genre, respected and well-liked at every stratum of society—a *muzhik* in Levis. In Moscow, where he is based as a journalist, he serves on rock festival committees, chronicles the development of Russian rock, befriends the musicians themselves, launches Russia's first discotheque, organizes concerts, and much more.[3] As *The Guardian*'s

---

2 Sasha Titov (famed bass player in Akvarium and Kino) in correspondence with author, December 2020.

3 Olga Slobodskaya in correspondence with author, January 2020. Troitsky was a member of the first Leningrad Rock Club (LRC) festival committee in 1983.

Moscow correspondent in the early '80s writes, "If the far-flung and chronically disorganized Soviet rock culture has a single focus it is Art Troitsky."[4]

Back in the USSR

Like Seva, Troitsky has also experienced the injustices of the Soviet system at many points in his life, not the least of which was when his father, Kiva Maidanik, a Soviet historian and political scientist of Jewish origins, was dismissed from the Communist Party in 1980 on tenuous grounds. Unlike Seva, Troitsky was born post-Stalin (1955) to intellectual parents—members of the intelligentsia—who did not send him into a Soviet military academy and actually raised him outside the USSR:

> From '63 to '68 we were living in Prague where my parents had been working on problems of peace and socialism for the international communist magazine. . . . I lived in an international community . . . and I had a lot of friends from all kinds of countries: Italy, France, of course Czechoslovakia, Romania—my first passion was a girl from Chile. Because of all these I had plenty of information . . . and I've been listening to this [Western] music all the time. You know, it was kind of new at the time. It was called ya-ya music or beat music and only later it was called rock music. And this is how I became obsessed with music. . . . I had access to these records, and I went to beat clubs in Prague . . . and attended concerts by local bands.[5]

Thus, he is a cosmopolitan, if not totally Westernized, thirteen-year-old by the time the political situation in Czechoslovakia and Brezhnev's actions with the Warsaw Pact force Troitsky's family to be recalled to Moscow in 1968.

Firmly returned to Soviet reality, he is overwhelmed by boredom and sinks into extreme depression. It is then that radio becomes his life raft. Whereas in Prague he had lived his life in the world and had no need of wireless to provide him connection, in Moscow it is the only window to a world he knows well and which he'd had to leave behind so suddenly:

---

4 Troitsky, *Back in the USSR*, 7.

5 Troitsky in discussion with author, June 2019.

> I can tell you that radio for me meant nothing until 1968 . . . when we'd been forced to return to Moscow. . . . Then, it was a very tragic period of my life. . . . No friends, no music, no sources. I was just sitting alone for days, just writing letters and sending letters to my friends in Europe. I was really desperate.

"The Critic" as a young man in his mother's Moscow apartment (courtesy of A. Troitsky)

By degrees he adjusts, makes some friends who have musical interests that more or less align with his, reunites with Russian musicians whom he had met in Prague, and starts attending underground rock performances.[6] However, from 1969 to 1972, he says, radio became the most important thing to him, the ticket to his mental liberation and continued education. He went from literally never listening to being an "absolute radio maniac" who retired to bed quite early every night just because some of his favorite radio shows would begin at 8:30. He listened via his small "but very good" German transistor radio until 2:00 in the morning:

---

6 It is possible these Russians had been granted passports to attend the Prague International Jazz Festival, established in 1964. Willis Conover wrote about his interactions with Soviet musicians, "young Komsomol members," and Radio Moscow presenters in '65 and '66. Willis Conover on Russia, 1967, Box 17, Folder 31, Willis Conover Collection, UNT University Libraries.

> I had a whole list of radio stations and their timetables, and I would be hopping from one station to another. . . . And some of the stations were very exotic. Ah, my favorite was Radio Free Europe in Romanian—Radio Evropa Libre. They had a fantastic DJ who as I found out later was also an absolutely massive cult figure in Romania and who got killed under mysterious circumstances, maybe even killed by the secret service of [Nicolae] Ceaușescu. His name was Cornel Chiriac.[7] There was news in Romanian and then there was Cornel Chiriac. And he was playing full albums and for me this was the main source of information. . . . I listened to his shows religiously every night, and I of course wrote down the names of the albums, names of the bands, and so on. . . . There were plenty of other stations on which I listened to daily shows like say . . . on the Voice of America in English . . . Radio Sweden in Russian, and the BBC in Russian. But at that time when I listened to radio there was no Seva Novgorodsev. . . .

Though this may already seem like a cornucopia of options, when Troitsky first visits his grandparents at their cottage in Estonia in 1969 he discovers that the radio landscape in this northern zone is "fantastic" and "much richer than in Moscow" because of the geographical proximity to the rest of Europe and the seeming absence of jamming. Therefore, the options are plentiful and diverse—Finnish radio stations that play rock music, Swedish radio stations, and Radio Luxembourg, to name only a few:

> [In Estonia] I went to bed with my transistor radio at ten o'clock or so and I listened to music until five in the morning, and this was one of the main reasons why I came to Estonia . . . for many years in a row every summer, to [listen] to musical radio and without jamming.

Radio is not only a pastime and source of information for Troitsky; it is also a constant companion for his parents and grandparents, as well as many of their

---

7 Chiriac was a famed music presenter even prior to his defection from Romania. His program was "hugely popular" and he was apparently feared by Nicolae Ceaușescu. See Eugen Tomiuc, "Memories of a Romanian Icon," RFE/RL, August 1, 2008, https://www.rferl.org/a/Memories_Of_A_Romanian_Icon/1187788.html.

neighbors and friends in Estonia. By his assessment, it is an absolutely common thing in this state to listen to Golosa Ameriki and the BBC, though not for music but for political broadcasts:

> There was a table by our house in the garden and the transistor radio was standing on this table [playing] the Voice of America from morning till night, and if there was something especially interesting my granddad came and then listened to it and sometimes also called his wife, my grandmother. . . . Their friends came to visit, and Voice of America or BBC was on and it was normal. It was absolutely normal. No one was afraid of listening to VOA and the BBC. . . .

Nevertheless, such liberal listening does not apply across the board, and certain stations are never tuned to, at least not in his grandparents' abode. Troitsky says: "I don't remember my grandparents listening to Radio Svoboda, and I also don't remember them listening to Deutsche Welle." Based on this anecdotal evidence, it seems that Troitsky's family's tastes or self-imposed restrictions (politically or personally motivated) converge with the great majority of Soviet radio listeners in Russia. For Troitsky, as for Seva over a decade prior, Western broadcasting to the USSR plays a powerful, nurturing role at a low point in his life, during some of his most impressionable years. Troitsky also has the benefit of a learned and loving father, a passionate and prolific scholar of Latin America, revolutions, and revolutionaries like Che Guevara. From Kiva, Troitsky has absorbed the qualities necessary to be an independent seeker of knowledge—to *think* for himself—and to embrace the spirit of revolution as his moral compass, that is, to reject a static society and pursue instead dynamism and transformation.

In short order, Troitsky becomes a recognizable figure in the cultural underground and, by his own admission, quite active on the black market. In 1972, armed with a head full of information and a passion for music, seventeen-year-old Troitsky and a friend launch the first discotheque in Russia—the first, as far as can be judged. "For fifteen rubles we rented a PA from musicians we knew and transported it to a café at Moscow University, where we would spin discs all evening." Although their aim at the outset is to replicate as well as they can what the West has been doing for decades, they discover quickly that imported culture takes on a life of its own in a new space:

> We wanted this to be a normal disco with new, trendy, ultra-cool western records . . . People get high and dance and scream and so

> on. But the students told us "Okay, that's fine, but what we also need desperately is information. We want you to tell us stories about those artists, about those bands. . . ." And I understood, I was into information, too . . . So, I said, "Okay, we can supply you with information; we can have this first part of the disco where I will play the records and tell you about the artists who sing these songs . . . and show slides also in this first part of the disco."
>
> People adored it, and this [lecture part] was no less popular than—or maybe even more popular than—the dancing part of the disco . . . I mean, some people they came for the first part, and then when the dancing got started, they left. And I can't explain it very well . . . Russian culture is very word-oriented . . . Therefore, people could be more interested in me talking or writing about Deep Purple than actually listening to the music . . . It was interesting for them, you know, how these guys live in England with their long hair and so on. Are they different from us or not? It was like watching scenes at the zoo through a hole in the Iron Curtain.[8]

In essence, during that first listening and lecture hour at the disco, Troitsky does what Leonid Pereverzev did in the '50s with his jazz lectures. Moreover, like Pereverzev, Troitsky's presentations are not given from a practitioner's standpoint and are not meant to teach the music itself, but rather generate appreciation, awareness, and portraits of a life off-limits. From 1972 to 74, Troitsky and his friend operate this discotheque, giving such information to the Moscow student crowd and Western-peering folks hankering to glimpse life on the other side.

Then, as the years pass, there is greater recognition of rock as an art form, as opposed to previously when rock musicians often felt like "outlaws" because the Soviet cultural authorities had pounded into them from infancy that classical music is the only true art form. Several other discos arise in other parts of Moscow, and Troitsky's lone operation gains company—some only holding lectures and no dance portions due to government discouragement of such frivolity.[9] However, as the nation becomes accustomed to rock and it sounds less

---

8 Troitsky in discussion with author, June 2019.

9 Troitsky, *Back in the USSR*, 33. These lectures are comparable to the "Rock Chronicles" segments of Seva's *Rok-posevy*, though what prompted him to employ this sort of lecture format is unclear. It may be seen as Pereverzev's influence.

rebellious and libelous, a shift occurs during the '70s, which leads musicians like Alexey Kozlov, one of the early venerable *stilyagi* of the jazz decade, to bravely cross "from the comparatively safe world of jazz towards the rock reservation." In so doing, Kozlov creates the concept of "cultured" rock, which is far more inviting to the "sizeable intellectual audience." And everyone breathes a collective sigh of relief: here is a chance to make the artless trash artful and even "prestigious."[10] This is in keeping with Seva's group Dobry molodtsy, which, like Kozlov's group Arsenal, had a brass section, singers, and a repertoire of easily accessible songs. The difference is that while Dobry molodtsy went for a more Western reimagining of folk songs, Arsenal refashions Broadway hit musicals for a Russian audience.

This is ultimately what Seva does on air, incorporate Pereverzev's and Troitsky's listen-and-lecture method—though, so far as can be gleaned, not on purpose. Meanwhile, Troitsky from inside Russia pushes the boundaries, somehow without getting into major trouble until the '80s, and holds the distinction of being Russia's first DJ within the USSR. Always searching for the edge and challenging what is considered music and musical, Troitsky is the chief *stilyaga* of the Russian rock world—hunting for the next thing according to his continuously evolving tastes, and the moment the next thing becomes the happening thing, he dismisses it like yesterday's refuse. Did Seva and Troitsky ever step on each other's figurative toes in rock broadcasting or rock proliferation? Apparently not, according to both men. Troitsky's answer nicely sums up the distinction between himself and Seva:

> I can tell you that there was never any rivalry between Seva and [me] because we have totally different approaches to music . . . I was always for alternative, I was always for the underground and so on . . . Seva likes good quality music, he likes jazz above all, and from rock music, he likes good quality pop music . . . Because of his very, I would say, safe taste, Seva became so popular with normal kids. I mean he was preaching to the majority who like Elton John, who like Queen . . . David Bowie, Prince, Kiss, Led Zeppelin, and Pink Floyd . . .
>
> I mean, Seva has good taste but a very safe taste, and I was always reaching for the outer limits, for the extremes. Like say even at this disco you know that we started between '72 and '74,

10 Ibid., 33.

> I didn't play the Beatles or the Rolling Stones or anything like that there . . . All my lectures were about (at that time) progressive rock. So, I was talking about Frank Zappa, King Crimson, Jethro Tull . . . you know, something that was on the cutting edge at that time.
>
> When punk rock and new wave started, I immediately rejected all progressive rock, all classic rock—I hate Pink Floyd, I hate Led Zeppelin, Deep Purple and so on can go to hell! And I was immediately, of course, with the Sex Pistols and Suicide and Talking Heads . . . But Seva avoided all kinds of crazy punk . . . didn't even consider this [to be] music. "Well, these guys they cannot even play!" *That* is what he would say.
>
> So, we have both been feeding two different fields, two different audiences, and this is also why I've always been more influential with the musicians and artists and journalists . . . whereas Seva is an idol of the general rock crowd. I was for the weirdness in the underground, and Seva was catering to the mainstream development of the art.[11]

Indeed, Troitsky does always seem to reach for the "extremes" and in doing so creates this eclectic persona for himself, this worldly, renaissance-type man who is more freewheeling and uncontained—making him an ideal example for the musician aesthetic. Seva, on the other hand, is the "True Gentleman," being the guide of the young male listener in particular and rock lovers in general—the "normal" kids, as Troitsky puts it. He writes in his book *Back in the USSR*, published towards the end of the '80s, that the tastes of the people—the "general rock crowd"—following the breakup of the Beatles run towards hard rock lines that favor Led Zeppelin, Deep Purple, Black Sabbath, Uriah Heep, and Grand Funk Railroad—all bands that Seva does indeed play liberally.[12]

Thus, it could be said that Troitsky prods from within the evolution of rock music according to his outer-limits, revolutionary appetite, while Seva from without popularizes the genre for the Soviet people with his cultured, mainstream, and BBC-safe tastes. Troitsky remains the rock critic, the journalist, and the engineer whose work fully complements and enhances the diligent efforts of the Russians' "Man in London."

---

11 Troitsky in discussion with author, June 2019.

12 Troitsky, *Back in the USSR*, 33.

"The Club"

It is most certainly thanks to Troitsky's "backstage" efforts that Russian rock has its momentous coming out at the beginning of the '80s. In 1979, with the official recognition of groups like Time Machine, "Russian Rock finally emerge[s] from the underground."[13] The timing coincides with the Soviet invasion of Afghanistan, which might be seen as a boon to rock's cause in that the government becomes increasingly preoccupied with this giant military undertaking.[14] For the people, youth entertainment serves as a useful distraction.

However, the official recognition of Time Machine is only the beginning of many changes that spring forth with alacrity starting in 1980. National radio starts "broadcasting songs that had previously been unacceptable," articles on rock start cropping up everywhere, no longer giving rockers an "anti-hero" image and appearing to open the door for collective conversation.[15] The same year, the crucial Tbilisi rock festival takes place, marking a historic moment in Russian rock history and causing a bureaucratic shift in attitude towards the genre—the Komsomol and KGB seem to adopt the slogan "If you can't beat 'em, join 'em." Finally, the port city of Leningrad, hundreds of miles north of Moscow, becomes the new epicenter of the genre where an emphasis on Russian lyrics and a "contemporary sound modeled on punk and new wave" grows.[16] As a result of this surplus of talent and the maturation of Russian rock as its own genre, the first successful rock club is established in Leningrad in 1981. Unlike the fleeting, shallow beat clubs elsewhere—fruitless attempts to quarantine popular culture—this club actually becomes the "cradle of Russian Rock" for several years.[17]

It's curious that rock should flourish in relatively quiet Leningrad when Moscow is the city with the electric energy and dynamic landscape. But as the cultural capital, far from Kremlin politics, Leningrad gives birth to a strong community of artists. By early 1981, more than fifty bands, by some conservative estimates, have emerged. But where to perform above ground, so to speak? There exists no sanctioned venue to address the popular demand for live music.

---

13 Troitsky, *Subkultura*, 142. Norwegian scholar of Russian culture Yngvar Steinholt disagrees, writing in *Rock in the Reservation* that Russian Rock had no official status with the government.

14 See Louis Dupree, "The Soviet Union and Afghanistan in 1987," *Current History* 86, no. 522 (1987): 333–35.

15 Troitsky, *Back in the USSR*, 61. Troitsky notes that an article he'd written in 1976 about Time Machine finally gets published in 1980 along with another one of his articles—a huge departure from previous years when his pieces were rejected or ignored.

16 Troitsky, *Subkultura*, 143.

17 Ibid., 142.

At the behest of the tight-knit Leningrad musician community, an official proposal and charter are drafted calling for a dedicated rock organization and space for concerts. The proposal arises through a conjoined agreement between the Komsomol, KGB, and the DST (or LMDST), the Leningrad All-Union House for Individual Amateur Performance. This is not the first attempt to create an organized venue for rock music, nor is it the second or even the third—it is the sixth.[18] Yet, the time is right, and Leningrad is ready. So, in spring of 1981—just barely on Brezhnev's administrative watch—the Leningrad Rock Club (LRC) is born, housed in the former Palace of Folklore at 13 Rubinstein Street.

Organized on similar lines to Lenin's original system for Houses of Culture, the LRC boasts neither its own equipment nor its own designated stage. Though the KGB has a hand in the initial formation and is a constant specter, it does not run the LRC or dictate its activities—at least not directly. Moreover, not all the administration are party members or related to KGB or members of the DST. One administrator, Olga Slobodskaya, who becomes secretary in 1985, is a genuine rock lover, an avid listener to Western radio and Western rock, and one of the young people who frequent the club for the concerts before actually coming into its employment:

> I ended up at the Rock Club quite by accident. I wasn't a musician. And, of course, it was not a government task. I came on my own initiative. . . . I went to the Rock Club asking for tickets to the opening concert of the 1985 season. So, I met the members of the board and its president [Nikolay Mikhailov]; they started giving me tickets to other concerts, and then I started helping them with their work, and so I became the secretary of the Rock Club.[19]

The first meeting of the LRC is held on February 7, 1981, during which the board is selected. As Slobodskaya describes it, "members of fourteen bands, among them Akvarium, Mify, Piknik, and Rossiyanye, participate." Akvarium founders Boris Grebenshchikov (BG) and Anatoly "George" Gunitsky and several other notable musicians are chosen for the LRC board.[20] Opening night arrives only a month later on March 7, despite disagreements among the members as to whether they should be an official organization modeled after Lenkontsert (a state concert agency) or

---

18 Troitsky, *Back in the USSR*, 71–72.

19 Olga Slobodskaya in correspondence with author, December 2020.

20 Ironically, both BG and Akvarium are banned from LRC in 1983, albeit, as with every punishment, only temporarily.

as free of government analogues as possible.[21] At this first historic but somewhat forgettable concert, the four bands chosen to perform are Zerkalo, Rossiyanye, Piknik, and Mify. Although the concert attendees purportedly perceive the presentation as "rather old-fashioned and boring," the main goal is accomplished. The officials watching from the balcony approve, or at least don't object. Rapidly, the LRC band roster grows to include a whopping thirty-two members in those early days, though not all have the necessary equipment—amplifiers, proper instruments, microphones, and so on—to perform in a real venue.[22]

Leningrad Rock Club, Aquarium performing (top), crowd packing the hall (bottom), 1985 (credit: Joanna Stingray)

---

21 Steinholt, *Rock in the Reservation*, 39.

22 Ibid., 38.

At first, the club restricts performers to Leningrad musicians only.[23] Although hundreds pay to attend the concerts, the talent receives no payment at all. According to Troitsky, this is the "official doctrine on 'amateurs' until the mid-eighties."[24] The main benefit then of the Rock Club is simply to give a platform and semblance of officialdom to a performing artist, to remove the stigma of attending a rock concert and normalize the forbidden, and thereby to widen the potential audience and reach of rock music. However, with a committee that includes Soviet officials deciding on what is permissible, what is "good" music, what is ideologically Soviet, the early offerings leave much to be desired. The club comes under the threat of shutdown more than once. Quickly, it becomes obvious that filling the six-hundred-seater hall depends on the presence of fresh and edgy acts like Alisa—a band that comes to national fame at the LRC.[25]

Then, in 1982, the group Strange Games (Strannye igry) debuts, focused more on performance and not as much on the music; they are "the first to get serious about arrangements and a stage show," according to Troitsky. Along with Strannye igry, but less dramatically, Kino (literally meaning "movies" or "cinema"), an attractive new wave group, steps onto the scene. Troitsky observes that Kino's exotic, handsome, and expressive lead singer Viktor Tsoi, who is ethnically unique with Soviet-Korean lineage, is at heart just "a teenager," without the "healthy cynicism"—healthy, per Troitsky's judgment—of contemporaries like Mike Naumenko (front man of Zoopark):

> His world is sincere, full of confusion, and rather defenseless. He wants to be grownup and sarcastic, but reality continues to surprise him. . . . Boris Grebenshchikov [becomes] Tsoi's main fan and benefactor, saying that no one's songs [have] so much tenderness and purity. . . .[26]

It is Kino that in the long run puts the LRC on the map. The group's performances, exuding Tsoi's brand of passion, innocence, and self-exploration are just what the youth need.

---

23 Evgeny Kozlov, "Spring Music Festival: Leningrad Palace of Youth. 15.3.1986," E-kozlov.com, July 23, 2019, http://www.e-kozlov.com/Rock-Festival-1986/index.htm.

24 Troitsky, *Back in the USSR*, 74.

25 Steinholt, *Rock in the Reservation*, 38.

26 Troitsky, *Back in the USSR*, 78–79. The sarcasm Tsoi seeks to embody is the same as that pervading the social climate, but he is less concerned with the lack of external changes in the country and more fascinated with internal metamorphosis.

Ultimately, Russian rock bands like Strange Games, Kino, and Alisa provide a space for young people to "feel" themselves, to embrace their Russianness while casting off the Soviet state of mind. Such concert gatherings make the Rock Club special and permanent, despite the political imbroglio. The LRC fills an intrinsic need for the youth, providing "a breath of freedom," according to Olga Slobodskaya. "Free music in a non-free country."[27]

Until the late '80s, Leningrad remains the mecca of rock, the place where anybody who is anybody (and anybody who wants to be somebody) must perform. Nevertheless, with KGB regulars at every single concert, the need remains for the LRC board to be careful and selective of which bands are given an official platform.[28]

The "Russian" Debate

While the Leningrad scene thrums in the early '80s, Moscow's rock underground, by contrast, is per Troitsky's typically crisp judgment "empty and boring" before 1983. *Mashinomaniya* has waned, and Moscow is waiting and watching the rising legends and motifs of Leningrad rock. The emergence of fresh talent is inevitable, yet it takes time for dynamic newcomers to appear. One notable band with a "cretinous aesthetic" seizes the spotlight with a curiously older, somewhat macabre front man by the name of Pyotr Mamonov.[29] Going by the name Zvuki Mu (Sound of Moo), Mamonov's group debuts in 1984 for an audience comprised of schoolchildren and established rockers like BG and Makarevich. From the outset, Zvuki Mu strikes a nerve with every level of Soviet society through its brittle music, its halting and strangely disorienting lyrics, and the cavernous depths of Mamonov's eyes as he stares unblinkingly at the audience, maintaining a clear stiffness—as if suggesting that life in the USSR has robbed him of his soul and reduced him to mere functionality,

---

27 Olga Slobodskaya in correspondence with author, December 2020. She also confirms Troitsky's role in the LRC: "He often came to us for festivals or important concerts. He helped our bands in the early 80s with organization of concerts in Moscow."

28 Ibid. Moreover, Olga writes that the KGB "wanted to expel me from the University, where I studied at the evening law school. But luckily, I wasn't expelled, though I do not know why."

29 Thanks to Troitsky, Zvuki Mu made a critical connection to Brian Eno and performed two US and UK tours, partially funded by Warner Brothers, proving that Russian rock groups (even the more bizarre and challenging acts) had an audience in the West. See Aaron Ouzilevski, "'A Folkloric Hallucination': Zvuki Mu, Soviet Russia's Most Glorious Band," *Guardian*, July 20, 2021. Mamonov passed away in July 2021 due to complications from Covid-19. Another Zvuki Mu member, Alexander Lipnitsky, died in 2021 after a skiing accident.

like a robot. This isn't too far from the truth. Mamonov, again being older than and without the sex appeal of a Viktor Tsoi, brings to the stage hard life experience. He had grown up in a neighborhood rife with criminals and alcoholics and had held a variety of jobs that made him into quite the Soviet specter in performance at least, terrifying and ghostly. It's as if Mamonov, a ghost howling into a microphone with sunken eyes, invites everyone to shake off their Soviet shackles before it's too late by chanting along with his repetitive, counterculture lyrics. Biographer Sergei Guryev writes that Zvuki Mu's concerts are a "shamanic ritual designed to drive out the demon lying in the Soviet consciousness."[30] Mamonov's band marks a huge departure from the developing sound of bands like Kino, Strange Games, and Alisa, which leads to the question of what in fact constitutes "Russian Rock"? Is there even a need for the separate categorization, and is the genre simply a geographic reference?

Zvuki Mu, like Strange Games, depends heavily on self-expression, which includes costume choices, props (like a goat), dramaticisms (breaking chairs or lighting things on fire), and more. This theatrical aspect characterizes Western rock as well—provocative movements and eye-catching visuals are inherent to this sensory genre. So, it is not the performative aspects of Russian rock that are its distinguishing feature, then. In terms of the music itself, the Russian bands largely do not make use of any melodies, scales, or chord progressions that are markedly different from Western tonality. In fact, they may be considered quite Western in this respect, though Russian rock seems to shy away from a full embrace of Western rock—or perhaps it can't achieve the same brazen clarity of sound because "freedom" is a key ingredient that isn't easily replicated in the USSR. So, if not the sound and if not the performance, what is the one true "Russian" aspect of the genre?

The answer is the emphasis and importance placed on lyrics. While Leningrad bands are hard at work striving to capture the unique Russian milieu through lyrics, Moscow is slower to catch on, even though the city has witnessed the work of Makarevich, whom Troitsky calls "the first and most influential designer of the Soviet school of rock lyrics,"[31] and also Mike Naumenko, the songwriter and founder of Zoopark. Everyone seems to agree that lyrics are important: "The lyrics represent the attitudes and philosophy of the rock community and are its litany."[32] Yet, there remains uncertainty and disagreement about what exactly the inspiration and guidelines for these lyrics should be.

---

30 Ibid. See Sergei Guryev, *Istoriia gruppy "Zvuki Mu"* (St. Petersburg: Amphora, 2008).

31 Troitsky, *Back in the USSR*, 40.

32 James Riordan, ed., *Soviet Youth Culture* (London: Palgrave Macmillan, 1989), 46.

A 1982 letter to Seva from a Moscow rock band calling themselves Juliet Mills outlines the conundrum that many young underground musicians are experiencing:

> It turns out to be an ambiguous situation. On the one hand, for example, "Time Machine" owes the lion's share of its popularity to the fact that its texts have a claim to meaningfulness. The Moscow rock audience is tired of countless *Zhek* groups savoring their compositions in pidgin English. We want to listen to something in our native language, but with meaning.... It is this desire that gives rise to the tendency [of bands] to compose songs based on the poems of good poets. This is the other side—[Mikael] Tariverdiev and [David] Tukhmanov model *chernukha*[33] on poems by [Marina] Tsvetaeva, [Anna] Akhmatova and Shakespeare as translated by [Samuil] Marshak. The sonnet of Shakespeare performed by Alla Pugacheva sold almost twenty million. And who needs all this? You can't even hear the music over this mess. So, the question arises: what to sing and how? And in what language?

Clearly, this issue bothers these young men greatly, and it's telling that they should cite composers like Mikael Tariverdiev and David Tukhmanov who both belong to the Union of Composers, and therefore are sanctioned by the state. Should rock depend on loyal composers and classical poets? Certainly "pidgin English" is not the solution. Seva replies on air:

> The answer: in England in English, in Mongolia in Mongolian, in Yakutia in Yakut. But seriously, that's why rock music claims the status of youth culture, because it is created by young people completely independently, without regard to the classics—even of Marshak's translation. Its purpose is to reflect the worldview and the views of its performers. That is why individuals in rock and roll are so popular—they speak with their own voice, express their own thoughts. Composing songs based on other people's poems, especially those written in a different era, turns into a kind of musical exercise—and this is better left to "professionals," in quotation marks. As Mayakovsky said: "I am a

33 *Chernukha* is a slang term derived from the Russian word *cherny* (black) that indicates artistic expression in opposition to official Soviet optimism. The word is supposed to have been a *perestroika* phenomenon and only popular among youth in the late '80s; but, clearly, here is an example of its use in the early '80s.

> poet—that's why I'm interesting," so you should be interesting in what you do. . . .[34]

It seems that his advice is more or less taken to heart by the young performers who learn to lyricize "with their own voice" in their native language and thus play a critical role in the emergence of Russian rock as a distinct, culturally specific genre rather than a poor copy of its Western counterparts and antecedents. Russian rock becomes a vibrant force that breaks the political grip the establishment has on the youth, particularly the young men who see in the rockers (the vast majority of whom are male) the kind of free and individualistic archetype of masculinity that suits their generation's need to spread its wings and soar above the system, rather than fight it. The movement—and it is a movement—sweeps the whole country, spawning bands in even the remotest regions with unique styles and approaches and a plethora of grim experiences:

> They all had sharp new sounds and hip, brazen names. . . . The guys were from places like Sverdlovsk along the eastern Ural Mountains and Novosibirsk in southern Siberia; the lead singer of DDT, a scruffy guy with big bright glasses and a gravelly voice named Yuri Shevchuk, was from Ufa, one of the old cities of the Mongol Empire's Golden Horde. It seemed like rock was spreading across all of Russia.[35]

Many listener letters that had reached Seva in the late '70s came from these precise remote regions, regions where radio is the one small but powerful window through which the world beyond the Iron Curtain may be experienced and explored. Of course, human connection plays a role in spreading rock music, but the distances in the hinterland are vast. It's safe to say that in remote areas, Seva (via the largely apolitical conduit of the BBC) is the youth's main source of information and inspiration. This inspiration then bears fruit, and Troitsky the talent scout plucks these new, fresh-sounding bands and brings them to Leningrad to test their mettle at the LRC. Russian rock thus evolves through Seva's steady voice and Troitsky's discriminating ear.[36]

---

34 *Rok-posevy*, April 2, 1982, radio broadcast, https://seva.ru/rock/?id=203.

35 Joanna Stingray and Madison Stingray, *Red Wave: An American in the Soviet Music Underground* (Los Angeles: DoppelHouse Press, 2020), 89, Kindle.

36 The initial rule that reserved the LRC stage for Leningrad musicians only obviously goes away, but when exactly or why is not known to the author; however, it seems apparent that if anyone had a hand in dispensing with this rule it was Troitsky.

Artemy Troitsky, the Critic (courtesy of A. Troitsky)

Featured Listener: Dmitry

I was raised in a family of so-called "technical intelligentsia" in the closed city of Gorky (present-day Nizhny Novgorod), which was prohibited to all foreigners and cultural exchanges, as it was rich in military institutions and factories.[37] It was basically a military industry disguised as a city, about one hundred kilometers to the east of Moscow on the Volga River. So, we listened to radio (since I was ten) for very many reasons, as it was one of the few things that could enter the closed city. The tradition of listening to Western radio—American, European radio—was a part of life in some circles of the Russian intelligentsia. Specifically, we heard best Radio Svoboda and, also, Voice of America. In fact, my mother who wasn't a dissident, who was a strong Soviet lady, would listen to Western radio at night. She couldn't explain why she was doing it; it was just an attempt to make her way to the truth because we lived in a society where you had nothing to believe. Maybe those radio programs would help her understand something.

She was an energetics communication engineer, and my father was a supplier in a transport company. Despite my parents divorcing when I was five and me living with my mother, I wasn't separated from my father; I had time with him regularly. Sometimes he used to bring in his huge JVC 4-speaker audio system for months so I could not only listen to his cassettes but catch some programs of Western radio: Voice of America, BBC Russian Service, Radio Liberty, and Deutsche Welle. Radio Liberty was the easiest to catch because it had the strongest communicator and didn't break up as much. It was not so intensely muted in this area as the others. Sometimes you could listen to it for twenty-four hours without having to change the wavelength. It was just the most available. But no one could tell you what you might pick up today—if you caught the frequency and it was a success then you didn't want to change the dial.

After 1983 I began to catch Seva as a name for me, and I made little marks on the scale for myself so I knew where I could find him. He was unique and that is not a figure of speech. Firstly, he was Russian, he was Soviet, and had the Soviet mentality—and he was a musician, which was also important. He wasn't anti-Soviet either; he wasn't the paid agent of England or the USA. So, when listening to him we didn't feel an agenda to fight with the Soviet [mentality], to replace in our mind what we knew. He spoke one language to us, a mutual language; there

37 Nizhny Novgorod is where Lenin initially ordered the first radio laboratory to be built and from where the first radio signals were broadcast. It makes perfect sense that this area remained closed and that there was less jamming in this region and better reception.

was no conflict. . . . He didn't fight, he didn't destroy what we believed (*whatever* we believed). He never intended to undermine the regime. His primary intention was to inform and entertain. Leaving aside ideological questions, he was the only source of music information.[38] The only other [trusted] source of such was the *Rovesnik* journal with Artemy Troitsky's articles, and that's all! From the early '80s that was all. Seva was our source of music, source of information, source of humor, source of ideological trends. And a way of thinking, a way of life.

That was a time when our parents, our fathers had no ability to tell us or answer very important questions for us. Because they had no voice, they had no firm use. So Seva replaced this ideological function for us.[39] We did see him as a father figure (or at least a close family member) because he gave us the answers that our parents wouldn't or couldn't. No one inside the USSR could be free from ideological enemies because just being here you couldn't. And Seva was "out," and so he could afford to be free himself, and he spoke to us from that position. Because of him, the "West" was a big smile with the Russian language who understood our matters. That was the representation of the West through the Soviet people's eyes. He was our agent in a Western environment.

Our Russian frame of thinking is based on this: you can evaluate something, some event only once you have some moral basis for it. So, you can tell us about medicine if you are a doctor. You can tell us about music if you are a musician. Of course, Seva was a Soviet and a musician, and we felt that. . . . He was authentic.

---

38 While it is not true that Seva was the "only source," it is worth asking why listener after listener remembers him this way. It is possible that he is specifically the "only source" to which the listener wants to subscribe or trust. Roth-Ey writes, "Even in terms of the enemy voices alone, 'Rok-posevy' was far from the only source for Western music and information: VOA and several other stations also offered pop programs. Yet many of Seva's correspondents described the show as something both unique and essential. 'You've become a safe haven for us; legends and songs are written about you,' wrote a young man . . . in Leningrad. 'We [his group of friends] listen to your Saturday shows greedily and call Friday *pre-Seva time*.'" Roth-Ey, "Listening out," 567.

39 A direct statement validating the absence of strong male guidance and confirming the assignation of that function to Seva—not even as a physical presence, but simply as a male voice—confirming Troitsky's observation that Russian culture is very "word-oriented." This also offers a plausible explanation for why *Rok-posevy* and Seva resonated so strongly with the Soviet audience at a time when Western music culture was more or less available to young people and being offered in controlled doses on state media.

CHAPTER 11

The Barbarossa of Rock 'n' Roll

> I'm still listening to you, by God. Marconi was such a good guy, inventing those most objectionable waves that penetrate, no matter what, into any iron curtain. They are not afraid of any artificial static. . . . Your iron rock and my iron will always emerge victorious.
>
> —Evgeny of Tula, RSFSR to Seva, May 4, 1984[1]

In 1981, as the Leningrad Rock Club launches, the new US presidential administration of Ronald Reagan places fresh strain on relations between the nuclear giants, leaving the Kremlin longing for the milder Jimmy Carter—rock-supporter though he was.[2] According to the long-standing Soviet Foreign Minister Andrey Gromyko, "tension" between Russia and the US increases with a "resultant cooling in the international climate" at large.[3] Gromyko does his best to pursue diplomacy with the US Secretary of State George Shultz, a bullish, one-note mouthorgan of the US White House. Shultz claims that "the Reagan administration is devoted to constructive dialogue with the Soviet Union," but his actions and aggravating manner convince Gromyko otherwise. "Problem number one," Gromyko says to Shultz, "is to avert nuclear war. . . . It is plain that the great responsibility for not allowing a nuclear catastrophe to occur must be borne by the USSR and the USA together."[4]

---

1 *Rok-posevy*, May 4, 1984, radio broadcast.

2 David Browne, "How Jimmy Carter Literally Rocked the Presidency," *Rolling Stone*, September 8, 2020.

3 Gromyko, *Memoirs*, 297.

4 Ibid., 299. It is in fact Shultz who is indirectly responsible for VOA's hiring of William (Bill) Skundrich circa 1984 to host *Pop Concert* on the Russian Service, which is significant because Skundrich is by all indications the most successful of VOA's Russian Service DJs in the twilight Soviet and post-Soviet era (Skundrich in conversation with author, January 2021).

Over the course of Reagan's first term, the Soviet fear of war, largely due to the nuclear threat that America presents, rises to such heights that the Soviet negotiators walk out of the Geneva arms talks in November 1983.[5] Per the story that runs in the *Washington Post*:

> The Soviet Union has now walked out of both sets of nuclear arms talks with the United States following the arrival last month of Pershing II and cruise missiles in Britain, Italy, and West Germany. On November 23, Soviet negotiator Yuri Kvitsinsky announced that Moscow was discontinuing negotiations on medium-range nuclear missiles in Europe and would not fix a resumption date.[6]

Not so coincidentally with the political and economic downturn, the '80s for the BBC World Service prove to be the "harvest years," and are especially a "golden age for the Russian Service" with the greatest audience achieved during this time.[7] The period of "great faith" (of the '70s) in the endurance and stability of the USSR—albeit cynical—wears away, and weariness and wariness become the pervasive emotions, leading more and more people to turn their radio dials to foreign voices, seeking solace and guidance. The fear of nuclear war is so great that the Soviet youth newspaper *Komsomol'skaia pravda* prints a form letter to Reagan that is essentially a protest against war. Apparently, though these are submissions in English to be copied verbatim, several Soviet citizens get creative and write personalized notes in Russian to Reagan and the White House. One letter compellingly implores, "Mr. President, why are you promoting nuclear war? Don't you realize what war is? We, the grandmothers, appeal to you."[8] The clear message is that Soviets truly believe the nuclear ball is in Uncle Sam's court, and that the USSR is, according to state propaganda, playing defense and signaling only peace.

While *babushki* are earnest in their pleas (and in their fear), *molodyozh'* don't appear to care much about an impending Armageddon brought on by America.

5 John F. Burns, "The Walkout by Moscow," *New York Times*, November 26, 1983, https://www.nytimes.com/1983/11/26/world/the-walkout-by-moscow.html.

6 William Drozdiak, "Soviets Halt Strategic Arms Talks," *Washington Post*, December 9, 1983, https://www.washingtonpost.com/archive/politics/1983/12/09/soviets-halt-strategic-arms-talks/5ec90e4c-8b95-4be0-9265-1e622f706176/.

7 Golomstock, *A Ransomed Dissident*, 172.

8 Don Oberdorfer, *From the Cold War to a New Era: The United States and the Soviet Union, 1983–1991* (Baltimore: John Hopkins University Press, 1998), 68.

Many young people use this essentially free mail coupon in the paper to write to their rock navigator at the BBC.[9] A Soviet citizen recalls the details of these campaigns and the wayward London-bound *otkrytki*:

> I remember that sometime in the first half of the 1980s, the officials from *Komsomol'skaia pravda* conceived a kind of protest against the aggressive policy of the American government. They suggested that everyone cut out from the newspaper a specially printed, ready-made form with an angry text (in English), denouncing the imperialist bourgeoisie. This clipping had only to be stuck on a postcard and sent by mail (free of charge). This kind of thing, in general, was familiar to our then-reality. The joke, however, is that after a while Seva Novgorodsev started to report with bewilderment that at his BBC address he was receiving a lot of similar postcards, beginning with the words "Dear Mr. President. . . ." In short, there were many clever people who made such "clippings" in the newspaper, inscribing their text in Latin letters and indicating, of course, not the White House address, but P.O. Box 76, Strand, London—they were able to get a letter to Seva without trouble. I lamented that I didn't think of such a trick myself. . . .[10]

It should be noted that this listener is referring to the second campaign that commences later in the decade and targets Ronald Reagan. But the postcard pictured here (indeed written in Latin letters and indeed addressed to "President V. B. Novgorodsev" in London) is actually from the first letter-writing campaign in 1980 to President Jimmy Carter in his final year as president.[11] What this suggests is that while many buy into Soviet propaganda and believe the nuclear threat from the US, many others, likely generationally divided, do not feel any great fear of the West and are more eager than ever to connect with the safe and smiling voice in London. If nuclear winter is approaching, better to spend their final days fulfilling personal wishes—like hearing their words read by Seva

---

9 While unverified, it can be assumed that DJs at VOA, RFE/RL, DW, etc. also received these postcards.

10 User "Andi," forum thread response, Beatles.ru, July 22, 2012, http://www.beatles.ru/postman/forum_messages.asp?msg_id=9617&cfrom=1&showtype=1&word=%D1%E5%E2%E0&headers=1&cpage=2.

11 *Rok-posevy*, January 23, 1981, radio broadcast. Andrey Polishchuk is a classmate of listener Yevgeny (see featured listener in chapter 11).

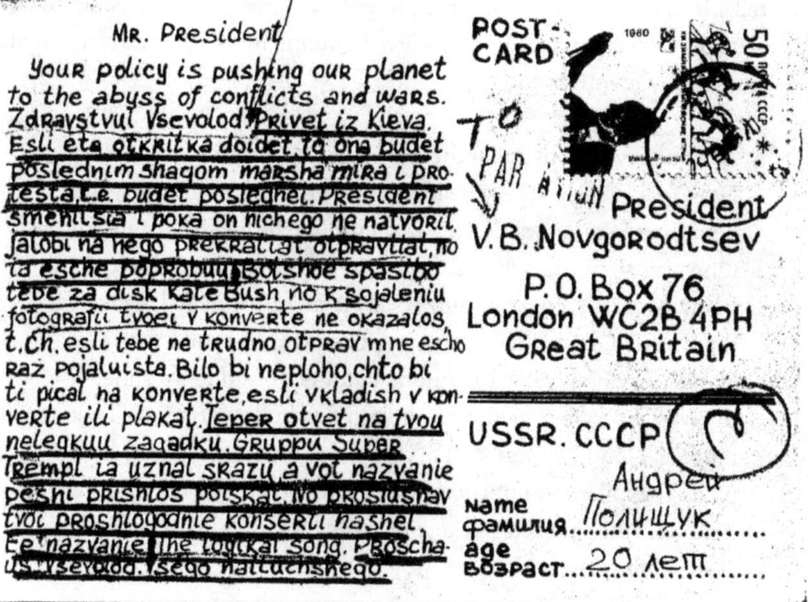

Mr. President
Your policy is pushing our planet
to the abyss of conflicts and wars.
Zdravstvui Vsevolod! Privet iz Kieva.
Esli eta otkritka doidet, to ona budet
poslednim shagom marsha mira i pro-
testa, t.e. budet posledhei. President
smenilsia i poka on nichego ne natvoril.
Jalobi na nego prekraliat otpravliat, no
ia esche poprobuu. Bolshoe spasibo
tebe za disk Kate Bush, no k sojaleniu
fotografii tvoei v konverte ne okazalos,
t.ch. esli tebe ne trudno, otprav mne escho
raz pojaluista. Bilo bi neploho, chto bi
ti pical na konverte, esli vkladish v konverte ili plakat. Teper otvet na tvou
nelegkuu zagadku. Gruppu Super
Trempl ia uznal srazu, a vot nazvanie
pesni prishlos poiskat. No prosiushav
tvoi proshlogodnie konserti nashel.
Ee nazvanie The logikal song. Proscha-
us Vsevolod. Vsego nailuchshego.

POST CARD
1980
TO
PAR
President
V.B. Novgorodtsev
P.O. Box 76
London WC2B 4PH
Great Britain
USSR. CCCP
Name
фамилия Андрей Полищук
age
возраст 20 лет

Postcard sent in 1980 by 20-year-old Andrey Polishchuk from Kyiv (credit: seva.ru)

Novgorodsev through their own personal radio. Acts of subterfuge to which youth resort in order to earn the attention of their broadcaster of "fascist music from the West."[12]

Death of a Beatle

Soon after the historic 1980 Tbilisi rock festival takes place, legendary bard and singer Vladimir Vysotsky dies, his funeral attended by tens of thousands of Russians. Then, in December of that year, another famous musician is murdered, and the rock world reels. It is, of course, John Lennon. The death of a Beatle receives diametrically opposed reactions in Russia—treated as nothing less than a family tragedy by Beatlemaniacs and a purposely muted nonevent for the Soviet government.

12 Ian Peddie, *Popular Music and Human Rights: 2-Volume Set* (Burlington: Ashgate, 2015), 151, 153, 155.

To tell his listeners the news, Seva presents a three-part series, the first of which airs on December 12, four days after Lennon's murder, while state media barely makes any mention:

> As you may have heard in the news, on December 8, at 11pm in New York, the legendary Beatles member, singer, composer, and poet John Lennon was killed. That evening, he and his wife Yoko Ono were returning home from the recording studio Record Plant. Several autograph hunters, as it often happened, were at the house. One of them, a young man with a round face and glasses, having received Lennon's autograph, suddenly pulled a thirty-eight-caliber revolver and fired five bullets at point-blank range.... John Lennon died of blood loss on the way to the hospital. The killer did not try to hide. "Do you know what you are holding?" the shocked gatekeeper asked him. "Yes," he answered, "I shot John Lennon."[13]

The Moscow bureau chief for US News & World Report at this time has a vivid encounter with a cab driver, which illustrates the fact that, even after Lennon's death makes headlines in the West, much of the Russian population has no clue:

> We were flagging down a cab, because you could never get a taxi in Moscow, so you just stood out on the street and raised your hand to get someone to stop his car and give you a ride . . . So [we] got in this gypsy cab, which I remember as being a Volga sedan . . . We told the guy where we wanted to go, then, I said, "Hey, have you heard the news? John Lennon's been shot." And the guy was so immediately affected that he had to pull over—initially he couldn't believe it, he said, it can't be true. And we said no, no, it's true; this is what happened. And the guy just completely fell apart . . . tears streaming down. He still got us to our destination . . . He was probably in his twenties, with that very working-class look of the day—the average *muzhik*, out making some moonlight money, maybe not even his car, but doing what people did at that time.[14]

---

13 *Rok-posevy*, December 12, 1980, radio broadcast, https://seva.ru/audio/rock/1982/r821217vv.mp3.

14 Jeff and Gretchen Trimble in discussion with author, December 18, 2020.

Then, as word finally gets around, doubtless in large part due to Western broadcasts like Seva's, people demonstratively honor Lennon by gathering unofficially in public areas, such as Moscow State University (MGU), and creating icon corners at home with lit candles, photos cut from Western magazines, and even Beatles records if they are lucky enough to own a real copy: "And it wasn't just a couple of people. It was like what people were doing in the age group of [those] we were hanging out with at that time. Now the authorities did crack down . . . about the gatherings like the one in MGU."[15]

But even with such a widespread reaction, there is still lingering disbelief in remote areas where Lennon's death seems barely more than a rumor, and few details are known or understood. For weeks, listeners who missed his December broadcasts continue to write in confusion to Seva, asking if the rumor (or even the published obituary in their local *Pravda*) is really true—in search of the truth, they ask the Voice they trust. In January of 1981, during his listener letters segment, Seva includes an epistle written from a girl living in Ufa, well over eight hundred miles to the east of Moscow:

> Good evening, friends. It has been a long, long time since we have read the letters that still come to us in spite of all the theories of probability, or rather, the theories of improbability. In December, we did not conduct any programs on letters and applications, because as you remember, John Lennon was killed in New York, and we devoted three programs to him. It is about this event that Masha from the city of Ufa wrote to us in her desperate letter:
>
> "There was a story in *Pravda* yesterday about Lennon's death. Vsevolod, tell me that this is not true, that this is just a mistake. Although newspapers have no right to lie, they can be wrong. Seva, just say "no" and everything will be all right again, eh? And well, who would have killed an innocent person? I don't believe it, I don't want to believe it!"
>
> To our great regret, Masha, this is true. There are no miracles, and there is nothing to dream about: there is Lennon, ashes, and hunched shoulders . . .[16]

15 Ibid.

16 *Rok-posevy*, January 23, 1981, radio broadcast, https://seva.ru/rock/?id=141&y=1981.

Rock Crops

As Seva's popularity peaks, his music program is renamed to *Rok-posevy*, in which *posevy* most clearly means crops. However, this is another instance of coded performance and wordplay meant to allude to Seva's name—*po Sevy*—where, following Russian grammar, the *po* means "on," "by," or "according to." Thus, *Rok-posevy* is not only translated as "Rock crops" but also understood to mean "Rock by Seva" or "Rock according to Seva," or, more colloquially, "Rock the Seva way," an accurate characterization because Seva sows in his listeners English ideas and music clothed in a Russian form.[17]

It is worth noting the BBC Russian Service's choice to change the name of this long-running pop music program to incorporate the program host's moniker (with clever wordplay at that). Not only does this give Seva much more prestige, elevating him beyond the émigré contract employee level, it also impresses upon listeners that the BBC places so much value on a Russian and former Soviet citizen that they have practically put the four letters of his name on their microphones.

Nevertheless, due to tensions between him and his bosses, Seva contemplates a hiatus from the BBC in favor of his thriving film work, a potential salve for his failure to achieve his dreams of being an actor in his youth. His timing to pull out from radio is poor, however, for rock in the USSR comes under fresh ideological attack, starting in 1983, with Brezhnev's successor Yuri Andropov, the KGB's top man: "It started with a campaign in the press; newspapers came down hard on rock groups for their 'greyness, 'bad taste' and 'lack of ideals.' . . . But a resolution adopted by the Ministry of Culture. . . . was directed not at the truly 'grey' non-talents . . . but at the rock groups."[18] The principal directive requires that eighty percent of the material performed by "any professional group" should come from the Union of Composers—a ludicrous stipulation when the average Union member's age is sixty and no new songwriter has been admitted into the Union's Moscow branch since 1973.

The main arguments, instigated by the Union of Composers, has to do with the oft-used keyword *education*: "rock musicians are 'illiterate' charlatans . . . and some of them can't even read notes!"[19] Of course, the illiteracy accusation is quite unfounded and even if true would have reflected more on the state and Komsomol for failing to ensure the universal education of young people. But as

---

17 M. Tabak, *RIA Novosti*, March 2, 2007, https://seva.ru/media/?id=148.

18 Troitsky, *Back in the USSR*, 95–96.

19 Ibid., 96.

it is the majority of rising rock musicians are actually engineers and enrolled in one technical program or another at the university level. And even if some drop out in favor of pursuing other passions, they can hardly be summarily dismissed as "illiterate." But the second part of the Union's gripe (about note-reading), whether or not valid, is a crucial lure of the genre for the general populace—rock music's accessibility, playability, and learnability make it much more of a democratic style than classical or even jazz. Perhaps one of the things that radio did is train people to listen, and by listening they learned, and many are able to figure out how to reproduce the sounds and create new ones, which technically speaking is much easier to do with rock than jazz (more like repeating an *anekdot* rather than regurgitating a hundred Pushkin poems). If the technical bones of the music are simple—a three-chord progression, for example—then it is much easier to concentrate on the lyrics, the passion of performance, and most of all connecting with the audience. And here is one of the main differences between jazz and rock at the highest levels. With jazz, performances are more of an esoteric, clever conversation among the musicians—like an exclusive *tusovka* or club—and the audience is invited to listen, but participation is not requested, required, or even expected. With rock, however, the audience is *everything*. And if jazzers' intellectualism sailed above the heads of the conservative and moderately educated Politburo, then freethinking rockers are most certainly frying the brains of the establishment.

The Barbarossa of the BBC

In 1984, confirming that political tides have turned, new blacklists of rock bands emerge as the anti-rock campaign only heats up. Troitsky is officially condemned despite the years he's spent quite openly engineering the rock scene—a truly fruitless expression of Soviet authority that coincides with yet another attack on Seva who has conspicuously just earned British citizenship.[20] Just as the "professional groups are in a panic" because they must appear before the Ministry of Culture with eighty percent Union songs, a protracted and theatrical editorial appears in *Komsomol'skaia pravda* concerning Western music as a tool of ideological sabotage.[21] This publication comes, ironically, at a time when jazz, the previously diabolized genre, has "long come out of the closet," now regarded as

---

20 Troitsky in conversation with author, June 2019.
21 Troitsky, *Back in the USSR*, 97.

a tame and accepted form of art.[22] Entitled "The Barbarossa of Rock 'n' Roll," this feature piece written by Yuri Filinov opens positively enough, admitting in the very first line that "modern pop music"[23] has become an "integral part" of life for youth.[24] But then the true agenda of the article quickly reveals itself as it draws readers' attention to the enemies of the USSR who take advantage of this rock "phenomenon" for their own dastardly plans. Filinov paraphrases *Der Spiegel* to substantiate his claims:[25]

> As the magazine stated, for the American secret service of the OOS (the predecessor of the CIA), popular American hits and Broadway shows of the 1930s and 1940s were a proven means of demoralizing the German population during the Second World War. Translated into German and arranged in a new way, they were broadcast by secret service transmitters in order to introduce the main tenets of the American way of life into the enemy's mind, reduce the will to resist, and thus remove negative emotions about the opposing side.

In the summer of 1944, Filinov says, eight records a week were released with hits and recordings of Broadway shows in German. This work, carried out in an atmosphere of deep secrecy, without exception bypassed American copyright laws. Therefore, if such were the practices of US broadcasting during the Great Patriotic War, how can the West at large be trusted *not* to have hidden and cancerous motives in their current broadcasts? To be fair, his general argument is not wrong: Western broadcasters indeed have a collective agenda, not only determined by the source of government funding but also by the employees themselves who have, to varying degrees, a common conviction that through radio they are liberating and educating captive listeners. Modern music (central to young people's lives all over the world), with "no borders or language barriers" or "customs checks," is a sharp, yet ostensibly harmless, weapon in countries where governments seek to control youth consumption and block their access.

---

22 Serge Schmemann, "Soviet Jazz Has Survived Politics," *New York Times*, March 25, 1984.

23 Troitsky, *Back in the USSR*, 97. The euphemism "modern pop music" is also a sign of this anti-rock fever; all press had to remove the term "rock" and find other ways to talk about the genre without *naming* it.

24 *Komsomol'skaia pravda* ironically published in March 1984 an op-ed by Troitsky that condemned the banning of rock bands and argued that these anti-rock actions will only deepen the underground movement. See *Back to the USSR*, 98.

25 *Der Spiegel* is a left of center publication based in Hamburg, Germany.

Filinov declares that while the BBC, VOA, and DW conduct music programs in an official capacity, the rest of the broadcasters who fill up the ten hours a day of jazz, pop, and rock music do so without "identification."[26] By this, Filinov most notably alludes to the US and UK, the former for covert CIA funding of RFE/RL and the latter for the Foreign Office's monetary support and use of Radio Luxembourg. He condemns the West as a lawless moonshine manufacturer, pouring rock culture down young Russians' throats to encourage an "independent, aggressive lifestyle," citing, tellingly, a NATO document:

> Here is an excerpt from just one document issued by the special body of NATO, the Council for Youth Affairs: "Special attention in this period should be paid to young people, who do not yet have a set lifestyle, who are susceptible to everything new, unusual, colorful, catchy in material and technical terms. It is our task to captivate the youth of the USSR with the ideals of the West."[27]

It may be apparent by now that the article title is a loaded declaration rather than a stab at sensationalism. By simply using the infamous word "Barbarossa," Filinov implies at least two important correlations. The first is the obvious Operation Barbarossa, which when applied to any context denotes treachery or a Hitler-esque anti-Russian, anti-Soviet crusade. "The Barbarossa of Rock 'n' Roll" suggests, in this context, a bold comparison between the Nazi agenda to bring the Soviet Union under the control of the Third Reich and the West's invasion of the USSR through the broadcasting of rock music. It is doubtful this could be the primary insinuation that Filinov or *Komsomol'skaia pravda* wishes to make, as such an equivalency would be a serious disrespect to those who perished during the Great Patriotic War. A second more likely meaning, that also complements the first, is that the "Barbarossa of Rock 'n' Roll" refers to a single person, not a campaign. The name Barbarossa has been carried by several historical figures, at least one of whom was a Barbary pirate in the Ottoman Empire. This pirate character with all his swashbuckling accoutrements and state sponsorship who conquers and seizes savagely, just as Hitler conquered and seized,

---

26 Exposed as a CIA operation in the late 1960s, even though it had claimed to be a nongovernment organization, RFE/RL eventually became openly government funded. But it was Oleg Tumanov, embedded in RL, who exposed the truth. See Oleg Tumanov, *Tumanov: Confessions of a KGB Agent* (Berlin: Edition Q, 1993).

27 Yuri Filinov, "The Barbarossa of Rock 'n' Roll," *Komsomol'skaia pravda*, September 16, 1984, https://seva.ru/media/?id=2.

is likely the narrative Filinov wants to create, targeting Seva specifically who has been referred to by listeners as their "Navigator" or "Captain." Filinov spends the rest of the article denigrating the wholesome image of Seva the Navigator and replacing it with Seva the Barbary Pirate who pillages the hearts and minds of youth at the behest of the evil Western establishment:[28]

> Seva Novgorodsev, the host of the program for young listeners in the Soviet Union who adore rock and pop music, reports on heavy metal—a direction of Western pop music characterized by pathological aggressiveness of performance and primitivism. Do not talk about this man who betrayed the Motherland. *Rovesnik* magazine described him quite vividly and eloquently in the article "Kto on takoi?" featured in the ninth issue of 1982. This renegade tries his best to impose on his listeners an antagonism of aesthetic tastes, doubt in the existence of moral norms.

Filinov knows that this published tirade will hardly present a new name to any reader. It is rather an attempt to discredit Seva—if any hope exists of doing so. Filinov scorns Seva for indirectly propounding the idea that "only we [the West] have a music worthy of you youth. Only the West brings progress to all mankind. They don't understand you 'there' [in the USSR], but we do." It is, then, not even the music the Komsomol fears, but the way in which it is smoothly delivered and packaged by a Russian voice from the West. For Filinov, Western radio DJs, but especially Seva, are only propagandists and spiritual pirates, nothing more.

The West's Trumpet Call

One final matter covered in the *Komsomol'skaia pravda* piece is that of religious propaganda and the ensemble Trumpet Call (Trubny zov), which rose to fame on what Filinov snidely dubs the "billboard" of Seva Novgorodsev.[29] Trumpet Call is the first Russian Christian rock group, which naturally brings them trouble. At home in Leningrad, the ensemble is not so popular, not because of its

---

28 *Rok-posevy* never claimed to be a program just for young people, as Filinov claims it to be. Apparently, the Kremlin and KGB viewed Seva this way, as a voice speaking to, being heard primarily by, and trusted by the youth.

29 Trumpet Call featured on several of Seva's programs and thus owes their renown to him. Seva brought Valery Barinov on *Sevaoborot* in November 1987 to discuss the band's history: https://seva.ru/audio/oborot/1987/s871128vs004.mp3.

religious bent but more because of a lack of musical appeal. But after becoming the victims of KGB designs, they gain fame when Seva starts to play their songs on *Rok-posevy* to draw attention to the band's plight. Filinov claims that Seva, "with pathos," calls the band's categorically offensive songs as the greatest achievement in the field of music. This is far from true.

The following is Seva's on-air account, given on October 21, 1983, of the first arrest of band front man Valery Barinov:

> On October 11, in Leningrad, at a metro station, Valery Barinov, a member of the Trubny Zov Christian group, was arrested . . . [and] was sent by ambulance to . . . the Skvortsov-Stepanov psychiatric hospital. All week, no one was allowed to see him; only his wife Tatyana could come to him by special permission. Valery Barinov was given daily injections of chlorpromazine, a drug used to treat schizophrenia and calm the violently insane. Doctor I.V. Künnapu, . . . the attending physician, told Tatyana Barinova that Valery, in general, is healthy, but his faith and views are so different from the views of "normal Soviet people" that he needs treatment. . . . It turned out that a capable musician, a working man, and a father of two children, by secret order, was deliberately maimed in the hospital by people of the most humane of professions! This became known in the West; first, we passed it on, then other stations—and on October 18, Tuesday, the chlorpromazine injections stopped, the head of the hospital told Tatyana Barinova that the commission would consider Valery's "character traits" for discharge. . . . Truly, as it is sung in the song—I don't know any other country like that![30]

After this first incident, which indeed becomes known to the international community, a second event involving two of the members takes place that seems more calculated on the part of KGB. This elaborate setup Seva describes colorfully as a "three-letter lunch":

> A year ago, [Trumpet Call] sent an open letter to the Supreme Soviet of the USSR with a request to allow them to perform on the concert stages of the country. In response to this appeal,

30 Seva Novgorodsev, "British Hits," *Rok-posevy*, October 21, 1983, radio broadcast, https://seva.ru/rock/?id=284.

troubles began: police detentions, calls from the KGB, difficulties with work, and, finally, the placement of Valery Barinov in a psychiatric clinic, though not for long. And now, the message I received: both Barinov and Sergey Timokhin have been arrested. What are they accused of? I'll read a listener's letter:

"A man approached Barinov, a young man, and said that he was a fan of Valera's music and talked for a long time with Valera alone. This man came from Murmansk. After a while, Valera and Sergey Timokhin took tickets to Murmansk and disappeared. On March 4, 1984, they were detained. On April 3, Barinov, Timokhin, and all those whose addresses were found in Barinov's possession during the arrest were searched. KGB officers who came to conduct the search stated that the reason [for the arrest and search] was an attempt by Barinov and Timokhin to cross the border in the Murmansk region. Valery and Sergey are currently being held in Kresty prison in Leningrad.[31] Searches were carried out on the same day, all at once, from eight in the morning to four in the evening. They seized items that had nothing to do with Barinov, such as a typewriter, all notebooks, cassettes, personal letters, a Christian science film, Christian bulletins, and a geographical map of Finland. . . ."

In this story, friends, several circumstances are suggestive: first, everyone who knows Barinov and Timokhin speaks about their devotion to their families, wives, and children, so it seems very unlikely that they could leave their loved ones to their fate, or even have thought about it. Secondly, the phrase "cross the border near Murmansk" is not very clear. I myself have been to Murmansk more than once, went there on tour, and before that, I served for several months in Polyarny at the submarine base. The terrain is familiar—there is no border in the Murmansk region. . . . More than one hundred and fifty versts to the border lies in a closed zone—you can see this on any map. . . . Thirdly, the month-long gap between the arrest of the guys in Murmansk and the search of everyone's homes in Leningrad is suggestive—none of their relatives and friends knew about the arrest. . . . And

---

31 For more on Kresty prison, one of the most famous pretrial detention centers in Russia, listen to the scripted podcast *Russian Limbo*, episode 1, CEPA.org, December 1, 2020, MP3 audio, https://cepa.org/russiann-limbo-kresty-prison/.

> then there's this certain young man, the fan of Valery's music, who apparently invited the guys to come to Murmansk—all this is familiar handwriting, as the criminologists say, a familiar three-letter lunch. The fate of Barinov and Timokhin is of great concern to many people . . . and the Western public is closely following their fate.[32]

On this point, Seva far from exaggerates. Trumpet Call becomes a martyr and is lionized by conservative Western Christians who jump at the chance to prove that religious persecution behind the Iron Curtain is very real. It is a slight misfortune that their token Russian Christian, Valery Barinov, is a rock musician, but "God works in mysterious ways."

A book, unambiguously titled *Valeri Barinov: The Trumpet Call,* written by a scholar at London's Keston Institute, appears in the West in 1985 whilst the eponymous hero withers away in a Soviet labor camp, separated from his family. Much is covered in this little volume, which draws extensively from S. Frederick Starr's work *Red & Hot: The Fate of Jazz in the Soviet Union* (Oxford, 1983) and includes Filinov's 1984 article. Despite the moving details of Barinov's journey that led him to his spiritual calling and joining the Baptist Church in Leningrad, the text is soured by the hypocrisy of the Western Christian community in the '80s—at no fault of the author—since the evangelical West has been experiencing a "Satanic panic" with regards to rock music (as they had decades earlier with jazz).[33] Nevertheless, the book gives more than a healthy nod to radio for its invaluable role in educating people on both music and religion—particularly, people behind the Iron Curtain. The author includes several mentions of Seva, owing Trumpet Call's rise to prominence almost entirely due to *Rok-posevy,* as most of the countless writers to Barinov mention hearing his name on Seva's program.[34]

Religion and KGB intrigues aside, can Trumpet Call be considered a real Russian rock band? Artemy Troitsky does not seem to think so: "I had no contact with [Trumpet] Call—because their work, in my view, was utterly uninteresting—and so I don't know the details of their 'crusade.' But . . . if [the band] had concerned itself more with the local audience and less with generating

---

32 *Rok-posevy,* May 4, 1984, radio broadcast, https://seva.ru/rock/?id=312.

33 See Anna Nekola, "'More Than Just a Music': Conservative Christian Anti-Rock Discourse and the U. S. Culture Wars," *Popular Music* 32, no. 3 (2013): 407–26.

34 See for example Bourdeaux, *Valeri Barinov,* 179, wherein a letter writer from an unknown location in Russia says that he first heard about Trumpet Call on Seva's program, which caused them to be interested and want to hear the band.

scandalous publicity in the West" they may have achieved more in Russia.[35] He compares them to English rock band Uriah Heep but with "reverb overdose" and "banal songs." Seva, too, despite being empathetic with their plight and the one to herald their "crusade" from Londongrad, says candidly that the group's musical contribution is "meaningless outside the persecution and beliefs context."[36] So, even for Seva's "safe tastes," Trumpet Call falls flat when held up to aural scrutiny, especially in the context of the Russian rock scene. Without radio, without the "Barbarossa of Rock 'n' Roll," Valery Barinov would hardly be a name at all.

The Pirate Departs

Even as Seva's name becomes virtually synonymous with the BBC in the USSR, his wife Gala once again divorces him and throws him out. This time, it's the end, and consequently, his relationship with his son suffers. With the dramatic reduction in familial obligations, he has the chance to moonlight as a Russian consultant for Western TV and film, relishing the creative opportunity to tangentially pursue his youthful acting ambitions. There are many productions underway at BBC Television that concern Russian reality and, as such, significant help is required:

> They didn't know what uniforms looked like, what they were supposed to say, what the backgrounds should be, how the slogans should be written and myriads and myriads of problems for production teams. So, I started helping. And my kind of memory, because I've travelled so much and seen so much, tends to retain the, you know, insignificant details, sort of mundane stuff, and it used to prove to be very useful and successful. . . . There was this film called "Englishman Abroad" about Guy Burgess, with Alan Bates, and it received five BAFTA Awards and I was a consultant on it. . . . Then the Americans got wind of it and started approaching me. . . .[37]

In his long days spent on set, he achieves a few roles here and there in major Hollywood productions for which he is the Russian consultant, including the

35 Troitsky, *Back in the USSR*, 74.
36 Novgorodsev in correspondence with author, January 1, 2021.
37 Novgorodsev, Museum of London interview.

James Bond movie *A View to a Kill* and the Chevy Chase espionage comedy *Spies Like Us*. "I have the dubious distinction of being shot down by James Bond in the opening sequence where I'm the helicopter pilot. I'm almost blown up as a Border Guards officer in '*Spies Like Us*' by John Landis, et cetera. You know, one thing leads to another." But the increasing demands of his consulting life directly conflict with his work at the BBC. The stress takes its toll, and familiar pains from being sick in the Arctic return. Thus, when the BBC tells him he can no longer have any time off to work with the filmmakers of the movie *Gulag*, he decides that a break is in order. Weighing the fact that such attention in the newspapers is making life hard for his parents and gaining them more unwanted KGB attention, he reluctantly parts ways with the BBC at the end of 1984, resigning from his job (and promotion) as editor of the Russian Service. Nevertheless, *Rok-posevy* lives on.

Featured Listener: Yevgeny

I was born on October 6, 1960, in the Soviet city of Baku in the Azerbaijan Republic of the USSR. Immediately after my birth, my parents Rosa Ayrapetova and Mark Gershoy moved to Kyiv, Ukraine to live permanently. I finished high school there, school number 2 on Kopilovskaya Street, which bore the name of General Dmitry Karbyshev. Then, I went to work at the same place where my father was employed, Kyiv OKB TM. It was in 1977. My father was a chief engineer there, but I was a lab worker, a sheet metal worker with a monthly salary of sixty-seven rubles. To say that life in the USSR was boring means that nothing was happening there at all. But modern rock and pop music provided us with tons of energy and fun.

I loved rock music (Grand Funk Railroad, Deep Purple, Nazareth, Slade, the Who, Led Zeppelin, and others).[38] I listened to all radio stations that had a Russian service including Voice of America, Radio Svoboda [Liberty], Deutsche Welle (in Russian Language), and others. Voice of America, BBC, and other Western Radio Stations brought a modern way of life and culture, and so the Soviet way of life and Soviet culture stopped existing for us. It was the most common way to pass evenings for me. For example, I go to the kitchen of our one-bedroom apartment where the four of us lived (me, my younger sister, and parents), turn on the shortwave radio (it was an Okean 214), and surf the shortwaves looking for rock music programs and Russian services. Only Voice of America wouldn't get jammed . . . Svoboda wasn't possible to hear at all, and I remember because there was some kind of Russian error, which allowed for about thirty minutes of clear listening to Svoboda. It happened one night and then it was over—noise again. At that time, I knew they were reading Solzhenitsyn's *Gulag Archipelago* on Svoboda, and I was interested to hear, but it wasn't possible to do. Still, I would try and try on different frequencies, and sometimes I remember I would get a few minutes of the clear voice of Svoboda news and other programming, which sounded shocking but true.

My parents didn't listen to music programs, but I'd learned about VOA in Russian from my father who had a shortwave radio and would sometimes listen. At first, my favorite music programs were rock music programs by VOA Russian Service. I perfectly remember they had them twice a week (Tuesdays and

---

38 With the exception of Grand Funk Railroad, all these are UK bands—the trend with the majority of Russians—which indicates that even if they listened to rock programs on all stations, like Yevgeny they developed their taste for UK rock very probably because of listening to Seva on the BBC.

Thursdays at 8:00 pm), and they would repeat them the next day at 10:30 pm. Also, VOA had one hour of music to dance to on Saturdays at 9:00 pm. I learned there about popular music bands and performers like Boston; the Eagles; Kiss; Blood, Sweat, and Tears; Alice Cooper; Gloria Gaynor; Donna Summer; and many others. Also, they would play British bands if they were on American hit lists like the Billboard. They played Sweet, Slade, Deep Purple, Nazareth, and all that was popular.

Then, one day in 1978, my former classmate Vladimir Kogut visited me and said that the BBC also had very interesting pop music programming, which airs each Friday exactly at midnight. The BBC wasn't clearly received in Kyiv on shortwaves then, but on Friday midnight all Soviet distortions would stop, and the pop music program would be very clear for thirty minutes. I tuned in and found out that it's hosted by Seva Novgorodsev, a former USSR citizen, and I heard him say that he would start sending prizes to all who write or call in the correct title and artist of the song played at the end of the program, which features listener letters—it happened once a month. (Other weeks Seva was playing British hit list performers and was telling about British rock and pop bands popular in USSR.) So, we started participating each time hoping to get the prizes: albums of British pop and rock performers. Yes, it was very dangerous and risky because of the policies then inside of USSR. But after discussing it, we (me and my above-mentioned friend) decided that we have nothing to lose and started writing and sending letters to Seva Novgorodsev, P. O. Box 76, London, England. We were signing our letters Vladimir and Yevgeny, using Vladimir's return address because we decided it would be safer because of his Ukrainian-sounding last name Kogut. (I carried my father's last name at that time, which was Gershoy. It was Jewish-sounding and I have to tell you that there was giant antisemitism in Ukraine during those years.)

We were having problems with getting our letters to the BBC as most of postal mail from within the USSR to the outside world would just disappear. In any case, we wrote two letters the next day, Saturday, and went to the central post office of Kyiv and sent one letter registered express with a return receipt and then we sent another as a regular letter with enough postage stamps for international shipping. On Monday, we returned to the same post office and sent another express registered letter with a return receipt. We were waiting for a month for the next pop music program about listeners letters and didn't hear any mention about our letter. We were shocked and disappointed. Seva said on the air that international mail works fine, but . . . Anyway, in the same program was the next song to guess, and we sent even more letters to Seva Novgorodsev. Two letters express registered with return receipts on Saturday from Kyiv central post office—each of us stood in line separately with different letters to send internationally, first my friend and then me and there was another person between us. (Only later I found out he wasn't an ordinary customer.) Again, we didn't get even a mention of our answers on Seva's next program.

We decided to criticize the BBC a little bit to let the letter go through KGB perlustrations.[39] For the next question we sent six letters total and mentioned our disappointment by the fact that Seva assured listeners of the perfect reliability of international mail services and mentioned that our answers for the first two questions [from previous programs] didn't get through. We tried to improve our international mail connection and decided to travel to another republic to mail our answers from there, hoping also that there will be higher fidelity of receiving Seva's program. So, we went to Vilnius, Lithuania, USSR, and I remember our first answer mailed from there got to Seva. He said that "to Vladimir and Yevgeny from Kyiv" he will send albums of ABBA, the Bee Gees, and Uriah Heep—the prizes for the last three months . . .

During all this, Vladimir attended a school, something between high school and college, and he mentioned to me that there were foreign students there. We decided to get our letters through them. First, we talked to a student from Iraq who said he was traveling to Europe. We paid him one hundred rubles, gave him the envelope with the letter, and asked him just to get postage stamps there, put them on the envelope, and mail it. He agreed and again we would listen to Seva Novgorodsev, hoping to hear our letters. But the letter got to the KGB instead, and I started to feel strange activities around me.

First, the head of the Personnel Department in OKB TM[40] suddenly tells me that I must present myself to the Soviet Army Department of my bureau (*biuro*). I went there, but after keeping me for an hour they simply told me I am free to go. However, there was another guy there who left at the same time, and we had to take the same trolley to go home and even got off the trolley at the same stop. He asked me what I thought about our visit to the Army Department, and I said, "I have absolutely no idea why they would call us and then just let us go." This man was carrying a big leather portfolio in his hands and, in the trolley, he raised it higher. At the end he said, "I heard the KGB caught some letter that two young

---

39 Since this critical letter reached Seva, it can be surmised that many of the letters containing criticism along with requests may be the result of writers' KGB-evasion tactics. See Roth-Ey's "Listening out."

40 In the USSR, an OKB—Opytnoye Konstruktorskoye Byuro, meaning Experimental Design Bureaus—were small, state-run, closed technical institutions working on advanced technology. According to GlobalSecurity.org, in Kyiv, the OKB established was for civil and transport aircraft, and it was here that many of the famed Antonov aircrafts were first developed and tested.

guys wrote to a Western country. Do you know anything about it?" I replied, "No." But still I wasn't sure what was happening.

After a while, the same person in OKB TM asked me to write a "character review" about myself for the Soviet Army Department, but I suspected the KGB wanted to check my handwriting. So, during lunch time, I went home, it was three stops away by trolley, and I asked my mother to complete my "character review" with her handwriting. Luckily, she was home that moment and did what I asked. I returned to work and gave the paper to the head of the Personnel Department Alla Gonchar. She said she needed to keep it. When I went to my place, to the lab, soon afterwards she came and said that someone wants to talk to me, and I would have to go with that someone to some place. I said, "Is it connected with the Army Department?" and she said, "Yes." I went to her office and saw a tall man who said that I had to go with him to talk, and I went along, asking on the way, "Where are we going?"

"We move toward communism. Isn't it true?" he replied.

"Yes, yes," I answered, and I saw a black Volga with a driver waiting inside. We got in and soon, after about five minutes, we stopped, and we all left the Volga. And the tall man rang the doorbell of a building and before we went in, I noticed a sign on the wall next to the door that read: KGB of Podol Byuro.

Now I knew what was happening.

Someone named Svatsky opened the door, and we went in. He brought me to his office, left me alone in the room, and said he will be with me soon. In five minutes, another person came in and said, "Tell me all now. Names, addresses, all the information you know."

I asked, "Concerning what?"

"Concerning your anti-Soviet activities. Concerning your letters to the anti-Soviet element Seva Novgorodsev . . . Who *else* has written to the BBC?"

I said, "It's only me and Vladimir Kogut." Apparently, the KGB got our second letter through another foreign student from Colombia. Her name was Lola, and we paid her forty rubles and she had sent the letter through Italy, when she went there. And the letter got to Seva, and Seva read it on his program, and we got a prize for it! But in that letter, we gave our full addresses because we were sure nothing bad can happen. Later, I also found out we were absolutely unaware of the fact that Iraq was a pro-Soviet country, and I learned that the student from Iraq went to the KGB and gave them our letter himself.

The KGB said to me to write down why I was writing to Seva, and I started writing and put down that the reason for writing to the BBC was for albums of rock music very popular in USSR, and we promise not to do it anymore. When I finished writing, Svatsky came in too and both of them said, "Vladimir Kogut is also here but doesn't say a word. Go talk to him and if he will sign your explanation, then we will let you go and make sure you keep your promise. Otherwise, we might send both of you to live one hundred kilometers outside of Kyiv if needed."

I said, "I will talk to Vladimir."

And they brought Vladimir Kogut, and I briefly explained what I had written and asked him to sign my explanation. We both did, and they let us go home.

It was dark outside already, and I said to Vladimir that we were fools for including our addresses, but I have to send this letter to Seva Novgorodsev anyway. But Vladimir Kogut didn't say anything. We couldn't continue writing using our names and Vladimir had to go into the Soviet military, to the navy, for a full three years. I advised him to skip the fall draft and he agreed. So, he went to Vilnius [to hide] . . . I at the same time changed my last name to my mother's last name of Ayrapetov. She was Armenian in nationality. This way I hoped to continue writing to Seva and hoped the KGB would think it is someone else.

While Vladimir was in Vilnius, the KGB took me in for another conversation during my work hours, this time to Obolon Byuro Headquarters, [the area] where Vladimir Kogut lived. They came in a Volga and inside their headquarters was a different figure asking me where Vladimir Kogut is. I said, "I don't know," I even swore I didn't know, and the KGB said that they were concerned that Vladimir might try to cross the Soviet border. I said, "He never mentioned anything like that." They took my explanations in writing and let me go. So, Vladimir went to the Soviet Navy as planned, but before that he stopped communicating with me, explaining that his father had ordered him to do so.

I remember I started to see strange figures on the street, figures I never saw before, and I knew that the KGB was watching me again. I went to the KGB Podol Byuro to ask if I am being watched and their answer was, "If you don't write to Seva Novgorodsev, then you are okay." But I continued to write to Seva using my new last name: every third month my letter would reach him. I continued to go to Vilnius to send letters from there but also from Kyiv Central post office too. But I wasn't able to go to college anymore. To apply to any place, you had to show your qualities and the info about yourself as written by a member of the Communist Party working in the Personnel Department. Since the KGB attacks, I started getting bad marks on my records . . .

I never saw Vladimir Kogut again.[41]

---

41 Yevgeny in correspondence with author, March 2019.

CHAPTER 12

Red Waves on the "Cinderella Hour"

> Good evening, friends . . . Letting your mind travel into the past, you remember the fifties, the struggle with jazz and tight pants; the sixties, the campaign against pop music and long hair; the seventies the fight with rock; in the eighties they took up disco. This process is constantly taking on new forms. . . . But I must say that the continuous thirty-year struggle on the cultural front has borne fruit: in terms of the number of rock groups and guitar ensembles, the Soviet Union today is one of the most developed countries in the world, . . . which arouses legitimate interest among the cultural lovers in the West. Last week, we started a story about a double long-play disc *Red Wave,* which features four bands from Leningrad. "Of all the arts, cinema is the most important for us!" is a well-known quote from the group to which we will turn our attention to today, called Kino. . . .
>
> —Seva, *Rok-posevy,* September 5, 1986

While the West is working hard to win the hearts and minds of Soviet citizens, the Soviets are also striving to win over Westerners. Radio Moscow, the international broadcasting arm of the Comintern, preaches the Soviet gospel to all the world while exchange programs bring the best of official Soviet culture into Western spaces. But do any of these efforts convince, for example, the average American patriot that there is nothing to fear from the Soviet people? Even the US tours of the Bolshoi Ballet or the small diplomatic trips to the USSR made by American youth debate teams and music ensembles have a negligible impact on overall public opinion in either Russia or the West. Such exchanges can only do so much, due not only to limited participation but also to a lack of true freedom of interaction between people.[1]

Circumventing these calculated, official interchanges, a young American rock singer by the name of Joanna Fields makes a lasting contribution to the perception of Russia in the West. In the summer of 1984, twenty-four-year-old Joanna accompanies her sister Judy on a week-long visit to the USSR, landing in Moscow's Sheremetyevo International Airport. Initially, she takes in the gray landscape and believes, for what feels like "the first time ever," that her father Sidney Fields is right: she should never have gone behind the Iron Curtain.[2] However, her outlook radically changes when she meets Akvarium's front man Boris Grebenshchikov, who introduces her to the musical underground of Soviet Russia. When she hears Russian rock for the first time, she is captivated. She realizes American propaganda is wrong. Her father, who had worked on the 1960s film *The Truth About Communism*, is *wrong*. Russian rock 'n' rollers, she observes, are, in fact, very similar to American rock 'n' rollers—they both "live for" the music:

> Rockers all over the world are bonded by their drive to express themselves through creative means. Real rockers are all about the process of just doing it, not about the result or fame or riches. Their passion for their art is all encompassing and there is a great camaraderie between them.[3]

Since America is already strongly romanticized in Soviet perception, Joanna is able to assimilate and make her way among the underground rock stars, though she feels inadequate, she says, as if in the presence of royalty.[4] Her surprise at finding "real rockers" in Russia—hearing top Leningrad bands like Strange Games, Alisa, Kino, Zoopark—makes her realize that the US is

---

1 Willis Conover notes that in 1957, in Prague and Moscow alike, he is visited by Russians in groups of three or more. He speculates that this is like a "checks and balances" system to ensure that nothing is said or done counter to Kremlin's agenda. Willis Conover Collection, Box 17, Folder 31: Russia, UNT University Libraries.

2 Joanna Stingray in correspondence with author, December 2020.

3 Ibid.

4 In correspondence with author, Stingray said that despite the poor situation of the average Leningrad citizen, she perceived a spiritual benefit to communism that the American Dream, which requires cultivation of wealth rather than creativity, couldn't provide. Communism, for all its downsides, allowed Russians to prioritize culture for culture's sake, not for monetary gain.

blind and deaf to its similarities with Soviet society. Joanna is determined to help correct the narrative; after all, Russian rock is a result of what first emerged in the West and should now be used as a uniting force, a common tongue:

> The underground Russian rockers had a voracious appetite for Western rock. The older rockers like Boris Grebenshchikov [Akvarium] and Mike Naumenko [Zoopark] knew all American 60s rock icons including Frank Zappa and Lou Reed, and the younger bands like Kino loved the new, indie British bands like The Cure, The Smiths, The Cult, and even Joy Division.[5] Kostya [Konstantin] Kinchev [Alisa] was a huge Marc Bolan fan. They all loved Bowie. Boris also liked Irish Folk music and bands like the Cocteau Twins . . . [T]he Leningrad rockers were not swayed by the Communist's propaganda of the West. They knew the West was a place that thrived with creativity.[6]

Inspired by the musicians with whom she bonds despite language barriers, Joanna flies back to the US, imbued with purpose and plotting her return trip to the place she now considers a "Wonderland." In subsequent visits, she bears gifts of musical equipment for the Russian rockers, despite the dangers to herself. She even gets David Bowie interested in Boris Grebenshchikov, and Bowie offers to purchase a brand-new Fender Stratocaster for Boris. As Joanna burrows "deeper into the rabbit hole," as she puts it, she notices the conspicuous lack of women in Russian rock. Other than the likes of Alla Pugacheva, there are few who have reached stardom. She asks Boris about it, but he has no answer either, chocking it all up to what he perceives as a backwardness persisting in their society. But Joanna sees something more:

---

5 All these British bands aired on *Rok-posevy* in the mid-'80s, which again reinforces the likelihood that Seva played an important role in the development of the '80s Leningrad rock scene, influencing the musicians themselves. This is even more the case considering that the BBC's main competitors Radio Liberty and VOA Russian Service were more likely to abstain from airing non-American groups inasmuch as the BBC wished to "project Britain" by favoring British hits. Also, Stingray's note about younger Russian bands like Kino favoring British artists is interesting because Leningrad rockers surfacing in the '80s grew up listening to Seva, unlike the "older" rockers like GB who in their formative years listened to VOA, that is, Willis Conover.

6 Stingray correspondence, December 2020.

> Unlike [in] the West, everyone under Communism had to work; so, all women worked, but they also still took care of the children and husbands, did all the shopping (which could take hours) and took care of the home and meals. I learned that Russian women were super-women, they carried the world on their shoulders, and I will always be in awe of them.[7]

Hoping to mend the grievous disconnect between their countries, Joanna and Boris hatch a plan. Together, they gather recordings of several Russian bands with the intention of getting a record deal in the US. Some of these recordings have been made in homemade studios with "archaic" equipment while, luckily, others have come out of the official recording studio where audio engineer Andrey Tropillo works:

> Boris and a couple other bands were lucky enough to record with Andrey Tropillo who . . . would let the bands sneak in after hours or on the weekends to record. Regardless, it was difficult to record, and the bands never had enough of the time that they wanted.[8]

When Boris and Joanna share with the musicians that they hope to get their music officially released in the West, the self-effacing vanguards of Russian rock invariably smile and shrug. It would be nice, they say, to be polite—but they have zero expectations. At great risk to herself, Joanna, determined to do these artists justice, carefully smuggles these recordings back with her to the US, just barely making it onto an airplane with the precious music.[9]

Big Time Changes

> Rock in its purest form is really an energy of freedom, the freedom of spirit. It helps people to feel and to find themselves. Rock gives people power.
>
> —Joanna Stingray[10]

---

7 Ibid. Another take on the gender issue comes from Steinholt: "In Leningrad, rock authenticity has traditionally been associated with the absence of women on stage. When Zoopark included a male-female backing vocal group in their lineup for the 1986 LRC festival, the band was immediately accused by rock purists of flirting with the pop mainstream" (Steinholt, *Rock in the Reservation*, 3). Rock was therefore linked to this new kind of masculinity, though it didn't forbid female participation.

8 Ibid.

9 See Stingray, *Red Wave*, part 2.

10 Stingray correspondence, December 2020.

On March 11, 1985, Mikhail Gorbachev becomes general secretary of the Communist Party and, consequently, international perceptions of the USSR begin to change. Well-educated, well-traveled, oddly optimistic, and deeply admiring of contemporary artists, Gorbachev is quite different from his predecessors. He breaks with typical Soviet practice and appears publicly with his personable and educated wife Raisa, claiming to discuss all with her. This very democratic image intrigues the West, which eagerly fashions Raisa into the role of "First Lady" of the Soviet Union—finally a Russian *couple* in the Kremlin. As Reagan and Gorbachev meet in DC, the threat of nuclear war diminishes and the prospect of a healthier relationship with the USSR seems attainable. Margaret Thatcher famously remarks in a TV interview for the BBC, "I like Mr. Gorbachev. We can do business together."[11]

This spirit of optimism isn't experienced at all levels, however, particularly in the intelligence community on both sides of the Iron Curtain. As Joanna actively shops around the original music from Russia, not just the KGB but the FBI red flag her activities. In their skewed but mirrored view, her conduct appears highly suspect—even though her earlier trips are through tour groups and always accompanied by her sister Judy:

> Quite clearly, both the KGB and FBI thought I was a spy. To them, there could be no other reason why someone, let alone a girl, would come in and out of the Soviet Union during the mid-eighties. I was really surprised by how similar both agencies dealt with me. They seemed to be trained at the same school and had real tunnel vision when it came to what they saw as "red flags," coming in and out of the country often and meeting with Russian citizens. Both sides seemed so fearful of what I could be doing.[12]

The FBI requests one-on-one meetings with her while she is stateside, leading to cold interrogations and her inevitable frustration. Neither DC nor Moscow will take her diplomatic efforts at face value, though it is somewhat understandable why a young American citizen nested in the Russian underground might be worrisome, or at least out of the ordinary.

---

11 "TV Interview for BBC," Margaret Thatcher Foundation, December 17, 1984, https://www.margaretthatcher.org/document/105592.

12 Stingray correspondence, December 2020.

After failing to get the big labels to buy into the Russian rock music, due in part to political and financial worries, Joanna finally sees the fruit of her labors pay off with Big Time Records, a US-based Australian company that isn't as concerned about losing business with Melodiya Records. Gratefully, she inks a deal as producer for the release of a double LP compilation that features several songs from each of four bands that Boris and she had selected for the wide stylistic range they presented: Kino, Strange Games, Alisa, and Akvarium. Elated at her success—producing the very first Russian rock album to be released in the US—she relays the incredible news to Boris and the rest of her Russian musical family through coded language and an alias, "Stingray."

Two major calamities hit the USSR before any records are officially printed. The first is the sharp and sustained dive in oil prices in January 1986, which cripples an economy that has hardly recovered from the 1979 oil price shock under Brezhnev.[13] Second, on April 26, 1986, the Chernobyl nuclear disaster occurs in Ukraine, "blasting radioactive fallout into the sky, many times more than was released by the atomic bomb that destroyed Hiroshima."[14] To its detriment, the Gorbachev administration doesn't immediately acknowledge the event, having themselves received inaccurate information from Chernobyl officials fearful of reprisal.[15] Gorbachev pushes the Kremlin to release a statement, but he himself does not even publicly speak the truth until May 14, via a televised address. Chernobyl opens Gorbachev's eyes to the putrefaction of the entire Soviet state, and from this point forward, he becomes a man of action, driven towards change, for he now sees that the "old system has exhausted its possibilities."[16]

Several bands, including Akvarium, had been on the verge of performing in the affected Ukrainian SSR region, and despite being exposed to radiation they are released back to Russia by the authorities. In May 1986, Artemy Troitsky

13 See Douglas Reynolds, "Soviet Economic Decline: Did an Oil Crisis Cause the Transition in the Soviet Union?," *The Journal of Energy and Development* 24, no. 1 (1998): 65–82, http://www.jstor.org/stable/24808741.

14 William Taubman, *Gorbachev: His Life and Times* (New York: Simon & Schuster, 2017), 240. For a detailed account, see David R. Marples, "The Chernobyl Disaster," *Current History* 86, no. 522 (1987): 325–43, http://www.jstor.org/stable/45315948.

15 Taubman, *Gorbachev*, 240.

16 Ibid., 242.

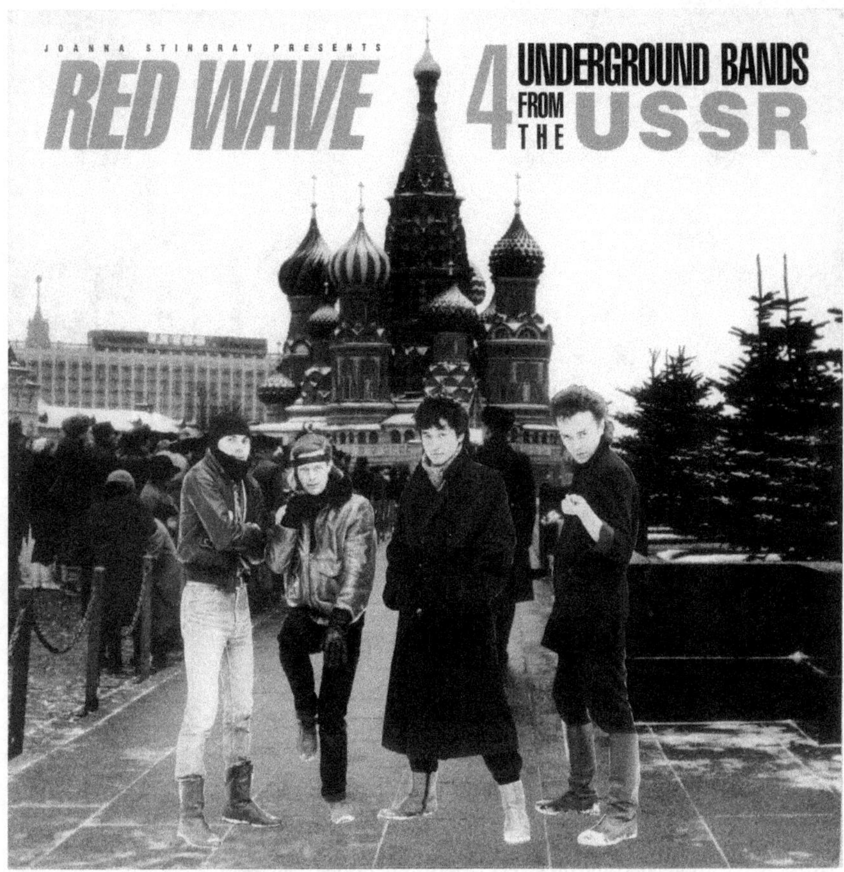

Red Wave album cover (courtesy of Joanna Stingray)

takes it upon himself to organize the first charity rock concert in the USSR for the victims of Chernobyl.[17] The nuclear disaster, on top of the economic downturn, thoroughly ties up the government and the KGB's resources, keeping them so busy that when Big Time Records officially releases the Russian rock album on June 27, 1986, nothing happens—at first. Then, as the media frenzy begins to ramp up, so does the political fallout.

17 Troitsky, *Back in the USSR*, 115–18.

Back of Red Wave album, Stingray center (courtesy of Joanna Stingray)

On the Air

For the US release, five thousand copies on red and yellow vinyl are pressed. Joanna sends fifty copies of these special editions to Russia through the Swedish Embassy for the musicians themselves. "I think all in all, 15,000 copies of 'Red Wave' were sold in the US. I don't know how many were sold when it was released in England, and I also do not know how many sold on the black market in Russia."[18] The record gets radio play in the States, but in the USSR, such a thing is impossible to achieve, and if Soviet citizens hear the music on their radios, it is largely because of Western broadcasts. While VOA does not air

18 Stingray correspondence, December 2020.

Red Wave, according to Joanna, RFE/RL does, though it's not apparent if these broadcasts are heard much in the USSR. However, via the BBC, *Red Wave* definitely crashes into Russian homes. Seva devotes a month's worth of *Rok-posevy* broadcasts to the album starting in August, indemnifying the album's place in Russian rock history:[19]

> Today we will talk about amateur rock 'n' roll, about international youth solidarity, about tourism as a driving force in musical progress—in a word, about everything that made possible the release of a new double album titled "Red Wave," which features four groups from Leningrad: Akvarium, Kino, Alisa, and Strange Games.[20]

Of his choice to broadcast four entire programs devoted to Russian rock when he has not played any Russian bands before, he says that he has always had to "act according to the BBC's rules." Everything he utters on air, all information and music that he provides, has to be verified by at least two reliable sources. Thus, nothing could be aired that is considered unproven information from the "deep underground." Now that Joanna has, in an official capacity, released *Red Wave,* the bands and their music are verifiable and may be featured on the BBC:

> [Russian rock] began to reach me after 1980, after the infamous Tbilisi festival, where [Boris] Grebenshchikov and Time Machine caused a scandal. After that they were smashed and beaten [in Soviet media]. But by the year 1984, they had nevertheless risen, and already they could not be kept by any censorship frameworks. . . . Then Joanna Stingray, an American, came to St. Petersburg and smuggled out the tapes of four groups: Akvarium, Kino, and two others. She published them in California as the *Red Wave* album. And since this album was published in the West, I could officially request it through the BBC. So, I received it and broadcasted it, because it was not me secretly digging up something there, and for the BBC it was very

---

19 Ibid. Stingray recalls the musicians and fans tuning into the radio, to BBC and also RFE, trying to hear their songs played, even as the state continued to jam the signals.

20 *Rok-posevy,* August 29, 1986, radio broadcast, https://seva.ru/rock/?id=433&y=1986.

> important [that it was official]. This was, of course, a significant breakthrough, because it was then that the underground rock music, officially released in America, was broadcast on the BBC for the first time ever.[21]

As usual, Seva provides not just the music but information about the artists. He prefaces songs with an opening story on how the album came to be, even reading the annotations on the album as written by Joanna. "Music knows no borders!" he says, quoting Joanna, a mantra with which Seva—and all musicians—can certainly agree. He also adds a bit of history for context:

> Curiously, in this sense, history repeats itself as about twenty-seven years ago, a record of Leningrad jazz musicians was released in the United States, and even then, Americans could be convinced of the existence of cultural pluralism in the homeland of the October Revolution. I myself have been collecting *magnitizdat* for the last four years, and this record is of interest to me, if only because the quality of the recordings is the cleanest that I have come across so far. At least for these reasons, the album deserves detailed consideration, and therefore we will devote the next four programs to each of the groups separately, starting today with "Strange Games."[22]

He begins with the song "Egocentrism" and warns his listeners not to dismiss the lyrics, which he then proceeds to read. He points out right away, to ward off any and all "critical attacks," that the poems used in this song were written by the twentieth-century French novelist, poet, and critic Raymond Queneau who died ten years prior to the release of the double album. The poems, Seva says, had been published in the USSR, and none of the six songs from Strange Games included on this album have any so-to-speak "homegrown" or ill-intentioned lyrics as all of them are borrowed from legitimate French poets. "Therefore," he declares, "there can be no accusations about the group either in the literary, censorship, or ideological sense." In his sarcastic, unironic way, he asks rhetorically, "Who are these rock wolves covered in French poetic scrawl?"[23] In answer, he

---

21 Novgorodsev, interview by Matthew Orr, March 28, 2019, in *The Slavic Connexion*, podcast.

22 *Rok-posevy*, August 29, 1986, radio broadcast, https://seva.ru/rock/?id=433&y=1986.

23 Ibid.

pronounces the names of each of the band members: Viktor Sologub, Grisha Sologub, Alexander Kondraskin, Nikolay Gusev, Alexey Rakhov, Alexander Davydov, Nikolay Kulikovsky, and Nikolay Olshavsky. Later in this program, Seva quotes the London magazine *City Limits*, which had published an article about Soviet unofficial rock a year prior, mentioning Strange Games and speaking of Sologub's search for rock freedom in the midst of "strange games" in the USSR. On the one hand, Sologub said to the magazine, the Ministry of Culture undergoes liberalization in response to pressure from Soviet youth. But on the other hand, the ministry wishes to retain the ability to regulate and maintain ideological control over rock bands, over lyrics, over young people in general.

Another point of interest in this first *Red Wave* broadcast is that Seva brings up a particularly infamous blacklist, albeit one of many, from 1984, which he undoubtedly obtained through personal connections, BBC Monitoring, or letter-writers themselves. This list Seva refers to for its inclusion of Soviet "unofficial" rock groups:

> In the famous document, published on October 1, 1984, by the . . . All-Union Methodological Center of Folk Creativity and Cultural Educational Work under the Ministry of Culture of the USSR, it is said that "in order to strengthen the struggle against the influence of ideology, it is recommended to prohibit the playing of gramophone records, compact cassettes, videos, books, posters, and other products reflecting the activities of the following groups . . ." And then follows a list of sixty-eight foreign rock bands and thirty-eight Soviet amateur bands.[24] So, in this list of thirty-eight, Strange Games is not included. But I think we shouldn't worry too much about this, first of all, because . . . the rest of the bands on the album *were* blacklisted—and we will listen to them one by one at our usual Cinderella hour, at midnight on Friday on the shortwave.[25]

---

24 This list is similar to one published in *Novaya Gazeta* from 1985, as included in Yurchak's, *Everything Was Forever*, 214–15. But the particular blacklist that Seva mentions is in Zhuk's "Popular Culture, Identity, and Soviet Youth in Dniepropetrovsk, 1959–84," *The Carl Beck Papers in Russian and East European Studies*, no. 1906 (June 2008) and pictured in the dissertation of Boris Von Faust, https://rucore.libraries.rutgers.edu/rutgers-lib/43919/PDF/1/play/. And indeed, Akvarium, Kino, and Alisa are listed.

25 *Rok-posevy*, August 29, 1986, radio broadcast, https://seva.ru/rock/?id=433&y=1986.

The main purpose of such a blacklist, which includes many if not all the Western bands that Seva plays regularly (such as Black Sabbath, AC/DC, Kiss, and Pink Floyd), is to serve as an internal memorandum, a guide for the Komsomol on the proper selection of music for the general discotheque movement. Thus, the sixty-eight Western and thirty-eight unofficial Soviet rock bands highlighted are banned for public performance within Moscow city limits. Sergei Zhuk notes:

> All these bands were now officially prohibited for cultural consumption by all Soviet youth. By the end of 1984 many regional Komsomol committees . . . were using these lists in their campaign to purify the pop music consumption of Komsomol members. They wanted to replace "bad" bourgeois music with "good," ideologically reliable, socialist music.[26]

It's difficult to say if this 1984 list had any direct impact on Seva's listenership or his selections, or if it had been conversely created in response to the groups Seva played on Friday nights. But it seems possible that the inclusion of mainly British bands in the "Western 68" serves as an indication of the greater influence that the BBC had over youth versus VOA or RFE/RL or DW. The omission of Strange Games from this list is quite curious and probably represents an oversight on the part of the list-makers, but as Seva says to his listeners with a hint of relish, "don't worry, three of the four bands are blacklisted."

On the following three Fridays, Seva features Kino, Alisa, and Akvarium—one band per program—and he no doubt takes great pleasure in doing so if for no other reason than that these groups are from his beloved St. Petersburg. In the final broadcast, featuring Akvarium, Seva goes into detail about Boris Grebenshchikov—expelled from Leningrad University for being "freethinking"—and about the name Akvarium, which implies "that its members live in their music like fish in aquarium water, and that like these fish, they are separated from their surroundings by a glass wall, but . . . they must remember that at any moment" their oxygen can be cut off by external forces. Like the previous bands, Seva names every member, calling out the already famous fish of Akvarium: Sergey Kuryokhin, Sasha Titov, Peter Troshchenkov, Seva Gakkel, Alexander Lyapin, Andrey Romanov, and Mikhail Feinstein. Seva draws from the liner notes of a compilation tape of unofficial Russian rock bands released in London the previous year, which focuses on Akvarium and its musical evolution

---

26 Zhuk, "Popular Culture," 38.

since creation in 1973, trying "all styles" from folk-rock to punk to ska to reggae before shifting into a "thoughtful sound, in the tradition of soft rock of the 60s." Seva adds his own commentary:

> In the early songs, I think there was freshness, intellectual mischief, philosophical depth of poetic and musical foolishness. However, satire and ridicule are destructive tools, nothing can be built with them. . . . [S]ociety is not free from the people who live in it; sooner or later it must notice those who have attracted attention and officially recognize those who are known officially. . . . Thus, comrades, we are dealing with a large-scale spontaneous process, and just as capitalism was born in the bowels of feudalism, and socialism was born in the bowels of capitalism, so a progressive musical system is now being born in the bowels of an obsolete musical order. . . . One thing is clear: the wheels of history cannot be turned back. And we'll end the program with the song, "Rock 'n' Roll is Dead."[27]

The press in the USSR is eager to castigate Seva for playing these Russian bands and readily lumps Seva into the same camp as the American, Joanna Stingray, who smuggled the music out of the USSR in the first place. However, counterintuitively, these same official mouthorgans now portray the Leningrad bands as innovators and forerunners of Russian creativity rather than the blacklisted urchins they have been in the very recent past. One article from *Smena* manages not only to accuse Seva of not "understanding" what is happening in the USSR today, but also to link badly organized charity for the Chernobyl disaster to Seva's developed radio-craft—mocking him as the "all-seeing disc jockey from London":

> Many of Novgorodsev's programs are full of sarcasm, anger, and most importantly, a clear lack of understanding of what is happening now with Soviet rock. You're amazed: what sources of information does he feed on, and where does he get his musical material? The London disc jockey himself admits to his difficulties—recordings of Soviet music come to him on occasion, and their quality is usually poor. . . . One can imagine what

---

27 *Rok-posevy*, September 19, 1986, radio broadcast, https://seva.ru/rock/?id=436&y=1986.

> a godsend the double album *Red Wave* was for Novgorodsev with recordings of four Leningrad bands. . . . released in the USA. He devoted several programs to it. . . . These groups are well-known—they cannot be classified as "underground," as the BBC DJ insisted. However, when releasing the album, the necessary publishing rights were not respected, but this conflict turned out to be insignificant and, according to a recent report by *Ogonyok*, it was settled—the American side, admitting its error, paid a fine.[28]

The "American side" that journalist Mikhail Sadchikov seems reticent to name is, of course, Joanna Stingray. Indeed, the KGB extracts a confession from her that this whole scheme was her idea, which she gives only to protect the musicians. As soon as she confesses, however, warmth blossoms on the faces of the KGB agents confronting her, and though she is fined a small amount, shortly thereafter, Melodiya offers *her* a record deal. She becomes essentially a Kremlin darling and receives due recognition from Washington, D.C. for her actions:

> It's been written that after *Red Wave* was released in the West, someone from the Soviet copyright company, VAAP, handed Gorbachev the album. After looking it over, he said, "If these bands are played in the West, why can't they be here?" The Soviets quickly tried to bring all the underground rock above ground and played all their songs on the radio and had them perform on TV. They also asked Boris and his band, Akvarium (and then the other bands), to release their album on the official Soviet record company, Melodiya, and agreed to put it out with no censorship, exactly as Boris wanted it. It was a game changer.[29]

Additionally, an article from *Komsomol'skaia pravda* published August 14 announces Melodiya intention to release a two-disc album of Time Machine and other rock bands like Bravo, which had performed at a youth popular music festival earlier this same year. Entitled *Panorama-86*, after the festival, the double album is nothing short of the Komsomol's answer to *Red Wave*.[30]

---

28 Mikhail Sadchikov, "Otkuda berutsia 'pomekhi'?," *Smena*, accessed August 25, 2022, https://seva.ru/media/?id=4.

29 Stingray interview, December 2020.

30 *Rok-posevy*, October 10, 1986, radio broadcast, https://seva.ru/rock/?id=439&y=1986. Visit https://thecorroseum.org/comps/panorama861.php for a picture and track list of the album, as well as the article, which was printed on the back of the record sleeve.

The fact that the BBC's coverage both earns negative Soviet press coverage for Seva and also fast-tracks official government recognition of previously abjured bands may safely be viewed as signs of the album's impact in the USSR. Thanks to Joanna Stingray who dared to swim against the dipole currents, *Red Wave* becomes a powerful connecting tool, opening up the Soviet world for the West. As a California paper writes on June 28, 1986, "Even though these bands exist in a different political system, what they express in their music: love, self-realization, irreconcilability with the threat of a nuclear catastrophe, striving for better in life—all this is strikingly close to the spirit of the rock around the world."[31]

Stingray pictured against spray-painted wall (courtesy of Joanna Stingray)

---

31 From San Diego Union, quoted in a letter from LRC bands (Strange Games, Akvarium, Kino, Alisa), secretary (Olga Slobodskaya), and president (Nikolay Mikhailov) to the Editorial Department of Moscow News, May 13, 1987. Provided to author by Joanna Stingray.

Featured Listener: Sasha Titov (bassist in Kino and Akvarium)

I grew up in the Petrogradskaya district of Leningrad, in close vicinity to the Peter and Paul Fortress. From my window, I could see the top of the cathedral spike with an angel showing the wind's direction, and I could hear bells chiming every fifteen minutes and a cannon bang every day at noon. My parents were both chemical engineers and they worked on many strategic missions and rocket fuel design. My mum never traveled abroad because of her job.

My parents had a plug-in-the-wall radio receiver in the kitchen, which would be playing the usual stupid programs every morning when I get up, wash my face, get dressed, and have breakfast. (Later my stepdad bought a shortwave radio and every evening in bed I would listen to Voice of America, Radio Luxembourg, and later Seva's program on the BBC. I had a shortwave radio while I was in army service from 1975 to '77 and listened to the same stations with the risk of being arrested for it.)

When I was about ten years old, I heard "Sunny Afternoon" by the Kinks. That was the first English song that really captured me. I still have a nostalgic pang every time I hear it. My first access to Western albums was through a classmate whose parents were wealthy opera singers and traveled a lot, bringing back all sorts of stuff including music albums.[32] Some of these, I copied for myself on a reel-to-reel machine. Later, I managed to buy a sex opera *Hair* LP and used it to swap for a day in order to copy from my friends' music collections. My hunger for the music was very strong. My first passion was American rock music.[33] I collected all the CCR albums, the Doors, Jefferson Airplane, Grand Funk [Railroad], Velvet Underground, Grateful Dead.

Then, British rock, such as Led Zeppelin and Black Sabbath, became my long-term obsession. I was fascinated by the bass lines and riffs of John Paul Jones and later they were the first lines I learned on the bass. He is my hero.

In autumn 1975, I interrupted my studies at the Leningrad Institute of Technology to do compulsory army service for two years. When I came back, I astonished my parents with the news that I wanted to quit the institute and become a musician. A huge row followed, and I moved out to live in a rented shack on the outskirts of a city called Ozerki. My best friend and musician,

32 It is this classmate who introduces Sasha early on to two future members of Akvarium.

33 Titov, as he stated, listened to Voice of America first, which explains his early love of American rock. However, as he goes on to say, British rock became his passion, very probably because he began listening to the BBC.

Misha Malin, had the exact same reaction from his parents and we shared the shed. 1978 was a very cold winter and we warmed ourselves burning old shoes given to us by our landlord in the fireplace. Black smoke blew from the chimney and the shack was filled with the strong smell of burnt rubber.

[W]ithin a year, I became the bassist in a band called Zemliane (Earthlings), playing stadiums all over the country. I became bored with it very quickly, played a little in the band August, and [then] decided to quit the professional music scene altogether by 1983. In the beginning of 1983, I was invited by Andrey Romanov [flutist and keyboardist for Akvarium] to record a track for Akvarium. There was a mobile recording wagon outside the Capella building where in secret they were recording material for the *Radio Afrika* album. In summer 1983, Boris [Grebenshchikov] asked me to join the band. One year later, I met my childhood friend Marianna who had started dating Victor Tsoi. She introduced me to him. Later that year he invited me to join Kino. I was over the moon. Both bands were equally important for our underground music scene. But there was very little [concert] activity, and [so] I could easily manage to play in both.

Kino in Leningrad, Sasha Titov on left (credit: Joanna Stingray)

Technical Matters

Many musicians of that era played on luthier-made copies of Gibson or Fender guitars through copies of Fender or Sunn or Ampeg amps. I remember buying two S2A9 speakers and making a plywood cabinet for them myself. Alexander Lyapin had a guitar, which was clearly the door of a wardrobe in its previous life. We picked fights with *gopniki* (lower-class street hooligans) for our long hippy hairdos and later for wearing earrings. Obviously, we were fascinated by Anglo-American culture. At first it was the hippies, R'n'R, R&B, and hard rock, then later it was punk, new wave, reggae, and jazz.

[Re: recording] There was no way to record multitrack at home. There was no such equipment back then. I used my home mono reel-to-reel and a cheap plastic "soap tray" mike. Andrey Tropillo Studio, which recorded the majority of Leningrad Rock Club bands, had two stereo reel-to-reel machines and with one bounce we could record three to four instruments and vocals. But it was an inseparable stereo recording, which could not be mended. Any mistake or level misjudgment and we all have to start again.

Leningrad, the KGB, and Fame

Leningrad was famous for its diverse and well-developed music scene. In the '70s and '80s there were only two jazz clubs, 81 and Kvadrat (Square). So, when the [Leningrad] Rock Club was formed in 1981, many of us attended gigs at the aforementioned jazz clubs, befriended jazz musicians, and some of them migrated to our scene as well. My friends Sergey Kuryokhin and Zhenya Guberman are just two examples. I mentioned above that I was used to playing five- to six-thousand-capacity venues from the very beginning of my career. So, the Rock Club main hall was quite modest and did not intimidate me. The audience was completely different though. Rock Club gigs were always full of excitement and rapture.

There were around twenty guys who were watching us; they were always the same guys. We knew them all and they knew that we knew. I had run-ins with the KGB after I started helping Joanna [Stingray] with her first videos. She brought a compact VHS camera and started filming gigs. I would cover her and carry the tape outside in my underpants. They stopped me a couple of times but did not think to check there. I was seriously busted a couple of years later one night when we were joyriding in the car of Philippe, a French cultural attaché. I remember they specifically told me, "You will disappear, and no one will ever know where to."

By the time Gorbachev came to power there was a blooming movement of contemporary musicians in Leningrad. Many of the lyricists of that era wrote protest texts, which influenced the masses. We started well before *perestroika.* We were different, we were anti-establishment. They [the government] claimed we were popularizing the Western way of life. We in turn hated them because they were full of lies.

At the beginning of 1986, the situation changed. Both of the bands [Akvarium and Kino] started becoming busier and more prominent and I had to quit one of them, so I quit Kino. [That same year] Akvarium played at the Yubileyny Sports Palace every day for two weeks, and every day it was packed. One evening we noticed that the police started forcing people down off their seats in front of us. We stopped the gig and demanded that the police let people go. There was a huge uproar in the audience, and they had to let them go. In 1987 we played the IPPNW festival and Steve Stills and Graham Nash were part of it. They invited us to be part of this event the following year in Montreal. That was unforgettable. This is shown in *The Long Way Home* documentary released in 1989 by CBS, directed by Michael Upted.

Radio's Role for Musicians

The radio was so important to us back then because it was the only regular source of new music. I don't think it would've been so important if we'd had more new music coming from elsewhere. Most of the musicians I know listened to some of the aforementioned stations. Seva was always my favorite broadcaster. I listened to him regularly. I think he has the ability to speak to our hearts because he is a Leningrad musician himself. He's been on the road and uses proper musician's lexicon. His stories are quick-witted and full of sarcasm. We all respect him.[34] I have been his guest on three programs as part of Akvarium. I am honored that my wife Alyona and I were invited to be his last broadcast guests.[35]

---

34 Sasha Titov in correspondence with author, December 2020.
35 Seva's final broadcast aired live from Pushkin House in London, September 4, 2015.

CHAPTER 13

(I Can't Get No) Satisfaction

> Seva, tell Mr. Director [Barry Holland] that . . . your program is still the most popular, because it is more lively, more dynamic and in a good way enticing. . . . There has still been no clear answer to the question whether it will be expanded in time limit. . . . I would just like to listen not only to music, but also to conversations with musicians, although I am aware of all the complexities of this undertaking and, in general, with interesting people. Your trouble, Seva, is that you are targeting fifteen-year-olds, but believe me, they are not the only ones (and not even the majority) who are listening to you. . . . I wanted to send you a disc by Valery Leontiev, so that you would play it . . .[1] [but] now there is no point in sending anything, because with the work of such active ladies in our country, the West will finally hear the heartbreaking cry of our avant-garde [rock movement] in stereo sound—loud, clear, and intelligibly. . . .[2]

In London, Seva finds that a career in the film and TV industry leaves him unsatisfied and just as restless as Soviet young people, even though he works for the likes of John Schlesinger and director Taylor Hackford. During this hiatus from the BBC, Seva continues to get letters, at least one even written in Braille and translated by the Royal National Institute of Blind People:

---

1 Valery Leontiev was a Soviet pop singer of significant renown whose popularity reached its zenith in the '80s.

2 *Rok-posevy*, October 10, 1986, radio broadcast, https://seva.ru/rock/?id=439&y=1986. By "active ladies," the letter writer is referring to Joanna Stingray, producer of *Red Wave*. The listener's statement about conversations with people may be the seed that eventually led Seva to the concept for *Sevaoborot*.

> I don't know if you've received anything like this in the ten years of your work on the BBC. I am one of your blind listeners in the Soviet capital and it would be difficult for me to write you an ordinary letter. Tomorrow, my friend will go abroad, and I cannot miss the opportunity to send you at least a few lines with the hope that they will reach you. But Russian is foreign for those living in London and finding someone who would read Braille in Russian is absolutely difficult, so I had to do the only thing possible.
>
> First of all, I would like to express my feelings about your program. For ten years you worked superbly, introducing Soviet listeners to modern rock music, for which I am grateful, because for a long time you remained the only reliable source of information, giving a small ray of light in the dark forest of our life. Young people tuned into your station wanting to hear not only modern music, but also the truth, unattainable within the country from their own media. Your jokes are always worth waiting for because they touch on the most real and, at the same time, the most forbidden topics in our hearts. . . .
>
> But things are now changing radically. I'm not going to tell you about our *perestroika*, you can judge about this even by the letters that come to you, so it's time to change your methods. Why didn't *perestroika* affect you? Your anecdotes and jokes are nothing compared to the materials that appear in our press every day. You look from afar and laugh sarcastically at everything that happens in the USSR, but we are working inside the country to improve our life. I am the secretary of the Komsomol organization of my school, and even I know this is *perestroika*. What do you know about it with your criticism?[3]

The fact that a Komsomol leader does not hide his devotion to Seva's programs (years of it) shows just how much *perestroika* has transformed daily life—perhaps especially for Soviet youth. At the same time, the writer acknowledges the continued difficulty of sending Seva letters by mail, which attests to continued KGB obstructions. Regardless, Seva feels the pinch of conscience, and,

---

3 *Rok-posevy*, January 15, 1988 radio broadcast, https://seva.ru/audio/rock/1988/r880115vb.mp3. Though read on air in early 1988, this letter was written and received much earlier (circa late 1986) judging by the emphasis on *perestroika* and reference to Seva's ten years on air.

both touched and chastened, is compelled to do something for his people that addresses the radical changes, or, at least, keeps up with the times. In earnest, Seva seeks a way back to the microphone.[4]

Gorbachev's "Rolling Stones"

Though the letter Seva had received from one BBC-raised Komsomol leader seems to suggest that the youth are, generally, united in support of *perestroika* and Mikhail Gorbachev, in July 1987, *The New York Times* publishes an in-depth piece on Russian youth, which strongly suggests the opposite. The article opens at the Maxim Gorky House of Culture in North Central Moscow, where on stage, beneath a stark red banner that exhorts all Soviet citizens to "fulfill the decisions of the 27th Party Congress," the Russian heavy metal band Chyornyi obelisk (Black Obelisk) deafens the packed historical hall.[5] The author Bill Keller observes that regardless of the chaperoning adults and the presence of plainclothes police, the youth go wild over the "blitzkrieg of electric guitars," undeterred by the dour watchmen. Such a concert that had until only recently been branded as "bourgeois decadence" is now a normal, run-of-the-mill event at this one-year-old experiment called *Klub "Vitiazi"*—the Warrior Club. Like the LRC, this club is a government-backed project, and in this case, sponsored by the Moscow chapter of the Komsomol. But unlike the LRC and its more normal board of both officials and musicians, the Warrior Club boasts an executive council of only Komsomol youth. Moreover, the council's official portraits show them proudly dressed in "full heavy-metal regalia . . . adapted from the Visigoths." The Warrior Club's manager Valentina Nedzvetskaya says of the changes:

> Even two years ago . . . the idea of Komsomol sponsoring a club where young people dress up like leather fetishists and listen to decadent Western music at earsplitting volume would have been inconceivable. These days it is inevitable, evidence of the lengths to which Soviet officialdom is going to regain its grip on a worrisome younger generation.

---

4 Kremer, "The DJ."

5 Bill Keller, "Russia's Restless Youth," *New York Times*, July 26, 1987, https://www.nytimes.com/1987/07/26/magazine/russia-s-restless-youth.html. This feature may safely be considered a result (direct or indirect) of the *Red Wave* album in the States, which even if not widely heard has drawn widespread attention from media and generated interest in Soviet culture.

Thus far, according to Keller, this "worrisome" generation, which comprises a quarter of the population, is not really responding to *perestroika*—in fact, they show "every inclination to abstain."[6] From "bricks" with which to build a "bright future," the youth have turned into rolling stones, developing ideas, identities, and insights that align with no political direction in particular. Part of the problem, Keller writes, is due to the fact that this is the first generation that has not had to work to support or supplement the family's income, and so they don't understand what it means to work or what a ruble is really worth:[7]

> Soviet analysts have discovered a general failure of the institutions designed to mold Russian children into bright-eyed young Socialists. Komsomol doesn't work, school doesn't work, the army doesn't work, even work doesn't work. . . . "Komsomol lost its ideals," said Zhan, a 20-year-old interviewed at the Warrior Club. "Now it is just a form of control. They're giving us rock music because they can't stop it. They have to support it, or things would be worse."[8]

Though there's a threat in Zhan's response, it is unlikely that "worse" would mean aggression, not when the Soviet war in Afghanistan has contributed to general "disenchantment" with the very idea of the military and of violence. Over five hundred thousand young men serve in Afghanistan with at least twelve thousand dead and many more than this returning home with wounds, addictions, or cynicisms (more so than before). "There may be no visible protest, but there is a deterioration of official credibility."[9] Essentially, the Great Socialist Experiment has run aground on its great socialist ideals. Gorbachev will *not* be able to agitate the youth to rally behind *perestroika*, much less rally behind *him* because he represents the system, and the system holds no attraction for the young.

---

6 Ibid.

7 Some scholars hold a different view, taking the industrialized sector into account: "Not only are most Soviet young people at an earlier stage of modernization and the 'rural-urban continuum' (as many as 40 per cent of young urban workers were born in the countryside), they do not experience unemployment (often said to be a major source of tension, alienation and social ills in the West)." Riordan, *Soviet Youth Culture*, ix.

8 Keller, "Russia's Restless Youth."

9 Ibid.

"We're just observers in this big arena. Understand?" one young man says to Keller. "If things change for the better, we'll be glad, of course. If nothing happens, then we'll have a good laugh."[10]

Small Seeds, Big Crops

Despite the *New York Times* article, young people, however they choose to align politically, are far from just "observers"; they are active and growing bolder in their activity. The Soviet youth are ready for more integration and connection with the West. Not long after Billy Joel accepts Gorbachev's invitation to the USSR to conduct a tour (that Joel himself partially funds),[11] the head of the BBC Russian Service, Barry Holland, approaches Seva and says that there's another hole in the air—would he care to fill it with music? However, Seva wants to do something different that will not only give him a way to creatively stretch himself but also better serve the general Soviet population. His need to make an impact on the "people" is conspicuously characteristic of the burden the Russian intelligentsia have shared from inception. But he is unlike the typical intelligentsia of old in that while they stood in fear of the immense gap between themselves and the "great unwashed" masses, Seva is not broadcasting in "ignorance" and has always operated with a sense of the audience acquired from his days as a touring musician.[12] He seeks to render the connection even more intimate and more relevant to the people, not only the youth, in the post-Chernobyl climate.

Inspired by the BBC's intimate broadcasting sensibilities and Gorbachev's wildly unpopular Anti-Alcohol Campaign (which had commenced in 1985 and actually results in an *increase* in the death rate), Seva proposes a wine-fueled chat show that brings the dinner table to the studio and combines Western culture with the chart-toppers of the era:[13]

> Gorbachev's campaign against alcoholism . . . the best method he came up with was the destruction of vineyards. In the Crimea, and in the Caucasus, the vineyards that had been growing for decades, perhaps for centuries, were destroyed by large

---

10 Ibid.

11 See Wayne Isham, *A Matter of Trust—The Bridge to Russia* (Los Angeles: Legacy, 2014).

12 Gessen, *Dead Again*, 7.

13 Leon David et al., "Huge Variation in Russian Mortality Rates in 1984–1994," *The Lancet* 350 (1997): 383–388.

> bulldozers. Some winemakers even committed suicide because it was the tragedy of their lives.
>
> In order to oppose this barbaric process, I asked to have a bottle of wine for the show. I had the idea to recreate the atmosphere of an English club where gentlemen are sitting, drinking, but not getting drunk. That is, to show that the process of wine consumption may be civilized. We wanted, so to speak, to become role models, to set an example. . . . The British management agreed, and for the whole nineteen years a trolley would come each week, with glasses and two bottles of wine. I remember the first time we asked: "Why two?" They said: "Well, while you will drink one in the studio, a technician who records the show can't just sit and watch you drink!"[14]

The Russian Service head loves the idea. Several pilot episodes are recorded, and the show is approved for airing.

Serendipitously, in September 1987, in keeping with *glasnost'*, the Soviet leader calls for an end to jamming, freeing up millions of rubles spent on blocking foreign radio signals and reselling the equipment to independent radio stations.[15] Moscow officially ceases obstructing both VOA and the BBC, though not yet Radio Liberty.[16] No doubt, this helps to erase much of the stigma of both being an "enemy voice" and listening to "enemy voices." Again, Seva occupies the airwaves at just the right time.

On November 7, the anniversary of the October Revolution, *Sevaoborot* launches, the name itself a cheeky stab at both Soviet agricultural jargon and the Russian word for "crop rotation"—*sevooborot.* Seva celebrates his return to the BBC studios with the clinking of wine glasses. In fact, listeners write and ask if the sound effect is simulated, but Seva assures them that the wine, the toasts, the laughter... they're all real. Unlike *Rok-posevy,* this program is not scripted, so for the first time the BBC is allowing Seva improvisational freedom and a liberty he has not previously officially enjoyed.

The success of *Sevaoborot* among Russian listeners transcends the BBC's expectations, serving as another wonderful example of the British broadcasting

---

14 *Sevaoborot,* March 28, 2019, podcast, https://seva.ru/oborot/archive/?id=1111.

15 Nelson, *War of the Black Heavens,* 198. Sam Jones (Yossman), who served at the BBC as a DJ, foreign correspondent, and producer for the RS, said, "Things in the USSR were developing at breakneck speed, and musicians, writers, actors wanted to jump on this cart and roll along with the restructuring." See Jones interview with *Radio Liberty,* May 6, 2016, radio broadcast.

16 Taubman, *Gorbachev,* 397.

model of radio diplomacy. Seva's status allows him to easily secure big names and controversial guests, as well as host live musicians and cultural figures for his chat show, and the popularity of the program vaults Seva to the top of the Soviet's list of dissidents, despite the warmer tides.[17] Many listeners heartily agree that *Sevaoborot* is "the best conversational program in Russian." One listener, Dmitry, says, "I listened constantly." He adds sardonically that his "moral decay" came about through the ever-present hiss of his Okean radio—as for millions of others. It is this collective "moral decay" that leads to something quite out of the ordinary, which begins appropriately with a young listener in a village in northern Russia who truly possesses only one window to the world at large: radio.

It Started as a Joke

In the remote town of Medvezhyegorsk, Alexander "Shurik" Fedorov, is an ardent consumer of "enemy voices." Music, primarily, is his listening passion, but not the "classical, patriotic stuff" that state radio plays; he loves rock. This practice of listening to Western radio began out of curiosity, not rebellion, when he was a child:

> Since I was nine or ten, I used it to play vinyl records of Soviet pop music, sometimes switching to longwave/mediumwave to listen to Soviet radio programs for kids. Sometimes I ventured to shortwaves, trying to catch something of interest. . . . It seemed funny to me. . . . Their repeated announcements like "This is Radio Tirana" or "You're listening to the Voice of America" or "This is Deutsche Welle speaking from Cologne." I asked my father why such broadcasts are so difficult to hear through all the noises. He replied they should not be listened to at all, because these foreign voices are all lies and they are so sophisticated that

---

17 Roth-Ey confirms the lingering concerns around listening to Western radio even though, as Yurchak proves, listening is normalized behavior: "Soviet sociologists who queried young people about their listening practices in 1987 found that half of respondents who answered in the negative to a direct question—do you listen to enemy radio?—would later answer in the positive to an indirect (or 'catch') question—where did you first learn about heavy metal music, say. Even in a period of comparative openness, *even in 1987*, many Soviet people were not completely comfortable disclosing their behavior." See Roth-Ey, "Listening out," 563.

> sometimes they can be mistaken for truth, and that's why our country tries to jam them.[18]

By fourteen years of age, radio is Shurik's constant companion. He becomes an active listener, writing a long letter to VOA with suggestions on how to improve its appeal to his generation—not enough music and too much talking, in his opinion.[19]

Then, in 1983, Shurik discovers the BBC Russian Service, catching through the fog of jamming a "delightful" program hosted by Seva Novgorodsev. Right away, Seva's unique, convivial, and markedly non-Soviet but truly Russian style resonates with the lonely Shurik:

> Obviously, these broadcasts could not avoid my attention: they had not only music, but also useful and interesting information about the artists, bands, and albums. . . . Seva articulated the Western names with Russian accent so you could pick them up, while the American DJs pronounced [names] in the native way, which sounded like unintelligible meowing to my ear. . . . He even translated the lyrics for youth.

Shurik feels as if Seva speaks to him directly, as if knowing everything about him and his life in the USSR. This respect and even love for Seva builds until in the summer of 1987, several years after his attempt to engage with VOA, Shurik sends his first letter to Seva "just to make sure that mail from the USSR does get through." He asks Seva to play a specific song and listens, expectantly; however, he never hears his letter. Did it even reach Bush House? Then, he thinks that maybe his letter wasn't interesting enough. Other listeners' letters, which Seva reads on air, are fun or poignant or even critical in some way. Desperate to make a connection, Shurik thinks to himself that he must be more creative than all other writers. So, on a dark November day, he writes a second letter to P. O. Box 76, London, and boldly suggests the creation of a fan club—as a joke—and solicits people to write their thoughts on the matter. Unconcerned about the KGB in his remote corner of Russia, Shurik waits anxiously in hopes that this idea is just outrageous enough to snag Seva's attention.

---

18 Alexander Fedorov, written testimony translated by S. Pantsirev, June 2019.

19 Another instance of a listener becoming proactive in his radio listening around or at the age of fourteen.

One month after Gorbachev and Reagan sign the historic arms control agreement, on January 8, 1988, Shura keenly tunes in to *Rok-posevy* while his parents are asleep.[20] Seva begins with his usual humor, which tonight waxes literary:

> Good evening, my friends. Our program today is dedicated to your letters and requests. These letters, departing to the Other World, fly out from your home as white doves. Their first stop is Postal Purgatory, where under-reformed cherubs pass them through all the Seven Circles of the Sorting System. Those found less sinful manage to make it to the heavens on a silver plane, while the unlucky ones go to the Underworld. . . . But the most likely to reach its goal are the ones that bypass the system altogether. No wonder: as an old proverb says, any curve taken around the bosses is shorter than a straight line![21]

Shurik listens as letter after letter is read. None of them are his. Then, just as he's about to give up, the very last one rings with resounding familiarity:

> Listen, Seva, I have an idea. Maybe your listeners might help. Read my address on air and let anyone write me—those who know only one way of entertainment on a Friday night: your broadcasts. We could organize, you know, a fan club, a Novgorodsev Appreciation Society, create an informal union of young people. I would love to reply to anyone: those who, like myself, eagerly listen to your midnight lectures and who like rock, not necessarily heavy metal, and also those who are ready to destroy me just because I dare to tune to a wavelength of a "hostile ideological radio center," and not to the waves of Soviet radio. But I will be most of all waiting for a letter from those who find an escape from hopelessness and loneliness in your programs, Seva. Those whose life is called life because there's a religion called Rock in it.[22]

---

20 "Gorbachev Mix on TV is Tough but Cooperative," *New York Times*, December 1, 1987, https://www.nytimes.com/1987/12/01/world/gorbachev-mix-on-tv-is-tough-but-cooperative.html?pagewanted=all&src=pm.

21 *Rok-posevy*, January 8, 1988, https://seva.ru/pdf/1988/880108.pdf.

22 Ibid.

Seva repeats Shurik's P. O. Box address twice so his listeners can write it down. But Seva doesn't comment on the message in any way, as he does for some others, and simply proceeds to play Shurik's requested song from American glam metal band Cinderella. An unimaginable thrill fills Shurik—it's a dream come true to become part of Seva's shortwave community, a dream he shares with no one in his isolated world, until more remarkable things happen . . .

Far south in the mammoth capital city of Moscow, another avid BBC listener Alex Tatishchev sits faithfully by the radio on Friday night like millions of others around the country and listens to Seva's dulcet voice read select letters he's received, anxious to hear his own. "On the one hand, you want Seva to read your letter, on the other hand, you are afraid, because of the consequences."

While Seva does not read Alex's letter that frigid January night, Alex still hears something that gets him, almost unreasonably, excited:

> He read a letter from a guy named Shurik Fedorov who proposed (as a joke, I learned later) to create a fan club for Seva. And Seva actually read Fedorov's address on air. I understood right away that this was a great idea, and I just had to send a letter to Shurik. But then, my second thought was that it might be a KGB provocation. . . .

Alex thinks it over agitatedly for three days—to write or not to write. Finally, he devises a plan despite his very real fear, like many around him, of the government:

> I had a friend in school who was (and still is) very pro-Soviet. I said, "Grisha, could you send a letter for me?"
>
> "To where?" he asks, "England?"
>
> I answer, "No, to Russia."
>
> "Of course," he replies. "What can they do for a letter to Russia?"

So, Alex writes to Fedorov in this very small town, very far away from Moscow, located between Petrozavodsk and Murmansk. He expresses his interest in the fan club idea and asks Shurik to contact him; however, he doesn't give his own address, but that of his friend Grisha. When a full week passes and no letter comes, Alex sees this as absolute proof that his first inkling was correct: it was a KGB ploy all the way. He thinks with only slight relief that at least the authorities will not know to come to him but will rather go to his pro-Soviet friend Grisha . . .

Shurik's expectations had been very low for a response to his missive, but soon not only a few letters reach him, as he had originally hoped, but hundreds from all over the USSR start to fill his previously lonely home. In one week alone, he receives an amazing seven hundred letters from listeners of Seva. After the first hundred, he realizes he can't possibly answer them all himself. Many who write to him are quite serious about starting a fan club and even offer their ideas of names and various activities—from publishing *samizdat* to staging gigs to organizing meetups.

"That's how a joke became serious business."[23] The decision is before him: dare he create this anti-Soviet thing? He has read all the articles in *Rovesnik* magazine, *Komsomol'skaia pravda,* and others that paint Seva as the "traitor of the Motherland." How can Shurik proceed with any plans without incurring unwanted "visitors"? He thinks it over. *Perestroika* means reconstruction, irreversible change, and so he decides he must make a big reconstruction of his life, too. He sits down and starts typing, possessing the rare and hard-to-obtain typewriter:

> I selected the authors of the most serious and detailed letters who proposed some plans and asked them to be a kind of regional coordinator of our Rock-Information Syndicate. I sent them lists of people from their respective regions so they could contact them directly and organize things quicker. . . . Ultimately, I had twenty regional branches. Not one of the people I selected to be regional bosses refused to take on this responsibility! That's how we all started this thing. . . .[24]

One of these twenty letters that Shurik writes is in fact to Alex Tatishchev in Moscow . . .

Ever the wary Soviet young man, Alex has not tried to make any more attempts to write to Shurik or pursue the idea of a fan club. He maintains his regiment of listening to Seva and somewhat apprehensively keeps an eye on his friend Grisha. KGB hasn't come for him—yet.

Then, as spring hesitantly comes to Moscow, Alex receives a surprise:

> We were sitting in class, and Grisha showed me an envelope, passing it secretly to me. It was Fedorov's reply, quite a long letter, many pages. He said that he had received seven hundred letters

---

23 A. Fedorov correspondence, June 2019.

24 This is in effect social media without the internet, as the big difficulty of the time is safely finding friends with similar views and interests and within travel distance.

> like mine in just one week and that he is physically unable to answer them all. He organized all those letters in groups according to regions, wrote down all the addresses of the people in one region (via carbon paper), and sent those addresses by letter to everyone in the same region.[25]

Overcome with joy and disbelief that this could be happening, Alex finds in his letter eleven or so addresses of people in his specific district of Moscow. With enthusiasm, Alex writes to the first two people on his list, and to his pleasant surprise, they reply. One of these is Igor Garashchenko—a twenty-five-year-old engineer with long hair who works in a secret technical institute. Of Igor's unconventional appearance, Alex says, "It would have been difficult to have long hair and be a Komsomol member, but otherwise in the '80s nobody cared . . ."

At their first meeting, Alex and Igor meet in Moscow and simply take a walk. Igor, unlike Alex, is fearless concerning the KGB and Soviet matters and is not paranoid at all despite his being older and more experienced than Alex. Igor feels that he isn't doing anything wrong, so why should the authorities come after him? Alex knows very well such logic holds up poorly in light of his personal experience: he knows of many incidents where young people who are merely listeners of the "voices" have been persecuted in some way, if not arrested. Thus, Alex harbors a real fear, though as a student he is less exposed to scrutiny than others. Nevertheless, he could be sent to the army, his parents' employment status could be affected, they could be arrested . . .[26] The pervasive sense of uncertainty and insecurity fills him—in the USSR *anything* can happen.

Like Shurik, Alex recalls the prominent, highly negative article in *Komsomol'skaia pravda* about Seva in 1984.[27] Is creating and participating in this club worth the risk? Despite his apprehensions, Alex agrees to Igor's idea of gathering all the Moscow listeners whose addresses Alex had received. Igor volunteers his parents' rather large Moscow apartment (while they are off traveling).[28]

---

25 A. Tatishchev correspondence, May 2019. For additional accounts, see also *Rok-posevy*, April 14, 1989, radio broadcast, https://seva.ru/rock/?id=570.

26 Alex's mother was working as an economist, but at a military secret institute, commonly known as *pochtovyi yashchik*, meaning mailbox, or just *yashchik* because there was no physical address and only a P. O. box—"He's working in the box, *yashchik*," they would say (S. Pantsirev correspondence, May 2019).

27 Filinov, "Barbarossa of Rock 'n' Roll."

28 Igor's stepfather was a prominent party member, and he was a leader of a party group on sports, which was very big following the Olympics. He actually played a very crucial role in Seva's return to the USSR in 1990 and was even there to drive Seva from the airport in Moscow (conversation with S. Pantsirev and A. Tatishchev).

Some two dozen people show up at Igor's place, about five or six are girls, and everyone meets each other for the first time. There is a lot of vodka and *zakuski* (snacks), and, inevitably, some romance.

The youth have a common stirring desire to do something, but no one knows what. Everybody loves rock music, and everybody wants to share their information about rock and make it publicly available. The idea forms to try to combine all the bits of information that everyone has into some kind of magazine—*samizdat.* Alex realizes, smartly, that there is something going on and these goings on demand to be documented. He starts to keep a diary.

Soon, everybody is writing to each other, not just those in Moscow. By the end of the summer, the club is a living, thriving structure, albeit one without a name. After much heated debate, Shurik pulls rank and reduces the options for vote. Even here, the Sovietness of their existence is inescapable. The winning name is an unwieldy acronym resembling those seen across the USSR and tellingly bears no mention of Seva or the BBC: *Nezavisimyi obyedinyonnyi rok-informatsionnyi sindikat,* or Independent United Rock-Information Syndicate. But the acronym is easy enough, and though not loved by everyone, the name sticks. Thus, what started as a joke, becomes tangible connection that changes not only the life of one young man in a tiny northern village, but the lives of many all over the USSR. As Seva puts it, because of Shurik's sheer "postal misery," NORIS is born.

Moscow NORIS club leaders circa 1989—Igor G. is 2nd from left (courtesy of A. Tatishchev, NORIS Archive)

Featured Listener: "The Programmer"

Back in the late 1980s, I was drafted into the army, narrowly escaped the Afghan War, and served on a small missile division near Kharkov [in Ukraine]. Of course, there were Seva listeners in the army as well—soldiers and officers—and I even tried to make a long-distance call to London once to ask a question for Paul McCartney when he was a live guest on BBC Russian with Seva as his interpreter. The call had failed, and of course had been intercepted, and as a result I was questioned by the internal security, but without any serious consequences.

At the end of my service, I returned to a totally different country. The first thing I saw in Moscow on my way home was a Swiss newspaper, *Neue Zürcher Zeitung*, freely on sale in a metro station's kiosk. That was a real shock. Many things had indeed changed during my army service, but Seva remained the same, and his broadcasts were something to hold on to in a changing—not to say crumbling—world. One of my letters to Seva, read on air, went like this:

> Hey Seva, this letter is caused by what you said in one of your *Rok-posevy* about the mutual feelings between the broadcaster and the audience, and about friendship being a two-way energy. Imagine: Friday, late night. Big city lights outside the window. On the top floor of a standard Moscow block of flats sit three friends—the Metalhead, the Programmer, and the Communist—playing Preference the night away, sometimes quoting Preference-related jokes from *Sevaoborot.* But the time is near midnight and the Metalhead turns on a radio, pre-tuned to the BBC Russian wavelength.
>
> "Oh, that's your Seva again, sod off," says the Communist, but nobody listens to him.
>
> The Metalhead and the Programmer are all ears, catching the voice they know from childhood: "Good evening, my friends" (the standard opening of *Rok-posevy*). And after hearing, "Take care, guys" (the standard closing phrase) and the outro jingle, the Communist asks: "What in the hell do you find in him?"
>
> "Hey, you don't understand anything!" says the Metalhead.
>
> I start to think, what to answer? How to explain to the Communist that Seva, a longtime ray of light in the darkness of totalitarianism, now, in time of uncertainty, maybe on the verge of return to their Communist dictatorship, still shines as

an example of something sane, kind, and—believe it or not—eternal, which is unaffected neither by the passing time, nor by propaganda, nor by the sheer squalor of our existence?

But not in the mood for arguing, the Programmer said something insignificant, as we returned to the game. So that's it about us, and about the friendship, which still works two ways, and still is very strong from our side. And we are—the Metalhead Yuri, the Communist Mike and myself.

Signed, the Programmer.

Featured Listener: Anna

I was born in Ukraine. When I was thirteen or fourteen, I started to listen to the foreign radio stations. With all the jamming it was difficult. At first, it was the BBC and then Voice of America in Ukraine. The BBC was in Russian. On VOA they also had a DJ named Fedinsky. And I was writing to that DJ, which was a crazy thing to do at that time. It was like 1983 or '84. I was sure that my letter would not come through. The address was just Voice of America, Washington, D.C. And I just dropped the letter in the mailbox, in a very small town in Ukraine (in the Kyiv region). But in a couple of weeks, I heard my letter broadcast on Voice of America! So it did go through, and that was unbelievable at the time. I don't remember what I wrote. But I dropped the letter in the box, thinking that tomorrow some KGB or police would come. It was more real than what actually happened.

And then, it was Seva. Also, around 1983.

So, I was listening to Seva very regularly, not missing any program.

It was not a breath of fresh air; it was a *hurricane* of fresh air. Because living in a small town in Ukraine was very boring.

Then, one day, I heard Alexander Fedorov's letter read on air [about starting a club], and I decided to write to him. By that time, I lived in Russia, the Kursk region. I found a few people in the Kursk region who listened to Seva. In principle, in Russia, rock 'n' roll was primarily listened to by guys, not so much by girls. Why? I don't know. That's a question for a psychologist or sociologist. Not easily answered. In America, was it any different?

My grandad was a dissident, so I was interested in dissent as a whole. Not just music. I liked rock but not heavy metal. I liked rock 'n' roll people, too, but not the heavy metal people so much. In NORIS most were interested in rock but not heavy metal. Maybe the metalheads were just more prominent in the pictures. Most normal people wore long hair, but they were not necessarily heavy metal fans. In St. Petersburg, there were more diverse members . . . There were directors, jazz musicians, etc. So, here in Peter there were more of the intelligentsia involved. And some Moscow people like Alex [Tatishchev] were not heavy metal people either. But if you see the *samizdat*, it's heavy metal. (It was fashionable at that time.)

I listened to other radio voices, such as Radio Svoboda. For me it was not as important because there was no music. I was fourteen, so I was interested in music in the first place. There was Solzhenitsyn on Radio Svoboda, and I was interested in that because he was in exile. But the politics and such didn't make any impact and I didn't understand it, nor was it interesting. It wasn't close to me. Voice of America, yes, because there was some music.

In my opinion, Russian rock was much more rebellious than listening to Western rock. And it was always underground from the start and going against the system.

I didn't listen to Sevaoborot either.[29]

I participated in all of the yearly NORIS meetings. Most of those who kept the spirit alive are unfortunately all gone.[30]

29 Another important note is that many of these *Rok-posevy* listeners who listened mainly for the music had little interest in *Sevaoborot* as a chat show with older co-hosts and guests (often nonmusical ones). Yet, *Sevaoborot* had a huge audience, which implies that the show brought in an additional swath of the Russian-speaking population.

30 Listener Anna, May 2019, St. Petersburg.

CHAPTER 14

Highway to Hell

> Hello, Seva. Today I listened to your program with great interest, because, due to the lack of a radio receiver, I had a three-month break. I've been listening to you since only recently, not more than a year, but in those three months [without radio] I missed your voice, exactly your voice. Now, I live in Düsseldorf, and of course there is enough musical information here. But your programs are so interestingly presented, listening to them is a pleasure. I don't think you should "re-adjust" [your style] as Soviet listeners advise. If you only talked about music, then, in my opinion, the program would feel thin—since you live in a free country, you can say whatever you want. Of course, your programs did not mean less to Soviets with the beginning of *glasnost'*, because the information [the government] presents to us is still doused in political sauce. . . . *glasnost'* is a good thing, but it alone is not enough. . . .
>
> —*Rok-posevy,* Listener from West Germany, 1988[1]

The trio of years from 1988 to 1991 gives little hint to the revolutionary and terminal path on which Mikhail Gorbachev has firmly placed the Soviet Union; it's hard to predict where this road will lead when everything is in constant flux. "Rather than continuing to resist change, both outside and within the Soviet region, Gorbachev propose[s] to accelerate the reform process."[2] Gorbachev optimistically relaxes restrictions, opening the door to the West and the world at large. He withdraws troops from Afghanistan beginning in May 1988, initiates free elections for the Soviet Congress of Deputies, and says openly "we can't go on like this" to the entire USSR. Referring to himself, he states: "The politician thinks about the next election—the statesman thinks about the next generation."[3] Though he genuinely cares about the people, Gorbachev still

1 *Rok-posevy*, February 12, 1988, radio broadcast, https://seva.ru/pdf/1988/880212.pdf.

2 Sheeran, *Cultural Politics in International Relations*, xi.

3 Taubman, *Gorbachev*, 642.

wishes to maintain his position and power while rendering the USSR more open, more international, yet distinctly Soviet. Is it possible?

The constant state of volatility and revelation—not overt revolution—emboldens the youth who eagerly ride the waves to their advantage. However, the older generation of *shestidesiatniki* and their elderly parents are stricken by uncertainty. As these citizens put it, "*glasnost'* revelations" cause them to see things differently and essentially terminate any lingering faith they may or may not have had in the Soviet system itself: "everything we believed in, everything that we considered sacred and holy, turned out to be not only unholy, but even the handiwork of the devil."[4] Citizens are forced to wrestle with themselves and all that they'd internalized as "sacred," leading to a pervasive and growing culture of conspiracy. "[I]t was as if there was deception everywhere . . . and the sense that we really could have lived through those years differently." As the revelations mount and implicate nearly every aspect of Soviet life, it becomes clear to many that nothing can remain, "for it turns out that there was nothing about us that was good."[5]

During this time of extraordinary changes, Margaret Thatcher agrees to be a guest on the BBC Russian Service to answer live listener questions in a thirty-minute segment. Many callers are from Leningrad, several lavishing praise on Prime Minister Thatcher, saying she is greatly loved in Russia—potentially because they associate her with the BBC and with Seva. Other callers bring up pressing matters such as the conference of the Soviet Communist Party (partly televised in the UK). To all questions, Thatcher's responses are graceful, sincere, and clearly delivered. When asked whether she has noticed the changes in the USSR and whether she thinks them significant, she replies most eloquently and passionately:

> I think that they are not [just] significant, they are historic. I think it's remarkable that after seventy years of what I might call the old-fashioned kind of communism . . . that Mr. Gorbachev should have been able to see that it was not producing either the standard of living that people wants or the standard of social services or the standard of technological development. Not only that he should see that but that he should have the courage to say so. And say then this is not good enough. We must not rely only on military strength for our place in the world. The people of the Soviet Union deserve more. And we must change the system to see if we can get more. . . . That will not only be good for

---

4 Raleigh, *Soviet Baby Boomers*, 284–85.
5 Ibid. See also Yurchak, *Everything Was Forever*, 7–8.

> the people in the Soviet Union, it will [also] be good for their neighbors, and indeed for the cause of human rights, freedom, and democracy the world over.[6]

What Prime Minister Thatcher expresses in these words is a genuine sense of metamorphosis that is stealing over the full breadth of the USSR. *Change,* as Viktor Tsoi's hit of this era heralds in smoky undertones, is coming. Not just coming—it is already here.

The Syndicate Grows

As the USSR evolves, so does NORIS. From inception, however, the club rouses dissent in the ranks of Seva's listeners. Many abstain from association with NORIS for fear that it is another kind of Komsomol, and also because, as some members note, the Western idea of a "fan club" is new to Soviets and not readily seen as separate from government-organized clubs. Even the most devoted avoid having anything to do with the club at all:

> When NORIS started, I wrote a grumpy letter to its founder Alexander "Shurik" Fedorov, saying, "You are trying to monopolize Seva, and you are trying to create another Komsomol. . . ." Time proved I was both right *and* wrong. NORIS indeed monopolized Seva's attention as Seva assumed every listener had joined (though in fact, NORIS was some 2–3,000 strong, a drop in the bucket). But I was wrong in that it wasn't a new Komsomol. In fact, NORIS was needed to create a network of like-minded people. . . .[7]

"Like-minded" is a word often used by the members themselves to describe the purpose of NORIS, though even nonmembers could appreciate that this club is

---

6 Margaret Thatcher, interview on BBC Russian Service, July 11, 1988, radio broadcast, https://www.bbc.co.uk/sounds/play/p033k7t4.

7 S. Pantsirev in correspondence with author, February 2019. His response is not unique in that quite a few interviewed for this book said they were never members (likely because of the Komsomol comparison) but ultimately believed that NORIS was "good" for Soviet youth. It was almost a way of categorizing Seva's listeners: if they were members, they were die hard rock fans (not just fans of Seva), if they were not members, they were almost always listeners because of Seva himself (several said his words were good literature or even poetry, though with typical Slavic frankness they said he wasn't *always* great either).

all about shared interests. Eugen from Krasnodar, the NORIS coordinator for southern Russia, the North Caucasus, and southern Ukraine, confirms:

> Rock fans in the USSR needed information and like-minded friends. There was no Internet at that time, the only channel of freedom was shortwave radio and western broadcasters. We needed an organized brotherhood that would allow us to exchange thoughts, information, and music. . . .

Eugen's referral to the club as a "brotherhood" highlights the fact that the average member is "a twenty-year-old male metalhead." Only about ten percent of the membership is female, a statistic that cannot be satisfyingly explained when there are many young women who consume rock music across the USSR. There are certainly several discouraging factors, not only for women, but also for men. Whereas listening to foreign voices has largely taken place in private, albeit lonely, spaces, now in a gathering of BBC devotees, there are many to witness the "crime" of consuming Western influences. Who can guarantee that one of these participants is not a spy or will not betray such activities to the KGB at the slightest provocation? The consequences and damage to life and social status might not be worth even the liberalizing connection. Nevertheless, despite the prevailing fears, Shurik Fedorov, the founder, continuously receives letters of application to the club as word of its existence spreads. He sends out even more lists of addresses to his region leaders for them to make contact. Alex Tatishchev in Moscow happily recalls meeting his "first love"—a girl from Crimea—through NORIS's correspondence system:

> It was very vivid communication that was going on during this time—I used to write ten letters per day, every day, and I was communicating with a girl from Crimea, and we hadn't even met each other yet. My parents didn't know anything about the work that was going on. I would be sitting at my desk, there was a small drawer in it, and if my parents came to my room when I was writing, I would just be able to drop the letter into the drawer. . . .[8]

The Moscow leaders decide they need to start keeping an account of members in a more permanent way. "We came up with the idea that we had to be some kind of official registered organization. But we were a long way to that."[9] So for

8 A. Tatishchev, May 2019.
9 Ibid.

now, keeping their own records will suffice. Igor Garashchenko, working in the aviation industry, has access to a huge mainframe computer. He is able to enter and store the addresses of the members as they are received from Fedorov and then print many copies. These copies are then distributed, sometimes with a note for various genre preferences whenever such a thing is known. If one likes hard rock, write to this address; if one likes new wave, write to this person; and so on. Consequently, many in proximity to each other, with aligned musical tastes, organize impromptu meetups to listen to Seva together on Friday nights, swap records, or simply drink and talk. Kostya, another key member, confirms:

> We exchanged records and photographs of rock groups; there were branches in many cities and also sections dedicated to specific activities, i.e., audio copying, radio amateurship, and so on. An average member was just the average lover of rock music. There were some who had long hair, like hippies, but they were the minority, and most looked like the average young man of that time. . . .[10] Many of us were from various cities in the European part of the USSR, and those from Moscow, like me, were those who had no such friends from whom they could obtain LPs from abroad.[11]

Everyone starts to understand that they all have a special love for music but not necessarily for the same bands or subgenres of rock. More importantly, they all want to do something to "realize themselves." They have "huge hopes" that they will actually bring about some change in society, proving that Seva did not raise a listless and indifferent generation. Rather, he taught his listeners to think for themselves; so naturally, invigorated and united, they want to follow their own moral compass, just as Seva has followed his.

At the same time, what these music-loving youth want in terms of "change" is largely undefined and hard for them to articulate. Freedom is their ideology and rock their religion, but what does this mean in practice, in the real world, away from the ether with its endless possibilities? Where will these open, uncharted waters lead?

---

10 Kostya is careful to disassociate the NORIS movement from the Soviet idea of "hippie," which he holds is more "redneck" and seldom encountered by or known to him and those in NORIS. This segregation is debatable as many of the rock musicians were in fact hippies. Pyotr Mamonov of Zvuki Mu was a hippie, and much of the aesthetics of hippies (hair, dress, etc.) was embraced by Russian rockers. For more on the Soviet hippie movement, see Juliane Fürst, *Flowers Through Concrete* (Oxford: Oxford University Press, 2021).

11 Email correspondence with author, March 2019 and 2020.

Shades of NORIS

One notable subsection of NORIS is in Leningrad, which is among the most active districts. This group of Seva listeners, interestingly, predates NORIS by a few years, having formed as a local society devoted to English band Deep Purple. They are proud of their distinction as the first Deep Purple fan club in Russia. Although Deep Purple is an old group dating back to 1968, this fan society only came to exist in 1986, not long after Seva does an in-depth three-part series on Deep Purple starting on May 3, 1985.[12] These three episodes are filled with history, member profiles, and many of DP's songs. Mere months later, in Ulyanovsk, hundreds of miles east of Moscow, on the Volga River, one DP fan, Konstantin Drigin, who hears these broadcasts, decides to start a fan club. However, it isn't until NORIS comes into existence that Konstantin has a real framework in which to build his group. Thus, it becomes officially called the "Deep Purple Russian Fan Section."

In early 1989, Konstantin reaches out to Seva himself, asking for help to attain real DP records and to possibly connect with the much older and larger Deep Purple International Fan Society in South Yorkshire, UK, run by Simon Robinson.[13] Seva obliges, knowing these people personally, and sends Konstantin the address as well as an "Illustrated Biography of Deep Purple." Thus, Seva's broadcasts and active connection with his listeners lead to Soviet interest in Western rock bands long past their prime, creating a resurgence of popularity, even in the middle of Russia, far from the cultural centers of Leningrad and Moscow.

One last curiosity about this section is that Konstantin has record of a member from Leningrad by the name of Dmitry Medvedev. He speculates with good reason that this might be *the* Dmitry Medvedev who eventually rises to the position of prime minister and then president of the Russian Federation. Russia Today (RT) admits that Medvedev—born, raised, and educated in Leningrad—has a strong love of "hard rock bands like Deep Purple," having become enamored with the genre while in college.[14] CNN notes the same: "He grew up listening to black-market copies of 70s rock bands like Led Zeppelin and Deep Purple."[15] As

---

12 *Rok-posevy*, May 3, 1985, radio broadcast, https://seva.ru/rock/?id=364&y=1985.

13 Alexei Kononov, "Deep Purple Russian Fan Section," DeepPurple.ru, December 2012, https://www.deep-purple.ru/fan_club/ussr/first_fan_club_ussr.html.

14 "Who is Dmitry Medvedev?," RT, March 4, 2008, accessed April 11, 2020, https://www.rt.com/russia/who-is-dmitry-medvedev-2008-03-04/. "During his student years Medvedev was a hard-rock fan with Black Sabbath, Deep Purple, and Led Zeppelin as his favorite bands. He still collects vinyl records and recently was pictured with Deep Purple during their visit to Moscow."

15 "Dmitry Medvedev Fast Facts," CNN.com, March 20, 2010, https://www.cnn.com/2012/12/26/world/europe/dmitry-medvedev---fast-facts/index.html.

does the BBC: "Whatever his political values, Dmitry Medvedev has Western tastes, being a fan of rock groups like Pink Floyd and Deep Purple."[16] Even if this is not the same Medvedev who is a member of record of the NORIS DP subsection, it still means that the future leader of the Russian Federation had to have been a listener of the BBC Russian Service to even learn about such hard rock, especially Deep Purple, since Radio Svoboda and VOA expectedly did not play such old British bands. Therefore, this points to at least one likelihood: Dmitry Medvedev listens to Seva.

Samizdat

As NORIS nets more and more interest, people are invited to make their participation official by providing the Moscow organizers with detailed information: music preferences, age, hobbies and interests, and so on. Despite reservations about their safety and KGB discovery, a brave and brazen few hundred out of the millions of Seva's listeners respond to the call with their profiles and in many cases even a picture. Alex Tatishchev transfers the information to membership cards and catalogues them according to their region number in the top left of each card:

1. Volgograd, Voronezh and Saratov regions
2. Dnipropetrovsk, Zaporizhzhia, Kherson, Nikolaev and their regions
3. Orel, Tula, Kursk and their regions
4. Kharkiv, Cherkassk, Belgorod, Vinnitsk, Kirovograd and their regions
5. Donetsk region, Ukraine SSR
6. Belarus SSR
7. Yaroslavl, Vologda, Kostroma, Vladimir and their regions
8. Bryansk, Smolensk, Kaluga and their regions
9. Gorky, Penza, Ryazan and their regions; Yoshkar-Ola
10. Kyiv, Zhytomyr, and their regions; Rivne, Lviv, Ternopil (Ukraine SSR)
11. Leningrad and region
12. Rostov-on-Don and region; Krasnodar Territory
13. Moscow and the region
14. Baltic states (Lithuania, Latvia, Estonia)
15. Addressees in military units
16. Odessa, Crimea, Chisinau, Severodonetsk

---

16 "Profile: Dmitry Medvedev," BBC.com, September 24, 2011, https://www.bbc.com/news/world-europe-15047827.

17. Ufa, Kuibyshev, Ulyanovsk and their regions; Naberezhnye Chelny
18. Sverdlovsk region; Perm, Barnaul, Novosibirsk, Tyumen and their regions
19. Kalinin, Pskov, Novgorod and their regions
20. Karelian ASSR, Arkhangelsk, and Murmansk regions.[17]

12 НОРИС
фио ЧИЖИКОВ ВЯЧЕСЛАВ
А: 353410 Краснодарский край, г.Анапа, 12 мкр. 46 – 51
г.р. 13.10.69г. / г.в. январь 1988г.
м.ф. AC/DC, I.M., Круиз, Коррозия М.
х. дьяволыщина, авангардное искуоство, фантастика

9 НОРИС
фио ГАВРИЛОВ ДЕНИС АЛЕКСАНДРОВИЧ
А: 171950 Тверская обл. г.Бежецк ул.Чехова 3 – 68
г.р. 1973г. / г.в. 1992г.
м.ф. Алиса, КИНО, НАУ, АКВАРИУМ, КРЕМАТОРИЙ, Г.О., Beatles, Eagles, T. REX
DX-RADIO, Боевые искусства, философия

10 НОРИС
фио Савельева Екатерина
А: 262012 г.Житомир ул.Михайловградская 68 – 29
г.р. 11.05.74г. / г.в. весна 1990г.
м.ф. D.P., P.F., AC/DC, J.P., B.S., Башлачев, Янка, Г.О.
х. рисование

4 НОРИС
фио КОБРИН НИКИТА
А: 310162 г.Харьков а/я 8195
г.р. 13.10.56г. / г.в. январь 1991г.
м.ф. Beatles, J. Baez, Jethro Tull, B. Marley, D.P.
х. нет

20 НОРИС
фио АКСЁНОВ АНДРЕЙ
А: 184700 Мурманская обл. Терский р-н, п.Умба ул.Беломорская 6 – 25
г.р. 25.05.71г. / г.в. январь 1988г.
м.ф. ACCEPT, I.M., METALLICA, HELLOWEEN
х. фотография, фантастика, рыбалка

7 НОРИС
фио ТЕРЁХИН ОЛЕГ ЕВГЕНЬЕВИЧ
А: 601550 Владимирская обл. г.Гусь-Хрустальный, ул.Чайковского д.7 кв.52
г.р. 05.06.70г. / г.в. 1989г.
м.ф.
х. история и политика

18 НОРИС
фио СУЛАКОВА НАТАЛЬЯ БОРИСОВНА
А: 633128 Новосибирская обл. Краснообск I – III
(383-2) 48-34-80
г.р. 25.12.73г. / г.в. 1991г.
м.ф. CINDERELLA, METALLICA, SCORPIONS
х. фотография, англ.яз

1 НОРИС
фио КУЗНЕЦОВ Сергей Викторович
А: 404102 г. Волжский, Волгоградская обл., ул. Мира, д. 2, кв.23
г.р. 24 мая 1967 / г.в. ноябрь 1992 г.
м.ф. Дж.Хендрикс, Дж.Джоплин, Лед Зеппелин, Би Би Кинг, а также блюзы, психоделика, кантри, немного джаз

NORIS member card examples—the top left number indicates region in USSR. (Courtesy of A. Tatishchev, NORIS archive)

17 *Rok-posevy*, April 14, 1989, radio broadcast, https://seva.ru/rock/?id=570&y=1989.

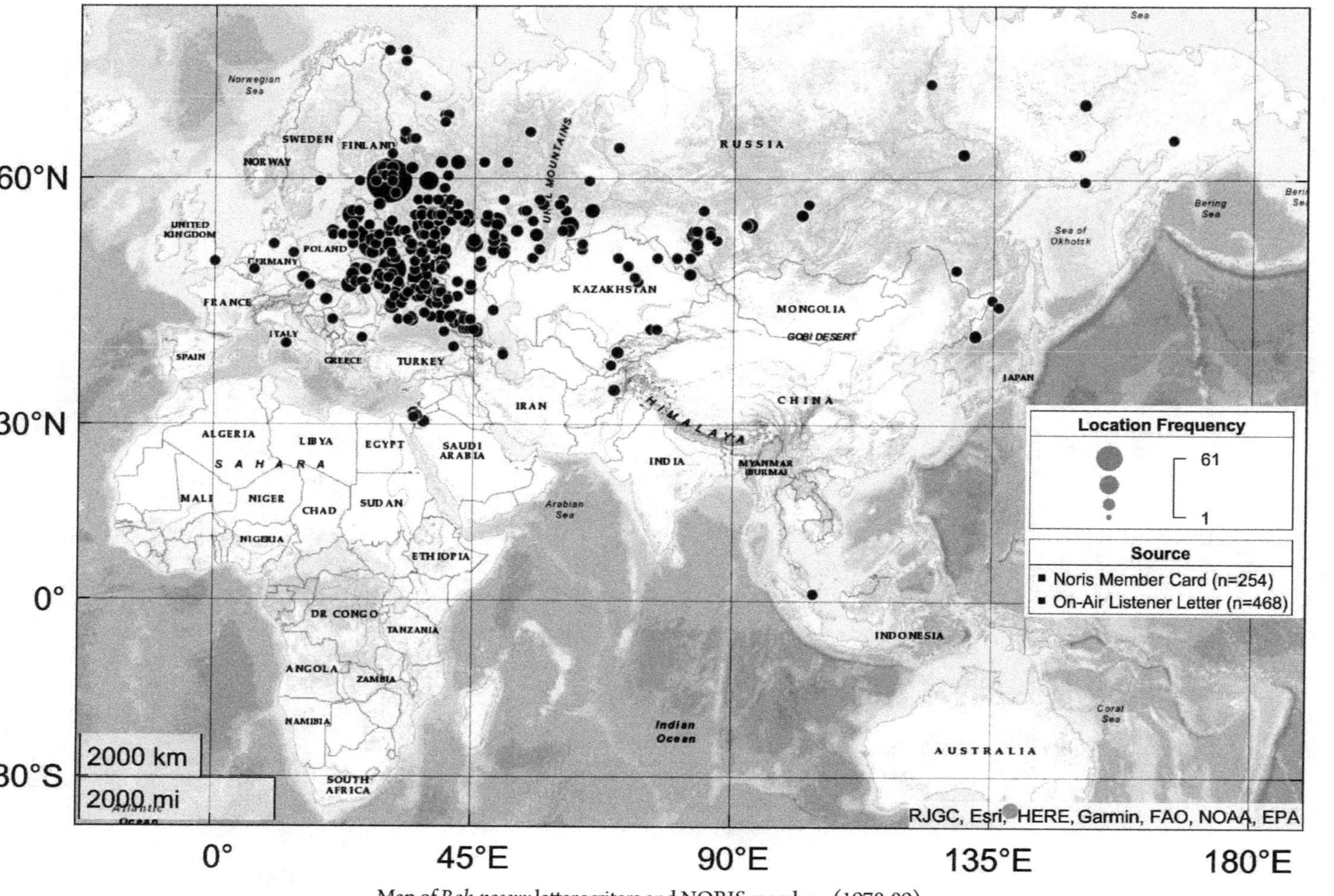

Map of *Rok-posevy* letter writers and NORIS members (1978-89)

The geographical data gathered from the cards quite closely matches the locations of many of the letter writers to *Rok-posevy*. Both NORIS members and Seva's letter writers appear to be heavily concentrated in the Western part of Russia, though this distribution cannot be conflated with the overall distribution of Seva's listenership, since it includes all those who write to Seva, those whose letters never reach Seva, and those silent participants who choose not to write at all. There are, of course, several outliers, which attest, if nothing else, to how far and wide the news of NORIS spreads.

To bring everyone in all twenty districts onto the same page, Shurik, Alex, and Igor decide to start publishing a zine for all of NORIS called *Novgorodtseva druzhina*—inadequately translated as Novgorodsev Squad.[18] Creating *samizdat* is not easy as access to copiers is strictly controlled, and even owning a typewriter requires special permission. They're successful, though, because in Soviet Russia someone always knows someone who knows someone.... The first bulletin is copied by the hundreds and mailed to each member of the club. It contains information about club activities, surveys to determine the top ten favorite artists and songs, specialized ads in each genre or band-focused subsection (like the DP Section), general music scene gossip, interviews with Russian underground bands, and classified ads sent by the club members (including for dating purposes)—all of which facilitates even more unlikely ties across the club. This becomes NORIS's central publication that everybody receives, though many regions also publish their own *samizdat* to serve their interests.

"NORIS had in total ten different publications," says Alex Tatishchev. Each of these are created, printed, and distributed by various regions, featuring interviews with Russian rock artists and also information about Western bands of interest. Some publications don't make it beyond their first issue, while others are far more successful and dedicated.[19] Most importantly, each publication serves the interests of particular regions and music preferences. For example, the Pink Floyd subsection has a fanzine called *Reds into Pink* to which even those who are not official members of NORIS, but still die-hard listeners of Seva, contribute.[20]

The DP subsection also publishes its own *samizdat* and manages to put out six full volumes for distribution to its members across the USSR before things become too difficult. The content of these volumes is purely apolitical and

18 This is another case of wordplay in the spirit of Seva's culturally specific style. *Druzhina* was the name for the old Russian military units, and the most famous was located in the city of Novgorod—Novgoroda Druzhina. So NORIS turned the unit name into their paper title: Novgorodseva Druzhina.

19 A. Tatishchev, May 2019.

20 Ibid. Also S. Pantsirev, February 2019.

focused on the music and the lives of the musicians. Understandably, the print quality is much poorer than the main NORIS publication, owing to the substantially lower conditions and resources in Ulyanovsk than in Moscow and Leningrad. Still, it is a triumph for Konstantin Drigin and his DP comrades. In fact, in the May 1991 issue of *Darker than Blue* (the official publication of the Deep Purple International Fan Society) Konstantin's subsection receives mention in the "Fan Clubs" portion of the magazine:

> We have heard from the land of the rising McDonalds . . . with a magazine from the Russian Deep Purple Society. They appear to be operating under conditions, which would make lesser mortals run and hide, and seemed quite pleased that we are able to help them a little. Konstantin Drigin is the man behind it all. We've parceled up some of our sleeve damaged/sticker marked, but otherwise fine, spares for him to do with what he will.[21]

The most active NORIS leaders in Moscow who are also the principal club organizers—Alex Tatishchev, Igor Garashchenko, and Andrey Kochebin—publish their own fanzine called *Rok-posevy*. Unlike *Novgorodtseva druzhina*, this fanzine is more clearly anti-communist with a punk rock and heavy metal slant. Concerning the correlation between anarchy and punk rock, which has noticeably dominated Western music culture as well, Shurik Fedorov notes, "Rock is essentially a rebel kind of music, especially heavy metal with its depth of expression, heavy rhythms, emotions, and untamed rage."[22] A piece in American magazine *Newsday* more than a decade earlier (in June 1972) reflects Shurik's statement, but also says that with few exceptions rock 'n' roll "usually implies an identification of male sexuality and aggression." This certainly seems to be the case with the *Rok-posevy* fanzine. These publications reflect a certain male dynamism and unbridled energy, if not quite rage, and exhibit a provocative sexual tone replete with sometimes graphic images. However, it should be noted that, in all cases, these *samizdat* are also word heavy, with some containing no pictures at all, which again reflects the priority placed on information and the cultural importance of words.

---

21 Kononov, "Deep Purple Russian Fan Section."
22 A. Fedorov, June 2019.

Rok-Posevy magazine cover, featuring Lenin decked out as a metalhead (courtesy of A. Tatishchev, NORIS archive)

The information within these varied NORIS publications is shared with Seva over the phone and through letters to give the club on-air publicity. Indeed, in this way, NORIS gains the attention of state media.

"NORIS is Recruiting"

The first piece about NORIS appears in a Kursk publication. Predictably disparaging, the author proclaims that the club is an agent of foreign intelligence and that Seva, of course, is recruiting young people for UK espionage. However, times *have* changed because the KGB merely gives Kursk members a warning about their activity, and no major harm is done. In fact, the article does more to help dispel lingering doubts about NORIS's nongovernmental status than discourage the youth from joining its ranks. As such, this critical coverage is hardly the last.

In Moscow, one afternoon, Alex returns home from a long day at work, and, as is his habit, he retrieves his copy of the day's *Pravda* from his apartment mailbox. He shuffles towards the elevator, starting to unfold the paper and peruse its contents like usual as he steps onto the lift: "I knew about the Kursk situation. . . . My lift from the ground floor to the fifth took only thirty seconds, and in that span of time I saw the words in bold: 'NORIS is recruiting.'" His eyes bulge and glaze over. Wisely, he decides his parents don't need to read *Pravda* today.

"Who should be blamed for this?" the article's author asks, continuing the Kursk storyline that NORIS is helping Seva recruit Soviet young people for Western intelligence services. Alex realizes that NORIS is in trouble because any critical article that appears in a publication with such a circulation as *Pravda* can only mean there is an organized campaign.

In November 1988, *Komsomol'skaia pravda* issues the Komsomol's official opinion on the club in a piece penned by the very same Yuri Filinov who besmirched Seva in "The Barbarossa of Rock 'n' Roll." This article entitled "Talents and Bureaucrats: Isn't It Time to Draw a Line under the Controversy of Rock Music?" seems to pull away from *Pravda*'s hardline conservatism, scolding officials for not serving the needs of the youth while at the same time disparaging NORIS.[23] Additionally, Filinov includes letters of harsh rebuke written by NORIS members to the publication's so-called Klub 33 1/3 address, a clear nod to Seva's own methods. The first letter writer criticizes the media system for either ignoring modern music culture or treating it only from a critical, educational standpoint, suggesting that because of the lack of reliable music information (either via print, TV, or radio), youths have to turn to foreign broadcasts. "In summary," the letter concludes, "if this continues, we will have no choice but to continue listening to 'voices' and especially to 'papa' [Seva]."[24]

The next letter is just as bold, coming all the way from Arkhangelsk, bordering Karelia and the White Sea: "Despite the fact that we, NORIS, listen to the 'agent' and the 'liar,' as the press has repeatedly called the DJ . . . of the BBC, our activities are exclusively musical, and in no way political." Of course, this writer is not only incorrect about NORIS activities being totally free of politics, he himself is being political by taking on the narratives that the Soviet system has constructed about Seva. "With this letter, we want to call our music officials to an open conversation on behalf of many, between the ages of thirteen and forty, and ask them when they will risk competing with the unsinkable Seva?"[25]

---

23 Yuri Filinov, "Talents and Bureaucrats," *Komsomol'skaia pravda*, November 27, 1988, https://seva.ru/media/?id=5.

24 Ibid.

25 Ibid.

Drawing by a "BBC-ist" (per the hat) and NORIS member from Kyiv. The radio is inscribed with AC/DC and "Highway to Hell," and must have had English labels since he writes in Latin letters "Volume" above the knob. The listener is wearing (as he indicates) a *Mitkovskaya telnyashka,* the shirt of a sailor but specifically associated with the art collective "Mitki" in Petersburg (since 1984)—a counterculture group and one of Russia's earliest protest art demonstrators. He sits atop a submarine branded Slava KPSS (praise to the Communist Party of the Soviet Union, which carries ironic and humorous connotation). The sub is both a reference to Seva's role as listeners' navigator through the ether and also a curiosity of Mitki because the group enjoys putting on floating demonstrations. At the bottom left corner, the artist includes some note with the chemical formula for water, which in itself is fine but that its oxygen component leads to oxidation and "because of this, corrosion begins." This holds huge significance because he is writing this in 1989 and directly implying that air (the ether) is causing the corrosion of the KPSS. Additionally, there is a saxophone peaking from the listener's back he feels he has to label as such because he writes that he has never held one in his hands—another indication that the saxophone is perceived at least historically as counter-Soviet. For more on Mitki, see *Mitki and the Art of Postmodern Protest in Russia* (2019). (July 1989, Seva Novgorodsev letters, Hoover Institution Archives, Box 2.6.)

Finally, a sardonic but indignant letter signed by two members from Kalach in Volgograd Oblast reads: "At present, units of the 'heavy metal division' are being created on the basis of NORIS, ready to go to any town of the USSR on the first call to protect the rights of rock music and its fans." Filinov wastes no time in ridiculing these earnest statements: "So you have a syndicate, a heavy metal division, and a single information center. . . . A rock plague is coming!"

He goes on to diminish their claim about the lack of information and objects on behalf of his readers (as if he knows where the millions stand), implying that NORIS members don't really read at all—a true insult. Then, he surprisingly starts castigating the "guardians" of Soviet culture and ideology for being slow to catch up with the times. He states that eighty percent of the music broadcast in the USSR is focused on folk, classics, and pop in general. For these officials, "there is no need to talk about rock, and because of this fact NORIS is recruiting our music lovers." A whole generation is driven into the underground and these fans of the "disgraced genre" are engaged in the ether—the youth are "swimming on shortwaves" guided by the "navigator" Seva Novgorodsev. He says with pain that the BBC is answering young people's needs faster than the communists who continue to call rock music a "Trojan horse" from the West. He sympathetically writes, "Rock music . . . has been reflecting for many years the troubles and hopes of the younger generation." As if the creation of NORIS has spurred the Komsomol itself to rethink their glacial response to the youth's demands, Filinov signs off with an urgent plea to the bureaucrats to act before it is too late.[26]

Despite this almost validating piece in *Komsomol'skaia pravda,* Alex's fears of a concerted anti-NORIS campaign prove to be correct. The mother of one of his known friends is summoned from her workplace to the '*perviy otdel*' (the first department, subordinate to the KGB) and there she's interrogated. Does she know what her son is doing and that he has had correspondence with some suspicious non-Komsomol members? Does she know that his activities will lead to trouble and her getting fired? NORIS leaders, even confident Igor, understand now that there may be serious consequences forthcoming. Yet, no one wants to stop; they know they are doing something important, both for themselves and for their country.[27]

---

26 Ibid.
27 A. Tatishchev, May 2019.

The First Congress

> I scribble out this message with both good news and not very good news. The good news is that we do not stand still, we are moving along the path of progress and prosperity with our Rock Syndicate. The presence of all sorts of troubles is sad, although inevitable. . . . In the Rostov region, guys with pitchforks went after our syndicators. . . . But the unseemly activities of some of our own guys is also alarming. Someone really wants to add tar to our rock drink. Well, nothing surprising—there are ill-wishers in every business. . . .[28]

From London, Seva makes frequent mention of the club, informing his listeners about its activities, featuring NORIS leaders (like Alex) on broadcasts occasionally, and even donating money for the production of a club pin. Several people, including Shurik Fedorov go to London to meet Seva, and together they create a logo for this purpose. The resulting circular pin and emblem is judged by some of Seva's listeners to be as "naïve" and "overly complex" as the name itself: an owl, an electric guitar, a soundwave, parchment, and the words "Seva Novgorodsev Fan Club." Why an owl? According to Alex, the owl is most probably selected because of a popular quiz show (an intellectual trivia sort of game) on Soviet TV during this time, which sported the owl as its mascot and logo.[29] The idea is thus that the owl, which represents knowledge, will suit their mantle stupendously when paired with a guitar. All members receive the badge free of charge.

NORIS membership badge

---

28 Letter from A. Fedorov to Seva, August 31, 1988, as broadcast on *Rok-posevy*, April 14, 1989, radio broadcast, https://seva.ru/rock/?id=570&y=1989.

29 The show is titled *What? Where? When?* It first aired in 1975 and continues in some variation to present day. A picture of an owl is indeed its logo, and underneath the owl are the words "Intellectual Club" in Russian.

With growing demand in the various regions, the *Novgorodtseva druzhina* bulletin naturally must increase its circulation. For this, Alex and his comrades-in-arms make the necessary changes to the magazine's output, though it's difficult and involves the (illegal) use of copy machines owned by the government. In Alex's place of work, there is a heavy-duty copier; a counter keeps track of every copy made, inhibiting the use of the machine without authorization. However, the Moscow leaders make use of the copier at night when every employee is gone, printing hundreds and hundreds of copies of their publication on government paper. Then, when finished, they reset the counter to precisely the number it was at the end of the workday. It is a mystery why the copy machine is so overheated the next morning. . . .[30]

By 1989, NORIS is one thousand members strong, at least, and has a case for becoming an official nongovernmental organization. On March 2, Shurik Fedorov writes to Seva of his hard-fought battle to move NORIS from an informal association to a formally recognized and registered cooperative with a proper charter. The process of going through the bureaucratic channels takes him two months, but despite the pioneering achievement (not just for NORIS but for Russian youth and rock in general), he is not sure if all the club's leaders will be happy about it. He himself doesn't seem at ease with the new status either:

> I had to fight for every line in the charter. Now we can say for sure that we've become official, become bureaucratized, acquired seals and a magnificent office. And you, Seva, wished this yourself, in your letter last year where you gave your paternal order—to organize things officially. . . . The guys in other cities may want to demote me to rank and file for this, so then you may have to come here to move things forward yourself. . . .[31]

In the wake of their officialdom, someone suggests a summit—a "congress"—for all Seva's listeners, members of NORIS or no, who are able to participate. Shurik resists the responsibility of organizing such a thing for the practical reason that his remote location will not allow him to make such a congress happen. He suggests Moscow for the place of gathering, as it is the heart of the country, politically, socially, and transportation-wise. Living in the capital, Alex, Igor, and a few friends agree to organize the grand meetup.

---

30 A. Tatishchev, May 2019.

31 *Rok-posevy*, April 14, 1989, radio broadcast, https://seva.ru/rock/?id=570&y=1989.

The first congress takes place on July 9, 1989—Seva's birthday. Youth from across the USSR, who are able to make the journey, travel hundreds of miles to meet in Moscow, as discreetly as possible for this unsanctioned gathering. Together, as a community of rock lovers, they venture out into the surrounding forest area with tents and radios—and little else—to listen to music, listen to Seva, and get to know each other. Embodying the spirit of hope and freedom, this first congress is truly, as one listener aptly phrases it, a "communion."[32]

When the people of the GDR shock the world by making a breakthrough in the Berlin Wall on November 9, 1989, the momentous event serves to encourage and bolster Russia's young people on their path to freedom. Seva reports on air that all the news is about Germany, Germany, Germany. "Now, there is a stream of people walking through the wall . . . at a speed of 450 people per hour. . . ."[33] The Iron Curtain is literally and figuratively coming down. Per Filinov's own words: "Thunder rattles. It is time."[34]

First congress, 1989 (Credit: K. Zaitsev)

32 S. Pantsirev, May 2019.

33 *Rok-posevy,* November 10, 1989, radio broadcast, https://seva.ru/audio/rock/1989/r891110vb.mp3.

34 Filinov, "Talents and Bureaucrats." For an explanation of the fall of the Berlin Wall, see A. James McAdams, "An Obituary for the Berlin Wall," *World Policy Journal* 7, no. 2 (1990): 357–75, http://www.jstor.org/stable/40209151.

Featured Listener: Igor

I have been a listener of Seva's since 1980, when I was twelve years old.

I included several photos for you. In these you can see my life. Seva's programs from various years, I recorded on audio cassettes and magnetic tapes from the radio receiver itself. You also see notebooks. They contain the texts of Seva's programs. I listened to the programs via the tape recordings and then transcribed them word-for-word in these notebooks. I am now a vinyl record collector and collect rare American psychedelic music produced from 1967 to 1969. I also collect American tube amplifiers from the '20s to '50s.

My life has been consumed by love for Seva. I listen to his programs every day, think about him, tell other people about him, remember many of his phrases by heart. He changed my life and shaped my language, my speech, my taste. I owe him a lot. In his broadcasts, Seva read my letters many times, and I even talked to him on the phone. I still remember these conversations. Those were the best moments.

My childhood in the '70s was spent in a small town on the edge of a big empire, in Belarus, the BSSR. Life was black and white, but my soul was full of color. I lived in a crime neighborhood—cigarettes, cheap bad wine, fights, and murders. Primitive life . . . Primitive communication about primitive material things. But I was a romantic, I could dream for hours when I was six years old, and once I'd learned to read I would read for up to seven hours a day. I immersed myself in words and heard nothing and did not see anything around me. I loved fantasy and adventure . . . When I was eight years old, I fell in love with music, and at the age of ten, I began to listen to Western radio stations. I listened to Voice of America, especially music programs, and Radio Liberty, Radio Sweden, Radio Luxembourg, Deutsche Welle. I memorized the news and passed it on to others I knew. I then gained a friend. He was my doppelganger, my twin. He and I talked for hours every day. We learned a lot about the USSR and began to hate the country in which we lived. We learned the truth about the terrible regime and policies of the USSR. We fell in love with the United States and the West and dreamed of running away there. I began to tell everyone the truth about the USSR, and because of that I had conflict with my parents. They were afraid I would be thrown in jail.

I moved to Kaliningrad twenty-nine years ago from this small town. I wanted to live in a city that was close to the western border. From Kaliningrad to Europe it was only thirty kilometers. I wanted to work on a ship and escape to America or Canada. Also, I knew that it was a seaside city, and there were many sailors.

They brought a lot of vinyl records and there were a lot of rock fans in the city. It was not quite a Soviet city. It has a different atmosphere.

On Radio

This letter will be about our friend [radio], without which nothing would have happened. It was in almost every home, although it was expensive. To buy one, you had to work one to two months. Everyone had different reasons for owning a radio. But the main reason is that it connected a person with the rest of the world.

Now I want to say why people listened to Western radio (our propaganda called it "enemy voices").

People in the USSR were divided into three categories:

1. They believed in communism, supported the government, loved their country.
2. Didn't believe, didn't support, didn't love.
3. They did not think about such subjects, they lived with their own worries (work, food, family).

But all people had one thing in common. They resisted the system.

So, people in the USSR received ten to twenty dollars a month for their work. But there were only the most primitive products (goods) in the stores. Everything else had to be acquired illegally, which meant paying more. Jeans (the biggest dream) could be bought by working 1.5 to 2.5 months. But the purchase was dangerous; jeans were not sold in the store. They were sold by special people—speculators. You could be deceived. It was the same with other goods. Therefore, in reality, the salary was even less than ten to twenty dollars. People didn't want to put up with it. They, as they were able, deceived their state.

So, all the people (ALL!) stole everything they could steal from where they worked. My parents stole, my father was a thieving genius, my neighbors, my friends. No one was ashamed; they were proud of it, that in this way you can punish your state.[35]

People knew that they were receiving insufficient and false information from their state. People resisted it. They obtained information themselves and

---

35 No other listeners made such admissions, but the question was not outright put to them either.

disseminated it to others. The more the state did not like such information, the more willingly people passed it on to each other. It was their revenge for the state lies. That is why people were so willing to buy a radio and listen to it at night.

I remember my father and I once were resting on the banks of the river. There were two men nearby. In the hands of one was a very expensive radio and the voice of the announcer was loud. It was clearly Voice of America. My father said that they were KGB officers. Later, I found out that KGB officers and even the military and leaders of the USSR listened. So, people listening to Western radio and relating what they learned to others was their soft war against the regime.

If you turned on the TV in the '70s in the USSR, you would see a tractor in a field or a worker in a shop on the screen. The films were usually about a tractor in a field and a worker and also a soldier who defeated all the opposition. The books were about the tractor, the worker, and the soldier. The songs were about the same. How do you like that?

But the radio receiver returned to the person what was stolen from—the truth.

In the USSR, there was monotony in everything, for receiver brands as well. The most popular were VEF and Okean. They were of poor quality, but they were loved anyway.

Even young criminals had receivers. Often on the street you could see them sitting on a bench and listening to music on Voice of America. Some wrote down the names of Western bands and songs in notebooks.[36] These names were unusual for us. Our bands [in the USSR] were called Smile, Friendship, or Hope—it was terrible.

There are almost no shortwave radio stations these days, but some people collect radios, many make special rooms where they are stored . . . They remember that radios once saved them.

[Now] I still read a lot of books, and many authors write that their fathers listened to Western radio at night. Also, I spend a lot of time on trains and (I have a peculiarity, I easily start a conversation with strangers) I constantly turn to the subject of Western radio and Seva Novgorodsev. Everyone I have spoken with has said that they or their parents were listening to the radio in those days . . . I have been especially pleased to learn that almost everyone knows Seva. Completely different people though they are, but they all know Seva . . .

---

36 This practice of writing down bands and songs and even copying album artwork into notebooks seems to be a trend among young people during this time. Virtually every listener interviewed had some personal notebook to show or speak of.

He's a unique person. He has the most magical voice. He is to me, the Man from the Stars, although he is earthly. He's a true gentleman. I've been learning from him all my life.

Western Objects

Although the radio voice was a confirmation that there was another world, the radio voice was intangible. Therefore, everything that came out of this other world was highly valued, something you could hold in your hands. Their magazines, especially music ones, even photos taken from such a magazine were highly valued. Their records were re-recorded and a photo was taken, then another photo was taken from this photo, and so on ad infinitum. Even packaging from Western goods [were valued]: soap, toothpaste, candy, chewing gum, empty beer cans, labels (tags, cartons from jeans and shoes with the names of Wrangler, Lee Cooper, Lewis, Montana). Understand, it was not the joy of a savage at the sight of glass beads, it was a spiritual joy.

As a child, I had a neighbor, Gena, and he had a brother who lived in the USA in the city of Erie. This brother fled to America after the Second World War to escape the communists. He fought against the Red Army during the war. He sent one copy for Gena from a 1970 American newspaper. A leaf of the paper was given to me by Gena. I studied this sheet, its every letter, and would not have exchanged it then for all the treasures in the world. Now I took it out to take a photo for you and cried. Sadness and nostalgia filled me. How much I remembered just looking at this sheet. Maybe a small hint of my emotions will reach you when you see the photos.

Best Regards from the Dark Side of the Earth,
Igor

CHAPTER 15

Welcome to the Jungle

> It cannot be overestimated, you know. The broadcasting in Russian from the west, really created the new atmosphere, they created an alternative voice to the totalitarian propaganda.
>
> —Vassily Aksyonov, Soviet dissident and writer[1]

> Without Western broadcasting, totalitarian regimes would have survived much longer. The struggle for freedom would have been more arduous and the road to democracy much longer. From these broadcasting stations we gleaned our lessons of independent thinking and solidarity action. When it came to radio waves, the iron curtain was helpless. . . . Frontiers could be closed; words could not.
>
> —Lech Wałęsa[2]

Winds of change warm the USSR, signaling the end of what has seemed like an eternal winter. Jamming has completely stopped. Western sources of information appear in newsstands, freely available to any Soviet citizen. People can now not only write letters, but also easily *call* in to Seva's broadcasts without consequence. Even as early as January 1989, when Paul McCartney is a guest on the BBC Russian Service hosted by Sam Jones (in English) and Seva, over one thousand phone calls come in from across the USSR to speak to the Beatle—a huge leap from the few hundred that Margaret Thatcher's guest appearance had solicited just months earlier in 1988. This is quite amazing considering the cost of a long-distance call for Soviet citizens, the youngest caller being a mere seven years of age.[3]

---

1 Vassily Aksyonov, interview by Brian Lamb, C-SPAN.org, November 1, 1989, television broadcast, https://www.c-span.org/video/?9801-1/say-cheese.

2 See foreword to Nelson, *War of the Black Heavens.*

3 N.a., "Granny's Chest—Paul McCartney," *Paul McCartney Club Sandwich Magazine,* no. 52, January 26, 1989.

Seva receives even a letter from Adelaide, Australia, where an émigré family writes to him about their Russian community of listeners. They say that their teenage daughter had already been listening to Seva without their knowledge while still in the USSR. After moving, it became a family practice to listen until the late '80s when the frequencies become harder to catch for them. But they write to Seva, telling him that even though they can't hear him anymore they continue to talk about him very often, quoting memorable lines from his programs and reminiscing about one song or another.

With things rapidly developing, the BBC schedules a tour—UK Days of Culture—to send Seva to the USSR for live broadcasting in May 1990. Once the incredible news reaches Russia that Seva is coming, the chieftains of NORIS start preparing well in advance for their second annual congress, knowing that many more people will come for the chance to meet Seva. The planning begins in the winter of 1989–90. The three Moscow leaders, Alex, Andrey, and Igor, put their heads together to think how they can make this visit momentous, the "event of the century." They refer to the first *iyul'ka*—July congress—for inspiration, but Alex sours at its memory: "As a kid from a good family, I was put off by the fact that everyone was drinking during all of those four days. Although these people were great to drink with, I understood that drinking cannot really be the agenda for the meeting, and we needed something more."[4]

Andrey is in the business of organizing gigs for rock groups, so he suggests having a big concert and inviting a few bands. Alex straightaway agrees as plenty of Russian rock musicians know Seva and owe him their success. "We expected they would come and play for free." Since Andrey is knowledgeable about such things, Alex and Igor give him their blessing to arrange matters however he is able.

Next, they determine that this event should take place in several locations, not just in Moscow, but also in St. Petersburg. They understand they have to have some sort of reception for Seva, as well as a quieter experience so people can *hear* Seva speak and talk with him. "We came up with the idea to hire a boat to go down the Moskva for everyone to have a peaceful meeting with Seva," Alex says. "We tried to figure out how much that would cost. So, we asked all potential participants to send us the same fifteen or maybe twenty rubles," just as they had asked for in the first congress, "and we sent the information out to all NORIS members" in a special bulletin.

Meanwhile, Andrey finds that while many well-known bands are willing to participate, there is nowhere to hold such a huge concert, since official locations

---

4 A. Tatishchev, May 2019.

are leery of opening their doors to NORIS. Even if such a place is found, where will they get the money to rent it? Member tributes will not suffice, especially when most can't or don't send the requested amounts. The same problem arises with the boat:

> I don't remember how we approached the director of the House of Culture [in Petersburg] where the concert did ultimately take place, but I remember very well how Andrey and I approached the boat company. We as a private group said we would like to rent one big boat. They were very surprised because that was the first time they'd been asked to rent out a boat. They asked what will happen on this boat? And we answered, "it's just for cruising." "Will you pay by cash?" they asked, and I answered, "Yes."[5]

According to Alex, *perestroika* has spawned "wild capitalism" in the metropoles and so everyone wants cash. Thus, the boat company agrees immediately. Of course, at the time, Alex and Igor don't have any cash—it's merely a good faith rental.

They determine for the day of Seva's arrival that the fans should meet him at the airport itself. They rent in advance two run-down city buses to accommodate two-hundred people. "We didn't know of course how many people would turn up . . . But we planned it for July 9, 1990. Seva's fiftieth birthday."[6]

Now all that's left is to invite the DJ himself . . .

Back to the USSR

"Tell me, has Seva arrived?" ask two out-of-breath boys, arriving at the BBC exhibition in Kyiv, Ukraine. "We overtook him in a taxi. He's out of the hotel just behind us. That means, it's—it's about to happen!"[7] Such hysteria over a mere radio DJ has surely not been seen or felt since Soviet audiences exhibited their love for Willis Conover during his visit to the USSR some years prior.[8] Indeed, at that moment not ten meters from these boys walks a man of medium height with a shoulder-length silvery mane, dressed in all black with teenagers flocking around in reverent agitation. A silver Coptic cross around his neck draws the eye immediately, lending to the impression he really is a rock star, past or

5 Ibid.
6 Ibid.
7 Ibid.
8 See *Newsweek* article on Conover's reception in the USSR: Charles Paul Freund, "The DJ."

present—or rather, a rock priest. But the boys are even more preoccupied with his footwear: "Look at what kind of shoes he has," they whisper.[9]

In the direction of the BBC mobile studio, the famed presenter strides unhurriedly, but even if he were in a hurry, it wouldn't be possible to go faster with so many energetic youth swaddling him.

"Seva! Seva! Seva, it's great you've arrived," they cry, peering into his eyes like puppies needing love from their master.

Rovesnik's B. Simonov, one of the many journalists covering this momentous event, describes the BBC setup in detail as some sort of "British industrial exhibition" with the studio itself an edifice of glass surrounded by a fence of metal pipes. "As in an aquarium," people are able to gawp at those working inside this ordered house: "reels spinning on tape recorders, people in headphones sitting behind the consoles, and some emigrant's Russian song sounding from speakers outside."[10] Simonov recalls in his piece about the last time Seva was the subject of the magazine, in the article from 1982, which featured Seva's mother and had been decidedly negative. An employee of the BBC Russian Service introduces Simonov to Seva, and Seva graciously consents to an interview "without any wariness, it seemed, without any emotions at all" despite the fact that the 1982 piece had greatly upset him.[11] Undoubtedly, Seva's reunion with his parents here in Kyiv, after nearly two decades apart, has put him in a generous mood, even towards *Rovesnik*. As soon as the interview time is settled, Simonov writes that a storm of fans swoops in on Seva again:

> He stands as an Indian at Disneyland, resignedly, with an unflappable smile, not noticing people's hands on his shoulders, poses in front of the cameras and hands out neat autographs. From behind the soda rack ran out the saleswoman in a white robe and also asked for a photo with an autograph. Pulsing on the artery blocked by fences, the visitors pushed in, but the boys, who rushed here by taxi, and several dozen more teenagers, like barnacles to the ship's hull, stuck to Seva. They came from different cities . . . came for him, to be near, to hear, to see him. These selfless people are fans from the All-Union Fan Club of Seva Novgorodsev's "NORIS."

---

9 B. Simonov in *Rovesnik* 12 (1990).

10 Ibid.

11 Ibid. Interestingly, 1982 is also the year in which Willis Conover visits the USSR with a US delegation.

The discrepancy in word choices between previous publications and this one is quite noticeable. NORIS is now embraced as an "All-Union" fan club, and the members are called "selfless people," apparently casting aside previous allegations about their fiendish recruiting for MI-5. Indeed, these youth have instigated real change.

NORIS leader Alex leaves Moscow to rendezvous with its founder, Shurik, in Kyiv. For Alex, this will be his first in-person meeting with Seva, as Shurik has already visited Seva in London—and even been in Bush House, in the studio. Throughout the train trip to Kyiv, Alex is filled with nerves, thinking, rehearsing what he is going to say to Seva, and wondering what the DJ is like. Alex has only seen pictures, and, for him, they convey very little about Seva's character.

Once at the site of the BBC exhibition, Shurik introduces Alex to Seva, specifying that this is the Moscow leader who "organized the first *iyul'ka*."[12] Seva invites both NORIS men to a restaurant for drinks in the early evening before the night broadcast. Alex remembers this moment keenly as he has never been to a real restaurant before. From Alex's point of view, Seva is a charming host, very accommodating, very approachable. "He was clearly touched by the whole story of the NORIS movement because this was his first chance getting to see and interact with listeners whom he'd never fully comprehended . . . and suddenly, they have materialized." A powerful experience, which may explain his subdued reaction when listeners swarm him en masse. Meeting Seva face-to-face changes Alex's whole world. "For me, personally, it was the event of a lifetime because I was meeting for the first time a person I'd listened to since I was fifteen."[13]

Other listeners echo Alex's sentiments: "I met Seva on his first return to USSR; it was in Kyiv. There was an English exhibition, and it included the mobile BBC studio. It was also my first experience talking English with a real Englishman, some technical studio worker. I studied German in school, so it was hard for me. Yet I had to translate for some other guy who couldn't speak English at all."[14] Still another listener, Yevgeny, one of Seva's regular Ukrainian correspondents but not a NORIS member, also remembers this time with great fondness:

> During *perestroika*, the BBC mobile studio came to Kyiv, USSR for a week of programming from the station VDNKh and for

---

12 A. Tatishchev, May 2019.

13 Ibid.

14 K. Zaitsev, March 2019. He notes that "English in Soviet schools was so badly organized that it made many of us suspect that it was intentionally contrived to prevent Soviet citizens of communicating with foreigners. (German was taught much better)."

> about one hour a day all week they were there on VDNKh for live programming. Seva Novgorodsev was there, and when I saw him, he asked me if I would agree to participate in his live program . . . and of course I agreed. The show took place on Friday, and I remember I heard "Fanfare for the Common Man" by Emerson, Lake & Palmer, while sitting inside at the table with Seva Novgorodsev. . . .[15] Seva asked me to say a few words and I told him about the KGB attacks. Two more guys were there participating too. One of them started the fan club of Seva, had been invited to London before, and told about his visit. . . .[16] Seva would step out of BBC mobile studio later in the show and would answer questions live and it was all a lot of fun![17]

Reporters and media outlets clamor for a few minutes with Seva during this visit to Kyiv, seeking his take on the political happenings and hoping for some kernel of reassurance and wisdom to give their readers. One publication called *Soviet Youth* (*Sovetskaia molodyozh'*) manages to nab Seva outside his BBC studio. The following is an excerpt of the conversation:

> **Vsevolod Borisovich, you well know our country, and I don't think that in fifteen years you have encountered revolution. . . . What is your view from London on the events in the USSR?**
> Seva: If you imagine the stage on which Gorbachev stands, on the right-wing sparkles an insignia representing tremendous power. According to my rough calculations, the Committee for State Security [KGB], in one way or another, employs roughly one million people. Plus, the army, the party apparatus . . . All of this creates a mighty fist in which is almost half the country. Now, on the side of *perestroika* at best there are 35–40% of the national forces, the rest are all on the right.
>
> **And what do you think about [Boris] Yeltsin in his current position? If I'm not mistaken, it's the English press that introduced this political figure to the West?**

---

15 A variation of this song served as *Sevaoborot*'s opening theme.

16 Undoubtedly, the two guys are Tatishchev and Fedorov, and the one who visited London is, of course, Fedorov, though strangely Fedorov's own written statement doesn't provide any impressions of London or his visit to Kyiv.

17 Y. Ayrapetov, February 2019.

> Seva: I think that Yeltsin's most dangerous moment is behind him. Because the moment to hush him up, trample, and destroy him has already passed. . . . And once the wave swept him upwards, it's always the trend in politics to move to the side of existing power. Yeltsin is already at the helm, and that's why those people who vacillated yesterday will join him today.[18]

The journalist, I. Danilov, closes his article with a most eloquent statement, summarizing the charged atmosphere and the unifying power of hearing Seva on the air:

> Night drew near, and Seva, apologizing to me [for having to abbreviate our conversation], went to prepare for his broadcast. Then, at the appointed time, the theme song of "Sevaoborot" sounded, heralding a new victory for Soviet democracy. Under the dark starry sky and the relentless gaze of the police, Seva Novgorodsev for the first time hosted his transmission from the Soviet Union, and the little house of the BBC became warmer and more welcoming for hundreds of eyewitnesses crowding near the white stone palaces of VDNKh.[19]

It is starkly apparent that Seva, once pilloried as an enemy voice but now allowed to broadcast from behind the Iron Curtain, carries almost more significance for the people than the reforms themselves. This is a powerful moment, tangible evidence of hope. The twinkling glass house promises new, open relations between Great Britain and the USSR; but for now, the only relationship that matters to anyone is that of the people to one Russian DJ.

For the few days they are in Kyiv, it is nearly impossible for Alex and Shurik to get any time with Seva around the BBC mobile station as crowds constantly pack the arena. However, Alex does get the chance before departing Kyiv to tell Seva that there are many things in store for him in Moscow if he will only come for his birthday in two months. Alex regretfully cannot send Seva a formal invitation or book a hotel for him due to NORIS's lack of funds. Still, Seva agrees

---

18 I. Danilov, "Seva-Seva Novgorodtsev, gorod Kiev, Bi-Bi-Si," *Sovetskaia molodyozh'*, July 10, 1990, https://seva.ru/media/?id=191.

19 Ibid. VDNKh of Ukrainian SSR is today the Expocenter of Ukraine National Complex in the Teremky district of Kyiv.

to travel to Moscow, buys his own plane tickets—British Airways, of course—to save NORIS the expense. Seva will fly into Sheremetyevo International on July 9.

The DJ Returns

Two days before the appointed date, Moscow's NORIS members start meeting groups of people arriving from all over the Soviet Union. They devise a method wherein they utilize the city's massive metro system and ask people to arrive at different stations and at different times where they meet a NORIS representative. In this way, they avoid crowding and thereby drawing the attention of the authorities. Then, on the day of Seva's expected arrival, all who wish to travel to the central Belorusskaya metro station where two dilapidated rented buses await. "We had 420 people who paid to participate—that is the official number," Alex says. Unofficially, though, many more arrive from the far reaches of the USSR, bringing little with them save the clothes on their backs. Once the word arrives that it is time to leave, the young people who have arrived load up into the rusted buses, packing in like sardines. The buses, practically bulging at their metal seams, trundle to the airport to meet their passengers' BBC idol.

Upon his arrival at Sheremetyevo, Seva deplanes and presents his British passport to the border authorities when it is his turn in line. But learning that there is a sizeable crowd of anxious youth waiting in the receiving area, passport control tells Seva to stay put. Shortly after, a pair of state police enter and come for Seva, not to arrest him but to escort him in a civil but urgent manner to a special exit reserved for VIPs such as Communist Party leaders and high-profile foreign delegations, bypassing the commotion. The passage is walled off by glass, and Seva can see the source of the cheering. Hundreds of youth, holding signs for him and playing music, crowd the passageway, making other travelers to the capital city uncomfortable with their rowdiness. Many have little clue what he even looks like, yet they are all sure when he comes down the tunnel, flanked by security, that it is him and start screaming and cheering. Seva gives them a small smile and wave. They roar his name in deafening cacophony.

Seva is floored by the outpouring, but he keeps moving, a true performer, giving nothing away. The youth chant his name and follow him out of the airport as if he has mesmerized them; security gladly chases them away. Seva is rushed into the back of a white Lada driven, in fact, by Igor's father, ready to take him to

Seva and youth at various moments in Moscow, 1990 (Credit: A. Tatishchev, NORIS Archive)

his hotel. A few have come to the airport, separate from NORIS, just to glimpse Seva, and for them this is enough. They leave, content to have put a face to the voice, even if from a distance. The youth see their icon drive off, but it is not over yet.[20]

Seva meets all those who can make it on the side of a highway just outside the city proper. On the grass, young people youth gather around him, clamoring for him to sign their rolled-up posters, scraps of paper, and anything else of Western origin. He tells them in Russian, "Sit! Sit! I will sign everyone's." But still, they press in, not, however, like mindless fans but like children seeking their returning father's attention.

Seva spends many days with his fans, discussing Western life, rock music, and the people's liberation. He hosts concerts in both Moscow and St. Petersburg that Alex and others had pre-arranged, which are so well attended that the rows of theater seating break from the thronging, rapturous young people.[21] During these concerts, Seva signs many an autograph and calmly emcees the events, which feature some of the most popular Russian rock bands of the day. The stage in Moscow has a huge NORIS emblem that backdrops every performer, every performance. Seva gives several interviews as well, and, in this moment, he is able to see with his own eyes some of the impact he's made; he is able to reflect on himself and on those years of broadcasting in relative darkness:

> I was saying things that all of them wanted to say for years, but never dared to . . . and in that sense, I was just following the British tradition of being slightly controversial. . . . I was actually bringing, in the Russian context, all the radio culture that has been accumulated [in Britain] over the years. Because I learned what I did by listening to different people . . . on British radio, and although I'm not copying anybody, the British broadcasting culture is actually the essence [on which] I based myself. . . . You don't talk down to anyone, you talk to people as if they were your friends. And you don't worry if they understand you or not, you

20 All descriptive details taken from over ten hours of raw video footage of the 1990 visit, filmed by NORIS member and Soviet magazine photographer Vladimir Ivanov (provided to author by Ivanov in May 2019).

21 From concert footage taken by Vladimir Ivanov, provided to author.

> know—the history will sort it out. You have to be completely honest and be on par. . . . I cannot explain what I do because it is steeped very deeply in the environment of Russian language and culture.[22]

Even here, in this freeing time, no one anticipates what will come next. No one really sees, just as Seva has been unable to see the results of his years of labor, what *perestroika* and *glasnost'* ultimately forecast. Most importantly, no one is prepared, but all of Seva's listeners are ready.

Seva and his "children" in Red Square, 1990 (Credit: A. Tatishchev, NORIS Archive)

22 From footage of Seva's July 7 Moscow visit by Vladimir Ivanov, provided to author.

Featured Listener: Oleg

I lived in Moscow. My father was an engineer, my mother was an editor. She was checking books before printing. My school was a regular Moscow school, No. 132. In 1982 I finished it and joined Moscow Aviation Institute in the School of Electronics.

I listened to *Rok-posevy* regularly for about ten years. First time I received this show was in 1979 or 1980 . . . I liked the style, but I didn't care about rock.[23] Later I discovered The Beatles and Deep Purple. I asked my friends at school about the show; they told me when to catch it. I started listening regularly since spring of 1982. I also listened to *Sevaoborot* sometimes, *Literaturnaia programma,* and *Babushkin sunduk* [Grandma's Hope Chest] by Sam Jones.

I started listening to VOA in 1982, host of the music show was Tamara Dombrovskaya. She didn't impress me at all. The KGB regularly destroyed the signal, but Seva's show was clear because broadcast was after midnight when all political shows were over. When Gorbachev got to power, they stopped destroying the signal, and I was able to listen to VOA again but with new hosts: Bill Skundrich[24] and Evgeny Aronov . . . (I also listened to Tommy Wentz's Rock salad from BBC English Service but did not understand much of what was said in those days. I managed to receive Radio Luxembourg, but signal was very weak, and the fading was horrible.)

One day, Bill or Evgeny of VOA received a letter from the USSR. The author asked about competition with Seva. He answered that there is no competition. Seva's show was half an hour per week, VOA's music show was one hour per week and on a different day. He also described American FM broadcasting—a lot of stations working at the same time. But he forgot about quality.

Soviet music was usually classical or official Soviet singers. There were only a couple of TV channels, and it was boring, showing mostly pro-communist shows and movies. We had a joke in our company, "Let's answer the John Lennon killing by killing Josef Kobzon." It was a parody on Soviet propaganda as no one wanted to kill Kobzon.

Michelle, I want to tell you one thing. Since about 1979, Seva started making jokes in a way that his English bosses would not understand them. It was because he had been blamed of breaking BBC policies. His jokes were very

---

23 Numerous listeners fall into this camp of listening for the sake of Seva's style and language, even if they abjured rock itself.

24 Bill Skundrich was one of the DJs interviewed by the author for this book.

important part of his show. They were about life in the USSR mostly. Can you understand them?

I am in the USA now. I have local broadcasting available plus Internet broadcasting. But the last show that I listened to regularly was BBSeva. Everything else is so boring! Seva is the best! He was very interesting, because there was little information about rock, and Seva was a very good host and entertaining.

Kind regards,
Oleg[25]

25 Oleg R., email to author, July 2019.

Featured Listener: Larisa

The following is a conversation between Alex Tatishchev, Sergey Pantsirev (webmaster of seva.ru), Sergey's wife Anna Pantsireva, listener Larisa, and the author.

Alex (re: Larisa): We met each other in the '80s. She always dressed in leather. She was coming to Moscow for the concerts, and I was living here, and every time I saw her, I was flirting with her—then *and* now. (*Laughter*)

Larisa: I was very interested in music. I was in a small town and had no information. Radio voices and friends from Moscow and magazines were all that I had. Alex was one of the first friends. To me it seemed that I must have been so annoying calling him on the phone over and over again, asking questions. And I had no phone at home and so I had to go to the station to use the phone. It was like 1988. I wrote to Seva Novgorodsev and once he sent me a letter with his signature. He never read my letters on air, but still he replied, which was a big deal.

I started listening to Seva (the exact year I cannot tell you) because I was very interested in rock music and heavy metal from when I was fifteen. My family was very simple. No one in my family listened to rock music or even had any connection with art. Moreover, I was never understood by my parents. I was a metalhead and looked like one, and my mother never understood that. And my mother always wanted me to look feminine and thought that I was not looking appropriate. She thought that all my friends were all alcoholics and drug addicts, etc. In my town, I had no friends, but I started to come to Moscow (it wasn't too far away) for gigs, and I made a lot of friends here because of music. And they were supportive and understanding.

Alex: When she was coming to Moscow, she was a true rock fan. And she would call and come often. And I had an understanding that she was in love with me. However, I was not a metalhead [like her], and I didn't know what to do with that. But I always liked her!

Larisa: The first time I saw Seva was when the BBC came to Russia on tour . . . I listened to all the stations. All the stations broadcasting music, Voice of America and Radio Liberty also. Everywhere

I could find music that I was interested in, all the sources, I listened to. Yes, Seva was special and he was close to me by his style of speech, by the music he chose for the broadcasts. None of my girlfriends listened to Seva, only my boyfriends.

Sergey: Nobody knows why it seems mostly males were listening [to Western radio].

Anna: I think there were two reasons: Girls were sticking strictly to housework more than guys. And they spent more time doing routine things—study, work, and cooking and such was *all* there in girls' heads. It was also difficult to listen to [Western] radio, and so you had to be a little bit of a technical person to have not only good sound but *any* sound. So, you have to understand at least some technical stuff, and not every girl had the time or motivation to do so.

MD: Marina Alexandrova said to me that this listening to rock on the radio (to Seva) felt like a man's world and listening to enemy voices was a man's thing. And she and her friends were more concerned with other things, including becoming wives and mothers and all the work associated.

Anna: Yes, my father told me never ever turn on the radio and listen to those voices. It was mostly because he was concerned for my safety. But it really was technical, it wasn't easy to do it at the time. Now, it's nothing. But back then . . .

MD: What was Seva to you, Larisa?

Larisa: He was not a friend or brother, but he was like a comrade.

MD: The age difference didn't bother you?

Larisa: No. I was interested mostly or exclusively in heavy metal. Seva was playing not only heavy metal, he played other music as well. So, he actually expanded my tastes, and I was listening to what he was saying. I wasn't listening to *Sevaoborot,* but I started later, not too long before it ended.

MD: Did your parents ever find out that you were listening?

Larisa: My mother was concerned that if I continued to listen to the voices, they would recruit me to some sort of spy network, and she was actually preventing me from listening.

MD: Then how did you listen?

Larisa: With a fight. It was never a mutual understanding, and from the beginning it was a constant fight, and then my mom started to realize there was no point in fighting, so she just gave up.

MD: What do you listen to now?

Larisa: Radio in general I do not listen to. I listen only to the records I have.

MD: Is there anything in Russia now that is filling the space Seva occupied?

Larisa: No. Of course not. Seva was a cult figure. But now, there is no need for such a figure. Everything is so accessible. Information readily available. It is not needed. Mostly it was our generation that needed him. He managed to become a conductor of this rock energy for a whole generation.

CHAPTER 16

It's the End of the World as We Know It

"The Soviet state, marked throughout its brief but tumultuous history by great achievement and terrible suffering, died today after a long and painful decline. It was 74 years old,"[1] reads the "obituary" on the front page of the *New York Times*. Russian youth celebrate; older generations wilt. It happened all of a sudden.

As late as August 1, 1991, things seemed to be business as usual with Gorbachev and George H. W. Bush signing a nuclear pact. But a few days later, on August 18, a KGB-led coup shocks the world. Gorbachev and his family are placed under house arrest in Crimea—a nonviolent comparison to the 1917 toppling of the Romanov regime. If the demoralized world leader hadn't appreciated the power of radio before, he certainly does now.[2] During the three days of his isolation, radio is his—and the rest of the country's—only window to the outside world. Strangely, the KGB does not resume jamming during the coup attempt. The head of VOA's Russian Service at the time reasons sardonically that if the KGB can't properly organize a coup, they're probably not up to jamming either, which, she implies, is far more difficult.[3]

> Gorbachev retrieved a few ancient receivers from the service quarters of the Crimean dacha where he and his family were temporarily incarcerated. They set up some antennas and listened to the voices from abroad describing the astonishing events in Moscow, where barricades outside the White House

---

1 Serge Schmemann, "End of the Soviet Union," *New York Times*, December 26, 1991, https://www.nytimes.com/1991/12/26/world/end-of-the-soviet-union-the-soviet-state-born-of-a-dream-dies.html.

2 Thomas Rosenstiel, "Captive Gorbachev Tuned in to the BBC, Voice of America," *Los Angeles Times*, August 23, 1991. Gorbachev had stopped all jamming on Memorial Day 1987.

3 Ibid.

> were manned by people also huddled around portable radios broadcasting from Munich [Radio Liberty] or London [BBC].[4]

It is a BBC reporter who placidly informs all Russians that the rumors are untrue: tanks are not breaking down the gates in front of the White House to seize Boris Yeltsin.[5] Gorbachev attests during his press briefing following the failed coup—which still results in his resignation—that the "clearest signal . . . was from the BBC Russian Service." An ecstatic BBC takes out a half page ad in all the London papers to let everyone know that the underfunded BBC had beaten the bigger Western radios in this one regard at least.[6]

It's tempting from a US perspective to simplify the end of the USSR to hard-line Western policies, holding that Reagan's Star Wars cracked the foundation of the USSR, or aggressive soft power tactics liberated the captive souls of Eastern Europe and Russia to act and act boldly. But there were many forces at work that go beyond American interventionism. Chernobyl was one. Sharply declining oil and gas prices was another. And a less trumped up but significant factor was the changing attitude that the Kremlin exhibited towards Eastern Europe coupled with the building of trust between Gorbachev and Western Europe. "These new levels of trust . . . made it easier for [Gorbachev] to accept the unambiguous rejection of Communism . . . in the Warsaw Pact countries" even though it is essentially a rejection of himself, for he is still a Soviet.[7]

During his final days in power, Gorbachev remarks with quiet indignation, "I led you all to independence and now you no longer seem to need the union. So, go ahead: Live as you wish and fire me."[8] And so it happens. Just three months after the Komsomol dissolves, on December 26, 1991 the USSR officially ceases to exist. Boris Yeltsin becomes the first democratically elected president of the nascent Russian Federation. For better or worse, Mikhail Gorbachev's name is inextricably linked with the fall of the USSR, which buried his greatest contributions—*glasnost'* and *perestroika*—"under the rubble of Soviet communism."[9]

---

4 Jo Glanville, *Radio Redux* (London: Sage Publications, Ltd.), 58.

5 Ibid.

6 Rosenstiel, "Captive Gorbachev." Note: the *LA Times* holds that this was a "quirk," as it claims that the BBC did not have a strong signal in the USSR. But the signal apparently had been relayed through Cyprus. See Nelson, *War of the Black Heavens*, 196.

7 Archie Brown, *The Gorbachev Factor* (Oxford: Oxford University Press, 1996), 242.

8 Taubman, *Gorbachev*, 626.

9 Zubok, *Zhivago's Children*, 361.

Rubble and Recognition

Eager to celebrate the dawn of a new era, the BBC tours the Russian Federation and the Baltic states in the most British way possible: aboard a bright-red double-decker bus.[10] Seva makes countless appearances on Russian radio stations and TV networks, doing marathon sessions with the press—the coverage of him is, without variation, positive now. He's a fully embraced icon. No longer the enemy, the traitor, the agent of the West. He is the acknowledged hero of the Russian people. The KGB doesn't bother him because the KGB doesn't exist, at least not in the way it did up until the failed coup; moreover, the KGB is subject to the new order, which as with the beginning of the Soviet Union, is a work in progress. In effect, 1992 presents a chance to reset and restructure Russia with the whole country tuned into what's going on as they were not at all in 1917.

Aiming to foster economic relations between the UK and Russia, the BBC participates in the first international business expo in St. Petersburg. When the default of '98 occurs, shutting down the Russian economy, Seva experiences the devastation firsthand:

> [T]he country obviously is in disarray, the old system collapsed, the new one hasn't emerged yet. All these colossi of industry which used to employ thirty or fifty thousand people no longer working like huge slave dragons lying on their side with a little smoke coming out of the severed head. And it'll take a long while before the new economy will just grow like blades of grass from these chunks of dead concrete, but it'll be new grass and new nature will emerge eventually. But the experiment that's happened in Russia is a tragic thing for the country and God knows how many years it will need until it's all healed and mended and forgotten. But Russians are dynamic people, fairly talented, reasonably well-educated, full of energy and initiative, they will think of something.
>
> All the recent troubles that have happened to the country are [because of] deeply entrenched corrupt practices that exist around the government and all the subsequent levels of management of the country. I don't know what's going to happen, maybe

10 John Peel, BBC Radio One DJ and by Seva's own admission a great influence of his, went on the BBC tour to the Baltic States and Russia in spring 1992; in particular, he loved Vilnius per his July 1992 broadcasts on BBC Radio 1.

> because there's no economy, there's no revenue to talk about, the central political leverage or power will dwindle, and we will see many centers of self-rule emerging. And I don't exclude the possibility of the country being split into parts in one way or another and that will be a price to pay for breaking the moral laws that every government should adhere to if they have God in their head.[11]

In Petersburg, Seva meets the vibrant and charming designer Olga Shestakova, who is his spiritual match in every way and whom he marries in 1999 in fashionable, London style. The following year, at the dawn of the new millennium, the young, blonde, and blue-eyed Vladimir Vladimirovich Putin, whose KGB affiliation and years stationed in East Germany cast doubt on his loyalties, becomes Yeltsin's chosen successor. In selecting Putin, the declining Yeltsin seems to signal his admission that he and others in opposition to Gorbachev were not properly prepared for building a democracy uncoupled from the stable, albeit decrepit, structures of the USSR. A firm hand is now needed to bring order to the Russian Federation.

On air, Seva welcomes the promise of democracy and stability that the new president brings, encouraging his listeners to take heart. Changes do come; however, it's apparent that stability will cost freedom and lives and that democracy—at least in the Western conception—has the merest footing in the new Russia.

Sevaoborot is in its own way a telling portrayal of Russia's return to authoritarianism as controversial figures begin to appear alongside the usual artists and musicians: Russian intelligence defector Alexander Litvinenko and American-born Russian journalist Anna Politkovskaya appear as guests on the show.[12] Both speak of Putin's Russia in unfavorable terms. While Politkovskaya talks about the work of journalists in war-ravaged Chechnya and reveals the war crimes committed by Russia, Litvinenko exposes the inner workings of the KGB's successor organization, the Federal Security Service (FSB). His book, coauthored with the historian Yuri Felshtinsky, entitled *Blowing Up Russia: Terror from Within,* is a stunning exposure of the FSB's involvement in the 1999 terrorist bombings of apartment buildings in Moscow that took place prior to the

---

11 Novgorodsev, Museum of London interview.

12 Litvinenko, *Sevaoborot,* April 6, 2002, radio broadcast. Politkovskaya, *Sevaoborot,* Jan 11, 2003, radio broadcast.

2000 presidential elections, purportedly as a move to justify the Russian war in Chechnya.[13] Understandably, this work is banned in Russia and copies confiscated for its incriminating content and implications for Russia's illiberal future.

Because of the measurable success of *Sevaoborot*, making the RS and thereby the World Service look good to government sponsors and external funders, the BBC offers Seva a contract for yet another slot on the air in February 2003, this time with a current affairs spin. Titled *BBSeva*, "News with a Human Face," a clear play on "Socialism with a Human Face," this weekday program seems more of a way to convey only inoffensive world news. The BBC-written tagline reads: "Offering an unorthodox view on the day's events not usually covered by regular news programming."[14]

Naturally, *BBSeva* is not as popular with Seva's Russian audience. According to one listener, guests are selected by the producers and Seva just walks into the studio, reads the script he's given, and interviews the guests. In other words, BBSeva lacks the same kind of quality, honesty, and artistic sensibility that Seva invested into *Rok-posevy* and *Sevaoborot*, proving that just because Seva's name is inserted into the title in a clever way, people will not flock to their radios in droves. His personality is the selling point, and listeners feel that he has sold out.[15] However, Seva is not so high in the BBC ranks (despite all appearances) that he is exempt from the need to proceed with caution. After all, with the new millennium, many presenters of a certain age are being (or already have been) taken off the air, and not just at the World Service. A BBC Radio 1 veteran, John Peel escapes the slaughter due to his massive popularity, but he dies suddenly of

---

13 Felshtinsky had also been a guest on *Sevaoborot* the previous year on September 1, 2001 to talk about the forthcoming book. In an unpublished interview provided to Lera Toropin and Thomas Rehnquist for *The Slavic Connexion* in September 2020, Yuri Felshtinsky recounts his discovery of the FSB's involvement in the bombings of 1999, a year in which Russia is by all accounts considered a "democratic country"; thus, his allegation of foul play by the Russian government is a "tough claim to make" and few were willing to buy it, neither in 1999 nor 2000 with Putin's election. Of the apartment building bombings that killed many innocent people, Felshtinsky said, "Really no one understood what was happening, what was going on. The government said this was done by Chechen separatists, and many believed this because Russia was in conflict with Chechnya . . . So, at one point, I decided to consult with two people in special services with whom I trusted, one of which was Viktor Suvorov . . . former GRU . . . who lived in Bristol." And the other, of course, was Alexander Litvinenko, who had fled from Russia in 2000 to the UK.

14 From the BBC podcast site description: https://mytuner-radio.com/radio/bbseva-from-bbcrussian-416235/.

15 Mentioned in several listener responses to author, without prompting, when referring to BBSeva.

a heart attack in October 2004, leaving Seva feeling that he is among the "last of the Mohicans" as he puts it.[16]

However, the very next month in November 2004, just after the RS ends *Rokposevy*, Seva receives an embossed, weighty envelope—the sender is in fact the office of the British prime minister. Inside is a missive stating he has been selected to receive the Member of the British Empire (MBE) in a ceremony the following year if he should choose to accept. Seva is astounded and overwhelmed to be honored in this way (as John Peel had also been in 1998). Though many notable awardees like John Lennon have rejected the honor for political reasons, Seva can hardly refuse:

> [I]t was not a matter of publicity, it was a matter of recognition; during the entire history of the BBC Russian Service, the only person to receive the MBE was Anatol Goldberg . . . who delivered his highly opinionated, often controversial "Notes by our Observer" for thirty-five years on the BBC. . . . The award would cement Seva's position within the BBC structure.[17]

And so it does, for a time at least. The BBC literally rolls out the red carpet for its Russian DJ—his recognition is another huge accolade for the World Service. On April 27, 2005, the BBC shuttles Seva to the palace to receive his MBE from Queen Elizabeth II herself in a grand ceremony (which poignantly contrasts with Seva's father's receipt of the prestigious Order of Lenin near the end of *his* career). Directly afterwards, Seva rushes to the studio to jump on the air for one of his weekly programs and then attends a private reception in the exclusive Carlton Club attended a number of Seva's colleagues and high-profile Russian friends. The event is covered in *The Times*:

> A unique gathering of former KGB spies and Russian dissidents took place yesterday in the heart of the Tory Establishment. They came together in the Disraeli Room at the Carlton Club to honor Seva Novgorodsev, the first DJ in the Soviet Union and BBC Russian Service stalwart, who was presented with the MBE

---

16 John Peel biography, BBC.com, accessed 25 August, 2022, video, https://www.bbc.co.uk/radio1/johnpeel/biography/.

17 S. Pantsirev, February 2019. It's interesting that the words "controversial" and "opinionated" are used to describe Goldberg's program when in fact at the time of Stalin's death the FO accused the Russian Service of being too pro-Soviet.

insignia by the Queen for services to broadcasting. At the top of the table was Oleg Gordievsky, the KGB London chief who worked as a double agent for MI-6 and escaped shortly before his planned arrest by his Soviet masters. There was Vladimir Bukovsky, the author, who was one of the first to expose the use of psychiatry against political prisoners in the USSR and spent 12 years in Soviet labor camps. Viktor Suvorov, a former intelligence chief, who defected at the height of the Cold War, made up the trio. . . . A portrait of Margaret Thatcher, the only woman member of the Carlton Club, who did so much to remove the Iron Curtain, looked down approvingly at the gathering.[18]

Seva and Queen Elizabeth II, April 27, 2005 (Credit: seva.ru)

Celebrations aren't only taking place in London. The World Service agitates the British embassy in Moscow to host an elaborate reception just a few weeks later—a very diplomatic move that begs the Russian people to remember that the BBC, that is, Great Britain, is a trusted friend:

18 Andrew Pierce, "Voice of Russia Hailed in a Tory Stronghold," *The Times*, April 28, 2005, https://www.thetimes.co.uk/article/voice-of-russia-hailed-in-a-tory-stronghold-2sls0lbvm23.

> The pictures of Seva's stylish arrival in a London black cab, wearing the same high hat and evening [attire] . . . circulated in the press, making the reception a publicly noticeable event, putting Seva's name on the front pages of glossy magazines. . . . Yet he remained the same Seva to his fans. . . . He said on his website: "This is an award not for myself, but for all of us. We did it together."[19]

Indeed, because of this high accolade, Seva's popularity—and his Bush House reputation—experiences a comforting resurgence for quite a while. He lands on the front page of *Izvestiia* and other big publications. It is around this time that RFE/RL tries to recruit him away from the BBC, but purportedly Seva asks for an "obscene amount of money," which rapidly sends the surrogate broadcaster packing.[20]

Unfortunately, political pressures begin to rise again the following year, revealing weaknesses in the BBC Russian Service that had been developing throughout the '90s as internal changes rock and threaten the World Service. Though the WS, thanks to a media campaign and public outpouring of support to protect its autonomy, emerges from the dispiriting '90s in somewhat better shape than before, the RS is not so lucky.[21]

In a changing political climate that's been shifting focus from Russia and the Eastern Bloc towards the Middle East, where it's harder to see the benefit of BBC overseas operations, the World Service is pressured to prove its usefulness and worth to the public and government. The House of Commons Foreign Affairs Committee begins an ongoing review of the WS to assess its usefulness, and this pressure has the unwanted effect of pitting BBC management against staff—*management* who are devoted to preserving the WS and *staff* who are devoted to preserving the service's journalistic ethos. From at least 1990, this dynamic plays a powerful role in the degradation of the Russian Service. It additionally appears that RS management's desire to appease Russia and to maintain rebroadcasting partnerships creates both a demoralizing work environment and diluted, unbalanced coverage for the Russian people, thereby muddying the BBC's core tenets

---

19 S. Pantsirev, February 2019.

20 Jeff Trimble, November 2020.

21 Jess Macfarlane, "BBC World Service in the 1990s," Open University, July 2014, https://www.open.ac.uk/researchprojects/diasporas/sites/www.open.ac.uk.researchprojects.diasporas/files/BBC%20World%20Service%20in%20the%201990s.pdf

of "impartiality, editorial integrity, and independence."[22] As with the fall of the USSR, the demise of this vital arm of the BBC begins long before it goes off the air.

The Decline of the Russian Service

The beginning of the end seems to be 1992, a pivotal year for the WS and one fraught with moral struggles for the RS.[23] John Birt, the newly appointed director general of the BBC, institutes sweeping changes, requiring a demonstration of "value for money and efficiency through performance measurement and other metrics." In other words, winning hearts and minds isn't enough; now, they must be numbered, too:

> Up to this point, while the World Service had of course been very much part of the BBC it had broadly managed its own affairs, including the relationship with the FCO. However, . . . John Birt [introduced] two major initiatives which revolutionized the way the BBC operated and assessed itself internally. . . .[24] [These were] Performance Review (the process by which each separate part of the BBC reported performance against a range of targets), and Producer Choice (in which budgets were no longer held centrally but devolved to individual program makers, giving the power to buy services from outside the BBC and creating a fully costed internal market).[25]

---

22 "Editorial Policy Guidelines for BBC World Service Group on External Relationships and Funding," revised March 2015, BBC.com, http://downloads.bbc.co.uk/rmhttp/guidelines/editorialguidelines/pdfs/250315-World-Service-Group-External-Relationships-Funding.pdf.

23 This is not to say that the RS was in any way experiencing "special" devaluation unique to the UK. The same was going on with VOA especially and also RFE/RL, both having to convince financiers that their services provided to regions considered "liberated" were still valuable, still needed, after Communism reached its ostensible end.

24 By the early '90s, the BBC adopted a partial commercial funding model across the umbrella World Service Group, permitting limited advertising and external funding partnerships as deemed appropriate. See "Editorial Policy Guidelines for BBC World Service Group on External Relationships and Funding."

25 Macfarlane, "BBC World Service in the 1990s," 2, 5, Whereas since 1984 the WS had enjoyed a rather strong position due to a "stable funding regime" with regular increases in budget, major cuts were portended in the early '90s when the government announced it would be

Such decentralization and emphasis on performance numbers and achieving targets create problems. For one, these changes potentially motivate middle management to "cook" the numbers so that the Foreign Affairs Committee will favorably assess the work of an individual service. For another, leaving budgets and power of purchase in the hands of program makers invests unreasonable trust in each service's management to act in accordance with the BBC's policies, inevitably opening the door for creative interpretation. All told, Birt's initiatives essentially provide management protection as long as they demonstrate "value for money." This, in fact, seems to be the root cause of trouble within the RS where the head in 1992, David Morton, appears to be doing his job well according to Birt's numbers criterion, but in fact is a poor manager and even a potential saboteur.

According to a May 1992 letter to the BBC leadership, written and signed by nearly two dozen RS staff members, morale has dropped to its lowest point in the service as a result of output quality issues and management's mistreatment of staff. The accusations are mainly levied against Morton: favoritism shown to certain managers, verbal abuse and repeat offensive behavior, demanding money from his staff, use of questionable characters from the former USSR, and termination of staff for minor infractions.[26] As one longtime RS producer phrases the turmoil in a separate memo to BBC Chairman Marmaduke Hussey: "there is a limit to what people can take, and this directly results in the declining standards of the work of the Russian Service."[27]

The May 1992 letter, signed by twenty-three service staff on pensionable contract, expounds on these declining standards. They claim that British current affairs content has been almost entirely dropped, and that those programs that convey "Britishness" have been replaced with reports done by journalists in the former USSR, which do little more than repeat their local news without any sort of British nuance or global perspective—in many cases, they are also subject to the political leanings of the reporter. These problems stem from the rebroadcasting partnerships that the WS has established with Russian stations, namely Radio Russia (launched by the Russian Federation), which by all indications

---

reducing the total budget of £135.6 million—of which less than five million went to the RS's budget. See Macfarlane, "BBC World Service in the 1990s."

26 After the successful Kyiv exhibition in 1990, Morton demanded payouts from staff (per accusations in the RS staff letter).

27 Memo from producer, RS to Marmaduke Hussey, complaint against head, RS, May 21, 1992. An earlier memo (April 3) to John Tusa from the producer states that in a meeting with David Morton on April 2, the producer was met with "a barrage of foul language and personal abuse before being thrown out of his office." Copy provided to author.

is purposely diluting the BBC's platform and threatening its valuable "political independence."[28] Firstly, Radio Russia presents BBC programs in such a way as to excise "Britishness" from the content, exercising "editorial and political control over BBC material." Secondly, according to a WS memorandum prepared for the Foreign Affairs Committee, Radio Russia carries weekly BBC live content "in exchange for technical assistance and work experience in London."[29] This caveat of the rebroadcasting partnership, which began in 1992, muddies and undermines the BBC's black-and-white brand. Seva himself confirms:

> After 1991 and the collapse of the Soviet Union an old BBC hiring principle of "fresh blood policy" came into operation. The new recruits had to be professional journalists with a good command of English and network of contacts. Soon our floor was filled with the kind of people we were trying to escape from. The then Head of Service David Morton played a significant part in the process. Some people went as far as calling him an "agent of Influence."[30]

Another letter sent to John Tusa, outgoing WS director, concerns the healthy-looking audience reports and also mentions partnership with Radio Russia:

> Suspiciously encouraging audience research reports can fool only those who have no contact with people inside the former Soviet Union. Quite often now despite dubious rebroadcasting on Radio Russia, people ask us in various republics—are the BBC still broadcasting to Russia?
>
> [I]f the situation is not rectified now, the BBC will soon be lost in Russia as a powerful British voice at a time when Russia badly needs British expertise. No flag waving exercises by the management . . . will make up for the great damage to British interests in the former USSR.[31]

---

28 Memo from RS members of staff to Marmaduke Hussey, BBC chairman, May 28, 1992. Copy provided to author.

29 "Memorandum submitted by the BBC World Service," Foreign Affairs Committee, October 12, 1999, https://publications.parliament.uk/pa/cm199899/cmselect/cmfaff/815/9101206.htm

30 Novgorodsev, correspondence with author, December 2021.

31 Ibid.

RS's David Morton quite forcefully defends himself against the injurious accusations, but it is impossible to overlook the statements of two dozen intelligent BBC-devoted, longtime employees. Yet, somehow, the World Service does.

John Tusa finally replies to RS staff in December 1992, expressing his views on the service's direction and chiding the signatories for refusing to attend a meeting set up with management to address their grievances. He points to journalistic changes throughout the WS, which he declares successful, and pointedly asks if RS staff will be "part of the problem or part of the solution." He finishes his letter with a kind of ultimatum: "The Service must decide if it wants to serve its audience in the best way possible in the light of current opportunities or if it wants to stay in a journalistic and editorial backwater."[32] As cold as his response is in the twilight of his tenure as WS director, John Tusa is hardly the downfall of the RS and is in fact one of its longtime proponents. Still, the leadership's willingness to dismiss detailed allegations against management proves that the World Service's loyalty—in this trying period, at least—is to management and not staff.[33] After months of internal drama, the matter is dropped but far from resolved.[34]

The Litvinenko Test

The declining editorial standards of the RS and the possible continuation of internal corruption bleeds into the new millennium, a small reflection of Russia's descent into a criminal maelstrom. Future US president Barack Obama tries to "reset" Western relations with Russia's new president, but the soft approach seems to only embolden and enable Putin's Russia. In 2004, Paul Klebnikov, founding

---

32 John Tusa, letter to RS members, cc: David Morton, Andrew Taussig, December 10, 1992. Copy provided to author.

33 Memo by RS members to John Tusa, November 24, 1992 (provided to author). Staff reference a meeting with Andrew Taussig, the controller of European services, in which he opened with the damning statement that "his first loyalty is to the Management of the Russian Service," reflecting the attitude of John Tusa himself and perhaps even Marmaduke Hussey, though Hussey kindly refused to reply and relegated the matter to Tusa to handle. It's possible Hussey gave Tusa some grief concerning these complaints, which may have led to his coolly phrased memo in reply to the signatories of the letter.

34 Seva himself holds Morton responsible for the decline of the RS, citing the same concerns of other staff who had signed the letters to BBC management. But also, with a loyalty that seems to be a trait of all longtime BBC broadcasters, he praises the institution for eventually ousting Morton. "As a credit to the BBC management, I can say that he was also quietly removed from his post. Early retirement with a golden handshake, I believe. But the damage was done." Novgorodsev correspondence with author, December 2021.

editor of *Forbes Russia* and an American citizen, is murdered in Moscow, and though promises of investigation follow, no justice is rendered.[35] Then, just a few months after Seva entertains NORIS members who had traveled to London for a July 2006 taping of *Sevaoborot*, Anna Politkovskaya is shot outside her Moscow flat on October 7.[36] Appropriately, *Sevaoborot* discusses her death the very same day with guest Sergey Nikitin, director of the Russian Resource Center for Amnesty International. In contrast, the official coverage of this hit by the RS current affairs department is suspiciously flaccid. When Alexander Litvinenko outright declares in a highly public speech that Putin killed Politkovskaya, the RS once again does not mention anything about it.[37]

The real test for the RS, however, comes when days later, on November 1, Litvinenko, a British citizen, is poisoned in London. His deathbed declaration that Putin is responsible makes BBC domestic and British print headlines but tellingly doesn't gain any airtime with the Russian Service. Knowing him personally, Seva provides insight into Litvinenko's background:

> I had Litvinenko as a guest on *Sevaoborot* on several occasions. Contrary to what you may read in the press he was neither a spy nor a KGB [sic]. He was an investigator in the Anti-Organized Crime [Directorate] (РУБОП). At the time criminal gangs in Russia through violence and corruption were running most of the country . . . so RUBOP [founded in 1992 under Yeltsin] created their own gang and gave it an informal license to kill so that the destruction of undesirable characters would look like a fall-out of a mafia war.[38] The process was remarkably efficient, and the top brass got the taste for easy results.
>
> Litvinenko was . . . given an order to eliminate Boris Berezovsky. He stuck to the rule book and asked for a written assignment. A conflict situation developed so as a last resort

---

35 Richard Behar, "Open Letter to Russia's Putin," *Forbes*, July 16, 2014.

36 *Sevaoborot*, July 8, 2006, radio broadcast. The trip to London was once again organized by A. Tatishchev as a sort of reunion of NORIS, though NORIS itself largely ceased activities after the '90s. The tour bus, which brought the whole group to London, is featured as part of a World Service documentary released in 2007, titled "London Calling: Inside the World Service," BBC.com, accessed 25 August, 2022, https://www.bbc.com/news/magazine-34157596.

37 Masha Karp, "BBC Plays by the Kremlin's Rules," *Standpoint*, October 21, 2010, https://standpointmag.co.uk/features-november-10-bbc-plays-by-the-kremlins-rules-masha-karp-bbc-russian-service-litvinenko/.

38 See Vadim Volkov, *Violent Entrepreneurs: The Use of Force in the Making of Russian Capitalism* (Ithaca: Cornell University Press, 2002).

> Litvinenko and his three colleagues went to the press (quite free at the time). Soon after the press conference, Litvinenko was detained for a year but released. It was then that he decides to flee, sending his wife and child to Turkey via Ukraine and himself crossing the Turkish border from Georgia. Berezovsky, by then in the UK, helped him to get plane tickets to Ireland with a stopover in London where he asked for asylum.[39]

After three weeks in the hospital, where doctors tried in vain to treat him, Litvinenko dies on November 23. The next day, Seva, who has retained contact with Litvinenko's family but is also fully aware of continued office politics within the RS, carefully speaks of the man's demise on *BBSeva* as an official investigation by British authorities launches. Seva pays homage to the late Georgi Markov, all the while managing to convey Britishness and objectivity:

> I'll say right away, I'm not going to blame anyone. . . . Before us is the fact that a young and healthy man in three weeks . . . dies in intensive care with the latest equipment and the best doctors. Gradually, the cause is drawn from the fog—radioactive polonium 210, found in the body of the deceased and, even more interestingly, in the alleged place of his poisoning. The British, who gave the world Agatha Christie and Ian Fleming, by their very nature are inclined to solve riddles, find clues and seemingly imperceptible connections. . . . His death has already entered the pantheon of other high-profile murders of dissidents, political opponents, and other objectionable ones, which journalists remember today. . . .
>
> For example, the murder of Georgi Markov on the Waterloo Bridge, to whom a tiny, invisible metal pill with ricin poison was implanted into his leg from a pneumatic gun in the form of an umbrella, and the gentleman, who allegedly stumbled upon him by chance, apologizing in obviously foreign English, went on his way—such a story a screenwriter cannot come up with. Even if they come up with it, they can't write it. Even if they write it, no one will believe such nonsense: a killer dressed in bowler hat and striped trousers—like a broker from the early 60s! It is clear that

39 Novgorodsev, correspondence with author, December 2021.

> the doctors could not believe in such a scenario for a long time, and when they did, it was already too late.
>
> In the case of Litvinenko, the doctors believed his story right away, and they gave him a drug against thallium poisoning. . . . However, it turned out that this was not thallium at all. . . . Of course, the past is not the basis for accusations of the present. In an English court, it is strictly forbidden to mention the previous convictions of the accused. You may be the last repeat offender, but you are judged as the one who committed the first crime. In justice, all prejudice is dangerous. . . . Therefore, we will not rush to the verdict, but we will not back down from the proceedings for anything.[40]

The Litvinenko case causes a great deal of political fallout in the UK. The BBC feels the heat of the newly surging political pressures and the Russian Service doubly so. *Sevaoborot* ends during these fraught days, though Seva himself attributes the end of his show to the internal moral struggle and not to international relations: "The termination of *Sevaoborot* in my opinion had nothing to do with big politics, rather it fell victim of the petty office politics. The new management was intent on budget cuts, [and] they considered some of our programs too intellectual."[41] The final episode airs on November 4, three days after Litvinenko's poisoning. The RS continues filling the time slot, however, until March 7, 2009, with repeat broadcasts of benign, apolitical episodes featuring interviews with musicians, artists, or other uncontroversial people—likely in part because of the need to play the numbers game.

As UK-Russia relations ice over, Western media and politicians accuse the RS of "being too soft on the Kremlin" yet again, just like it was after the death of Stalin.[42] The RS is said to only interview pro-Putin elements and even the interviews with Putin critics, which they do include, are not exclusive, as if to keep Radio Russia editors from taking offense—though this happens

---

40 *BBSeva*, November 24, 2006, radio broadcast. In correspondence with author, Seva conveys that he believed the Crown Prosecution Service's announcement that Litvinenko was killed due to poisoning by the FSB, and it is certainly the case that he believed as much even before the official verdict (why else mention the case of Markov in his comments?). Seva could not be overt, especially when considering his own safety and the editorial restrictions that the RS management had on anything that was critical of the Kremlin since roughly 1992. So, using Markov was a coded way to say what he really believed without getting caught by RS reviewers. This was the same technique he used during the Cold War.

41 Novgorodsev, correspondence with author, December 2021.

42 Steven Eke, "BBC Russian Radio Hits Off Switch," BBC.com, March 23, 2011, https://www.bbc.com/news/world-europe-12820788

anyway. *The Times* reports that RS broadcasts are temporarily taken off the air in St. Petersburg and Moscow from the moment the "Litvinenko affair" erupts. Russia officially cites "technical difficulties" and the Kremlin says nothing of Litvinenko's death-bed accusation that Putin is his murderer.[43] According to Seva, the reason for the kid-glove approach to Russia is the RS management's fear of a loss of rebroadcasting:

> At the time of his poisoning the BBC Russian Service had a number of contracts for rebroadcasting with the local radio stations in Russia (the shortwave radio transmission being abolished . . .), and our Editor, a former Soviet journalist, an Arabic speaker, and a TASS correspondent in Iraq in the 70s, deliberately softened the tone of some reports on [the] Litvinenko affair citing a possible loss of rebroadcasting. Some of our colleagues (of the dissident generation) saw it as a political and moral sellout. The story finally got to the British press and the Editor was quietly demoted.[44]

One particular joint letter of complaint to the BBC editorial department from academics at the University of Glasgow and Russians of note—Viktor Suvorov and Oleg Gordievsky—presents documented evidence of the decline of RS impartiality and balance in coverage of world events in comparison to the BBC's domestic coverage. The signatories even go so far as to say that they had hoped Litvinenko's murder would properly provoke the RS and inspire the editors to declare the truth, especially after the official pronouncement of FSB involvement in his poisoning. However, their hopes had been dashed:

---

43 N.a., "Buried in Lead in Londongrad," *The Times*, December 10, 2006, https://www.thetimes.co.uk/article/focus-buried-in-lead-in-londongrad-9m93f5s5mrv. Additionally, the RS was accused of failing to exclusively interview many of Litvinenko's closest contacts—people who had been in fact guests of *Sevaoborot* previously and who had attended Seva's MBE reception—and leaving out important details and the official announcement by the Crown Prosecution Service that the FSB poisoned Litvinenko. *The Times* prints an exclusive with Gordievsky who revealed that Litvinenko was poisoned not at a sushi bar, as had been previously thought, but at a "hotel where he met some Russian visitors." See "Letter to the Editorial Complaints Unit of the BBC," Select Committee on Foreign Affairs, https://publications.parliament.uk/pa/cm200708/cmselect/cmfaff/50/7062714.htm.

44 Novgorodsev, correspondence with author, December 2021.

> The BBC Russian Service seemed determined to undermine any news items or programs produced by the main BBC channels that seemed to its editors to be too critical of the Russian authorities. For example, on the eve of the BBC Panorama program about Litvinenko's murder (22 January 2007), the Russian Service thought it necessary to post an article on its website alleging that British journalists do not understand the case. . . . It used an exclusive interview with Andrew Jack of the Financial Times to say that the British media do not understand Russia properly and, therefore, will not get to the truth about Litvinenko's murder.[45]

However, the letter does praise one worthy RS program produced by Masha Karp entitled *The Life and Death of Alexander Litvinenko* that aired in mid-December 2006. As the writers tell it, the program was quite balanced and the first example since Litvinenko's murder that had featured not only Putin's spokesperson but also exclusive interviews with Kremlin critics:

> However, shortly after it was first broadcast, its repeats were cancelled, and the audio file was quickly removed from the Russian Service's website. We have recently learnt that the producer, instead of being congratulated on an excellent program, was actually reprimanded for it![46]

Per Masha Karp's own words, she had received a call from a senior editor at RS on the night of December 19, right after her program had been aired, who had told her the program was "biased" and had asked what the "man in the Kremlin" monitoring the broadcasts might think of the feature. Her answer: "I do not work for a man in the Kremlin. I work for the BBC."

In keeping with the BBC's guidelines for balanced and fair reporting (giving God and the Devil airtime, as it were) she gives voice to both sides. Yet, that's not okay, the editor replies, because the anti-Kremlin speakers sound more intelligent. She further says that the RS had been in possession of "an exclusive 50-minute interview in Russian with Litvinenko" from 2002, which the BBC

---

45 "Letter to the Editorial Complaints Unit of the BBC," Committee on Foreign Affairs Minutes of Evidence, November 19, 2007, https://publications.parliament.uk/pa/cm200708/cmselect/cmfaff/50/7062714.htm.

46 Ibid.

would have loved to have had translated into English. But the RS management hadn't wanted to air it, so Karp used snippets in her program, one of which included Litvinenko saying that Putin killed Anna Politkovskaya. "As it turned out, it was precisely the voice of the murdered man that my bosses did not want to hear."[47]

Thus, after two airings, the program is completely pulled from the schedule and the BBC website, and the RS dramatically fails the Litvinenko test in that they cannot muster the journalistic bravery to stand up to Kremlin pressure and Russian criminality. The BBC World Service itself betrays its new dynamic in not supporting Karp and not backing its own policies.

In the end, RS's soft approach to Russia results in nothing of benefit. The BBC's "partner stations in Russia" announce one after another "without explanation" that collaboration is off the table. This unfortunately eliminates "a big chunk of the audience, in a country where people will not return to the culture of short-wave listening."[48] The BBC loses its immense Cold War-era popularity in Russia and most of its post-Soviet successes and investments—the "consequences of being caught in the crossfire during the diplomatic row" following the murder of Litvinenko.[49] Finally, after huge budgetary cuts to the WS, which portend 480 job losses, on March 26, 2011 the Russian Service, which had begun broadcasting to Soviet Russia on this same day in 1946, goes off the air, retaining only an online presence. A listener in Russia writes of the very moment: "Transmission stopped abruptly . . . and it was (ironically) on Seva's talk show."[50]

The End of an Era

It must be said that whatever blame may rest on middle management or even such figures as David Morton at the Russian Service, ultimately the director of the World Service at this time, Peter Horrocks, shoulders huge responsibility for questionable leadership, shortsightedness, and, what John Tusa understatedly refers to, as a "strategic error":

---

47 Karp, "BBC Plays by the Kremlin's Rules." Karp mentions that listeners have written to the RS complaining that there are too many journalists who are working for Russian media, a concern also raised in the 2007 letter alleging the RS's use of journalists of "questionable past."

48 Eke, "BBC Russian Radio Hits off Switch."

49 Glanville, *Radio Redux*, 59.

50 Eugen Neumann, March 2019.

> When [Horrocks] appeared before the Commons foreign affairs committee on 9 March 2011 . . . MPs repeatedly offered to mount a campaign to help him to ask for a better settlement for the World Service. Horrocks repeatedly declined their offers of support, insisting the BBC as a whole must accept funding reductions. That looks like a strategic error, as does the earlier closure of direct broadcasting to Russia and central Europe on the grounds that pluralism of communication and information was now freely available in those countries.[51]

The committee meeting Tusa mentions is one that is specifically called to address the implications of cuts to the World Service. MPs ask Horrocks why he would cut shortwave to countries like India where eleven million tune in, or China where it is critical that access stay "risk-free" (not so for internet sites), or Swahili-speaking nations where exists a very large audience. In total, ending such shortwave services means losing thirty million listeners—"30 million regrets," Horrocks says, insisting that these distribution changes are "forced on us by financial circumstances," even though the committee offers to keep the services afloat. Horrocks's cuts to the WS and BBC Monitoring even attract the attention of US Secretary of State Hillary Clinton who expresses her concern about the changes, knowing how important the BBC is as a supplier of news and entertainment worldwide.[52] For motives that are not readily apparent, Horrocks seems willing to let the World Service and BBC Monitoring "deteriorate."[53]

Despite the termination of broadcasting, the RS continues to provide programming and content online at bbcrussian.com, following in the footsteps of VOA Russian Service, which had been defunded and discontinued in 2008.[54]

---

51 Tusa, "The BBC World Service is Not an Arm of the Foreign Office."

52 Moreover, Horrocks wants the WS to become integrated within the BBC, rather than "grant-aided by the Foreign Office." The MPs prompt Horrocks for an answer about why he does not fear the WS getting throttled and shriveling up because of the funding structure of the BBC; Horrocks answers that shortwave is no longer as important as it once was and that there are other mechanisms by which to reach the audience. Similarly, former director general John Birt had tried to completely restructure the BBC and merge the WS and domestic news departments to detrimental effect in 1996. Parliament had retaliated, and the *Guardian* started a campaign to "save the World Service." Macfarlane, "BBC World Service in the 1990s," 5.

53 Foreign Affairs Committee transcript on "The Implications of Cuts to the BBC World Service," March 9, 2011, https://publications.parliament.uk/pa/cm201011/cmselect/cmfaff/849/11030903.htm

54 Bill Skundrich in conversation with author, January 2021. As a result of the end of VOA Russian Service, Skundrich departed VOA, feeling disappointed in the decisions of US lawmakers.

Even then, this web-only presence is far from secure. In 2014, *Izvestiia* publicly warns the BBC that the Russian Service website may be blocked because of a "provocative interview" with a Siberian activist about plans for a "march for the federalization of Siberia." *Izvestiia* claims that the Russian Service has "ignored" repeat warnings to remove the article after purported citizen complaints, and, as a result, Russia can easily obstruct access to the website: "If we go down this path, we could fully block the website of the Russian Service . . . in the territory of our country. Not only can we do that, but we are obliged to do that because the Office of the Prosecutor-General has ordered . . . [blocking of] access to services and websites that publish information of this nature."[55]

With all the job cuts and the Russian Service in a fragile and demoralizing position, Seva reasons that even if the winds of change are not blowing directly at him right now, eventually they will, for the world is turning against Russia and Russia is turning against the world. He wisely decides it is time to *end* on his own terms. He sets a date—September 4, 2015—the relationship between Russia and Britain reaches "its most strained point since the end of the Cold War."[56] As expected, this last broadcast is an elaborate, much-celebrated affair.

From Pushkin House in London, in the presence of many friends, colleagues, and VIPs, Seva delivers his final program at seventy-five years of age. His well-seasoned Russian tenor melts over the air. He announces his retirement, banters with the invited audience in his personable yet gentlemanly style, and then plays Stevie Wonder's "Sir Duke"—a fitting way to conclude his radio career: right where he began.

---

55 N.a., "BBC Russian Service 'warned' May Be Blocked Over 'Provocative Interview,'" BBC Worldwide Monitoring, August 5, 2014. *Izvestiia* says this is according to the requirements of federal law No. 398-F3. The parallel can plainly be drawn between jamming of radio broadcasts and the blocking of websites, except that with blocking sites it is easier and cheaper to do so completely, while with jamming it is not absolute and not ubiquitous, tremendous costs aside.

56 "The United Kingdom's Relations with Russia," Report, Foreign Affairs Committee, February 21, 2017.

Featured Listener: Alek

It all started with Anglomania. I was listening to the BBC World Service. The first time I heard Seva on the radio was 1978. It was just like a miracle because . . . my parents were divorced when I was two years old, so Seva was sort of a father for me. And it was the greatest time because punk rock, new wave was concentrated in one time. And Seva was in London in the right time, right place, you know . . . Between you and Seva there is no distance—compatriots, like friends. No difference. So, these warm memories stay in my heart till today . . .

Yes, I was listening to all those—Voice of America and Radio Svoboda—and to this day I still listen to Radio Svoboda on the internet. But the BBC was so special. It was special, first of all, because of Seva. I was listening to both the Russian Service and World Service. Their English, the way of putting the news, no judgment, it was their policy . . . and I liked it. [Also] the British rock music was much more interesting for me than American rock, though I love Styx, etc. But British music developed American rock in their special British mentality. Seva is a gentleman, he is not a rock 'n' roll man. He was forced to listen to it. But I am only rock 'n' roll, I'm of the rock generation. I'm still digging the pearls of rock today . . . But Seva was . . . his humor, his knowledge of Russian life was a first, it made him a unique presenter of radio. (Seva's programs make no sense nowadays. Only that time—right place, right time.)

I dreamed of working on the radio. I was working on [state] TV as an editor with Mr. Artemy Troitsky. He was my boss. But he is so well-known, and I'm . . . [*smiles and shrugs*]

Troitsky interviewing Seva in London as host of Program "A". Seva's 1st appearance on Soviet TV since emigration. January 1, 1990. (Credit: seva.ru)

So, this is life. Maybe I've had no drive, I've had no ambitions to reach something. This meeting gives me hope. It's essential for living. I have no aim for my life. Right now. I'm just living for the process of living. So, I don't look for what is in the future. But rock 'n' roll still holds me. I am fifty-eight. I was running marathons and playing basketball, hockey. I drink, I smoke. It's so Russian. [*Everyone laughs.*]

I was [involved] in *samizdat*. I invented the magazine title *Urlite*. And I brought Seva these editions of *Urlite* magazine, for which Vladimir [Ivanov] was the photographer. My second meeting with Seva was in 1990. And in 1990 he was on our TV channel with Mr. Troitsky. Troitsky was the first man who came to London and this piece of interview was shown on Russian TV. So, I saw Seva thanks to the TV program . . . Before Seva, I listened to Voice of America's Yevgeny Aronov. Seva said himself Aronov was his first rival.

MD: How would you say Seva was different from VOA's presenters?

Alek: I mean, humor. This special, pleasant voice. And the music was . . . the music was better. It was mostly British rock. Top 20s. Some albums that were mostly from Britain. And the letters from the listeners . . .

MD: But didn't VOA do that as well? And others? What about Radio Luxembourg . . . ?

Alek: I was listening to Radio Luxembourg, but it was hard to hear.[57] Radio Liberty was jammed most of all. The BBC was maybe in-between, maybe less. You would have one day where it was absolutely clear, another day . . . not so much, and then the next day you would try to discern all the words that Seva said. But once I was living in someone's house, and the reception was good. I was recording on tapes and bringing it to my high school. Some guys invented special receivers to hear better . . .

The rock programs of the '70s and the '80s were the most precious for me. By the '90s I was listening to Seva routinely, to be honest. The music was great, but it wasn't the peak. Rock and pop music was best in '70s and '80s.

Sergey: *Rok-posevy* was different from other programs because it was scripted and that was critical. It was very good Russian literature . . . a masterpiece.

Alek: We remember all his jokes and everything.

---

57 Another listener, Vladimir, said that since Radio Luxembourg was on medium wave; it was easiest to listen to in the dark and bright light caused significant interference. Vladimir Ivanov in conversation with Sergei Pantsirev and author, May 2019.

Sergey: He concentrated on creating some quality content for *Rok-posevy*, and he succeeded. Most of the time. Sometimes I was like, "Well, what's that?" But most of the time, he was interesting, he was engaging, he was very . . . you know, you couldn't switch off at any point. Because you were like, what is he going to say next, what is the next song? Even if it was cheesy pop of the '80s or '90s, he could pick out words that we could relate to. So, say he was talking about, I don't know, Amy Winehouse. And it was interesting even though we couldn't relate to the music . . . He was still able to find the right words for this music. When I say right, I mean something that we could understand, relate to, and laugh to.

Alek: [*singing*] "Those were the days, my friend" . . . and now there is nothing.

Conclusion

> Seva Novgorodsev represents the best the BBC has to offer. Informative, witty, relevant—his broadcasts have been truly legendary. For decades, they occupied a very special place in millions of hearts. Seva is signing off as a broadcaster, but we are not saying farewell. . . .
>
> —Artyom Liss, BBC World Service European Hub

> I must confess, I never listened to rock music. . . . In general, any person prefers to listen to the music that they listened to when they were 18, 19, 20. This music remains with us forever. For me, it's those American jazz singers with beautiful voices and the big bands. . . .[1]

If the Soviet story can teach the modern world anything it is this: no matter how sophisticated a closed system, state oppression cannot perfectly isolate a society, especially not under conditions of increasing globalization and community building. The long hard struggle that played out between popular music and politics since the interwar period proved time and again that politics is weaker and inferior to the will of the people. People *wanted* to listen to foreign voices, so they did. People *wanted* to listen to blacklisted bands, so they did. While it is unlikely that another truly closed system can ever exist, oppression is timeless and information, education, and entertainment remain effective ammunition against authoritarianism. As international relations scholar Paul Sheeran writes:

> The communication of ideas and the transport of materials (technology transfers [included] . . .) that occurred between former Soviet Union and the West . . . contributed to a fluid change that could not be contained within the confines of a rigid social plan, irrespective of its sophistication.[2]

Therefore, in terms of the cultural and emotional impact to the citizens of Soviet Russia, it cannot be doubted that Seva Novgorodsev had a profound

1 Novgorodsev, interview by Matthew Orr, March 28, 2019, in *The Slavic Connexion*, podcast.
2 Sheeran, *Cultural Politics in International Relations*, 173.

effect on a large swath of the population during the late Cold War.[3] Most critically, he understood the culture, understood the challenges of Soviet life, and understood that to be Russian meant alienation from both the West *and* East. Moreover, he spoke in a language, in a vernacular, that Russians readily *heard* because it was familiar to them, their experiences, their frame of reference. In this way, Seva's transmissions retained their intent and integrity, despite being compressed, caked in distortion, and overwrought by fading. For even with high fidelity sound, a listener can hear but not understand or properly receive, as was certainly the case with Willis Conover, who was much loved for his voice but could not have captured the average Russian listener in the way Seva did. To cite one listener: "I felt there was no hope living in the Soviet Union, but [Seva] showed us a way of life within the system without having to have something in common with it."

While Seva would never claim to have been political in his broadcasts, he indirectly gained political clout in Russia by currying the favor and trust of millions, making him a revolutionary nonrevolutionary. To this day, he enjoys continued fame and popularity throughout the former USSR, conducting tours, making TV appearances, recording podcasts, and giving, as he humbly dubs them, "one-man shows" in halls that "keep getting bigger every year."[4]

Historian Kristin Roth-Ey calls Seva a "legendary" figure of the Cold War culture wars:

> *Rok-posevy* was one of the most influential Western broadcasts to the Soviet Union, to judge by its levels of audience engagement and by its cult status to this day. . . . *Rok-posevy*'s promise to Soviet audiences was not only new music and information, and new ways of thinking about media [but also] new avenues for thinking about themselves as individuals and about the nature of authority and community afforded by its very particular sonic experience.[5]

As several listeners suggested, Seva made informed, thinking, broad-minded gentlemen out of the disenfranchised, lost, and searching young men who tuned

---

3 Ibid., 172. "The broadcaster Seva Novgorodsev and his weekly rock show was particularly influential in both popularizing Western 'popular' music and prompting Soviet citizens through humor and satire to reflect on their relationship with the Soviet regime (the import of it adding to the existing disillusion)."

4 From various correspondence between Seva Novgorodsev and author.

5 Roth-Ey, "Listening out": 558, 576–77.

into this "sonic experience." This included societal misfits who didn't understand themselves, didn't have any positive role models, couldn't comprehend the frustrating lack of connection to the previous Soviet generation, and cared nothing for the Kremlin's politics. The spiritual and intellectual change that took place over the years in listeners—listeners who recall beginning to tune into foreign radio at around the age of fourteen—is evidenced in the letters Seva received: "You really can notice through the things that people allowed themselves to write in the letters how their state of mind changed and broadened during that period. [This] was the thing I was always interested in."[6]

Young people on the fringes of Soviet society and in danger of being branded dissidents could find comfort and empathy in Seva—an émigré and product of the USSR who himself had once stood inside the Motherland with eyes and ears curiously probing the West. His programs focused indirectly on building one's sense of self and identity, which agreed with freedom-seeking rock, with the very nature of the music.[7] He gave many something to live for, something to hope for, and something to do.

Seva in his BBC studio (credit: Seva.ru)

6 Tolkunov, "Seva Novgorodsev."

7 Ilya Smirnov, "Rock 'n' Gertsen," *Русская idea*, November 3, 2014, https://politconservatism.ru/experiences/rock-n-gertsen.

Rock, Radio, and Legacy

Regarding radio (internet, FM, and AM) in Russia post-1991, all listeners interviewed gave negative responses. One listener, Kostya, elaborated on his answer, saying that radio (from Russia itself) initially improved in post-Soviet Russia, with several new stations cropping up that were reveling in the new freedoms and flexing their broadcasting liberties. But in the final decade of the twentieth century, things started to go downhill. Another listener commented far less generously:

> Radio in Russia [today] is not for intellectual people—it is filled with stupid ads, imbecile blabber, chauvinistic propaganda, sewage pop, and sometimes corny pub rock. There is nothing for me. Russian radio hasn't improved since the collapse of the USSR, it has drastically worsened.[8]

What do these former BBC Russian Service listeners tune to now? Internet radio was a popular response: "I listen to various metal stations on the internet . . . Radio Metal (Ukraine), Radio Hellvetia (Switzerland), Metal Heart Radio (Czechia), Radio Shadow of Convulsion (Germany), Black Eagle Radio (Germany), and Epic Rock Radio (Canada)."[9] Many others stated that they switched from the BBC to Radio Liberty online (despite being averse to listening to RL during the Cold War), on which Artemy Troitsky hosts music programs and podcasts. Interestingly, though Seva's young listeners in the '80s were largely apolitical, or claimed to be, they have grown up to be clearly anti-Kremlin and suspicious of the state. Cynicism among those interviewed about the current state of politics in Russia ran strong. When asked how their view of the West changed towards the end of the '90s, as radio in Russia begins to go "downhill," listeners recalled their dismay in finding that America, particularly, did not turn out to be their friend in peacetime:

---

8 Eugen Neumann, February 2019.

9 Ibid. A limited anonymous radio survey conducted by the author in 2019 (across Russia) revealed similar responses; all have navigated away from any Russian media offerings, searching other countries for content via the internet. Interestingly, all respondents to the survey indicated, without exception, they were male.

> We understood even then that NATO countries are not the best friends for us, that we were situational allies . . . like previously we were situational allies in WWII. . . . It was not communism which they fought against but Russia in any form it would take, be it the Russian Empire, the USSR, or the Russian Federation.[10]

Overall, though these once young-and-restless are tired of the way things are today, there remains little of the spirit of activism or hunger for change as had existed in this generation when Gorbachev was making waves. They are established and set in their lives and express their displeasure with the government and the international order in muted ways. These people look to the past—the '70s and '80s—with a gleam in their eyes and a wry smile. Those were the good times, the *best* times, when the air was thick with hope and crackled with the BBC. It's a complex amalgam of post-Soviet nostalgia, pride, and, at the same time, regret that things didn't continue on in the right direction. While these people certainly have no interest in resurrecting the USSR, there is still this longing for the feeling of freedom rushing in through breaking walls. The collapse of the USSR wasn't the pivotal moment for them; it was the rapid metamorphosis before and after the USSR officially ended that empowered them and encouraged them to not just dream of being part of a better and open Russia, but to actually reach out and actively make it happen through the building of community. "Post-Soviet nostalgia" is, thus, the admission that the gray and alienating system of Soviet socialism nevertheless enabled, through disabling conditions, vivid creativity and alternative societies and spaces. Rock music seized Soviet youth in the late communist period because the genre in the '70s and '80s exuded a defiant, hierarchy-spurning, angry optimism that perfectly expressed and encouraged young people's fervor as Gorbachev himself rocked the USSR.

When asked about the role of jazz and rock in the eventual collapse of the Soviet system, those interviewed gave a variety of answers, but across the board, whether they thought a direct connection between music and politics existed, they did agree that society was forever changed by the music. Joanna Stingray said, "underground Russian Rock helped bring down the Iron Curtain in that it was a mass force of individual expression, the kind of force that drives democracy."[11] Jazz musician and educator Andrei Solovyov echoed Joanna's words:

---

10 Ibid.

11 Joanna Stingray, December 2020.

> I believe that jazz and rock have largely changed the social and ideological role of music in general. Both brought to the forefront an artist who, here and now, performed under his own name, from within himself. Before that, the musician and singer were only performers, transmitting what the composer and poet composed. A spontaneous ideology of freedom and personal responsibility for one's actions, both creative and social, developed around this.[12]

As might be surmised, Artemy Troitsky said that rock played an unquestionable part in transforming the mindset of Soviet youth, which in turn liberated them well before the end of Lenin's Socialist Experiment:

> I think that the Beatles played a bigger role in the breakup of the Soviet Union . . . than the CIA for instance, or many others. Because music was the main source of soft power in the '60s, '70s, '80s. It made . . . an unlikely dissident movement. . . . Rock music, Western culture in general like Hollywood, [reached] tens of millions of Soviets, and totally corrupted their belief in the communist system, because their favorite music was Western . . . you know, the things that they really fancied came from somewhere else. . . .
>
> And so, how can you manage a country where the majority, or at least the majority of the young population, don't give a shit about your communist culture, about your communist beliefs, about your communist everything . . . *And this was mostly because of music.*
>
> I wouldn't say that this music brought Western ideology like capitalism right to Russia, but rather it brought another form of idealism which is simply named *freedom*.[13]

At the very least, Western radio's impact on the development of rock music in Russia should be without question. Whether Seva himself shaped the Russian rock scene is another matter. It may safely be concluded that he certainly affected the musicians of the late '70s and '80s—at least those who listened to foreign radio—to such extent that many remain indebted to him. Boris Grebenshchikov

---

12 Andrei Solovyov, December 2020.
13 A. Troitsky, June 2019.

stated in recent years that Seva opened the English world to him; when visiting London, Seva—a "hero" to the Russian people with a name that was "legendary"—was more than hospitable to Boris.[14] Though Artemy Troitsky was indeed a critical musical guide for developing musicians, Seva was still the spiritual navigator for many rock lovers and rockers alike, despite the fact he was a jazz musician of an earlier era, a *stilyaga*. Listeners have even declared that this '80s generation of youth are the "children of Novgorodsev," or at least his students.[15] If Seva is from that part of the Russian intelligentsia who sought equality, reform, and human rights, but without violating the rules of the system, without political polemics, then it seems to make sense that his listeners, the young people of the '80s, would make their protest in peaceful, nonpolitical ways as well. In essence, they are Seva's spiritual heirs. This is why today his voice and persona still hold sway with this generation and remain closely connected to the music that served as the soundtrack of the late Cold War period.

The DJ-Russian Rock connection: Makarevich, Seva, and Sasha Titov, London, 2015 (Credit: seva.ru)

---

14 From a video clip (unpublished) provided to author from Novgorodsev's archive. Interestingly, in 2021 Grebenshchikov and Akvarium gave a concert in Kyiv, which billed Seva as the special guest—"legendary BBC radio host."

15 Seva said he always saw himself as more of a teacher who comes to the classroom three hours before the class actually starts to prepare. (Interview by Matthew Orr, March 28, 2019, in *The Slavic Connexion*, podcast).

The Battle Continues

In spring 2020, COVID-19 broke out and a pandemic claimed the world, serving as a great equalizer to the global (dis)order for a while. One of the more surprising and disheartening consequences of the pandemic was that instead of building international unity, the virus exacerbated and uncovered divisions on micro and macro levels within democratic and nondemocratic nations alike. In the post-Soviet space, two major protests occurred during the tenure of the pandemic, prompted in part by poor government handling of the virus, which showed the continuing role of rock in revolution. The first were the anti-government protests in Belarus and the second were the protests across Russia in support of the opposition leader Alexei Navalny and what Navalny represented—free and democratic elections.

In the Belarus protests, beginning in August 2020 and continuing into 2021, the song "Peremen" (Change) by Viktor Tsoi in 1986—already banned by Belarusian state radio in 2011—became the people's anthem. The song came up for the first time at a pro-government event on August 6, three days prior to the presidential elections, when the incumbent Alexander Lukashenko, the "last dictator of Europe," essentially forbade the opposition candidate Svetlana Tsikhanouskaya from holding her rally in Bangalore Square. Through social media, supporters of Tsikhanouskaya communicated a new agenda and they marched to Kyiv Square where the pro-Lukashenko concert was taking place. As it happened, two sound guys—the DJs—at the concert realized what was happening and, clearly betraying their loyalties (or lack thereof), they "sabotaged proceedings" with Kino's "Peremen."[16] In moments, the pro-government concert turned tide. The supporters of Tsikhanouskaya, and more importantly for a free and democratic Belarus, started chanting the words to this song, words they *all* seemed to know.

Joanna Stingray commented on one particular video broadcast by BBC World Service that showed Belarusian protestors singing "Peremen"—long after the sham of an election ended, and the days and days of nationwide protest began—as they march through the streets of Minsk:

---

16 Brendan Cole, "Belarus Opposition Hijacks Pro-Lukashenko Festival, Plays Revolutionary Song," *Newsweek*, August 7, 2020, https://www.newsweek.com/belarus-lukashenko-election-protests-rally-opposition-revolution-1523516. See also Andrew Roth, "Belarus Goes to the Polls," *Guardian*, August 7, 2020, https://www.theguardian.com/world/2020/aug/07/belarus-goes-to-the-polls-with-longtime-leader-lukashenko-feeling-the-heat.

> It's interesting because Viktor didn't write political or protest songs . . . he always said that his lyrics were about each person's inner struggles, that we all have a kind of psychological cage trapping us from doing things, and he wanted people to find ways to break from this and do what they wanted, what makes them happy . . . Once in a while, a song takes on a life of its own and "Peremen" is one of them . . . I got chills seeing the footage of the Belarus people blasting and singing Viktor's song. It was powerful![17]

Despite Tsoi's original intentions, his song became the anthem for an entire nation. Belarusian people did not show signs of faltering despite forecasts that bad winter weather would diminish the will of protestors; demonstrations, in fact, continued strong into 2021.

Overlapping and inspired by the Belarusian protests, a second demonstration erupted across Russia to protest the corruption of the Russian ruling elite and the repeat jailing of the Russian opposition leader Alexei Navalny, following his unsuccessful poisoning by the FSB in 2020. The protests began in the Far East on the morning of January the twenty-third and continued until late at night at the high-security detention center, *Matrosskaia tishina,* in Moscow where Navalny was held. Thousands from St. Petersburg to quiet islands near Japan participated, over 112 cities in total according to a BBC estimate.[18] An unbelievable crowd in Yakutia braved temperatures of minus fifty degrees Celsius (minus fifty-eight degrees Fahrenheit) to show their objection to the status quo of Putinism. This demonstration of solidarity with the forty-four-year-old anti-corruption leader was met with an egregious and disproportionate use of force by Russian authorities. In many cities tear gas and other instruments of violence were used to disperse the crowds and punish any who questioned arrests. Conservative estimates of the number of arrests made by OMON and *Rosgvardiia* (Russian National Guard) hover around 3,100, with people detained in 937 cities. A particularly sad case took place in Khabarovsk, which had been conspicuously protesting

---

17 Joanna Stingray, December 2020.

18 "Alexei Navalny: 'More Than 3,000 Detained' in Protests across Russia," BBC.com, Jan 23, 2021, https://www.bbc.com/news/world-europe-55778334. See also none, "As It Happened: Tens of Thousands Rally for Navalny's Release Across Russia," *The Moscow Times,* January 23, 2021, https://www.themoscowtimes.com/2021/01/23/as-it-happened-tens-of-thousands-rally-for-navalnys-release-across-russia-a72705.

Putin around the same time that Belarusians began protesting Lukashenko, wherein detained protesters were "lined up against a wall and beaten" by police.[19]

In retaliation, and to explain away the forty thousand protestors in Moscow, the Russian authorities accused diplomats at the US embassy in Moscow of "publishing routes of planned demonstrations in support of Navalny," after the US State Department issued a statement decrying Russia's violent response to citizens exercising their "universal rights."[20] Even Nizhny Novgorod, the former closed technical city of radio laboratory fame, experienced protest numbers in the ten thousand range. The protests had the unfortunate consequence of ensuring Navalny's subsequent sentencing to two and one-half years in prison.

Today, many of the Russian rock musicians who supported change in the USSR back the plight for freedom in countries like Belarus and, of course, Russia. They do not forget what they fought for with power chords. But it is telling that in this modern age of information overload, protestors and activists have to reach back into Cold War history to find songs with meaning and relevance to resurfacing struggles for freedom. Seva has expectedly abstained from speaking to the protests in Russia, but his many thousands of followers on Facebook were not afraid to discuss his apolitical public face. In response to someone asking why Seva would not speak up directly about the unfolding political situation, a young Russian (younger than the majority of Seva's modern-day followers) retorted: "Leave him alone . . . He saved more lives than anybody else. He was a voice of hope."[21]

It is understandable why Russians and Ukrainians today would expect Seva to speak freely and clearly on matters of importance, on the injustices without mincing words. However, given Seva's decades of practicing coded performance—where little was said directly that couldn't be said indirectly and more thoughtfully—why should he suddenly change his brand? Just because the USSR is no more, the Russian Federation is not any better—in fact, it is worse, proving its antagonism to the West and to the world with an unjustified and unprovoked full-scale invasion of Ukraine, launched on

---

19 Ibid.

20 Ibid.

21 Seva's Facebook account, on which he posts short pieces, is a sign of his continued popularity. His average post receives eight hundred to one thousand likes (often much more) with a great deal of engagement (commentary or sharing or both). He remains an influencer.

February 24, 2022, for the ostensible purpose of denazification.[22] In response to the fresh smoke of war, Seva wrote on his Facebook account the very day of the invasion in a manner that resembled one of his *Rok-posevy* scripts but with bolder language, using the term "war" rather than Putin's "special operation" euphemism:

> A long time ago, even under Soviet rule, my jazz friends and I joked that the symbol of the USSR is a triangular wheel. Any upswing is inevitably followed by collapse. The triangular wheel of Russian history spins slowly—the last half-turn took thirty years. How glorious everything rose [in that upswing]—the freedom to travel around the world, currency exchange, foreign cars, instant communication via the Internet, parmesan, scotch, Yves Saint Laurent, Gucci, Dolce Gabbana . . .
>
> But in the depths of the people, deprived of all these charms and regularly suffering from a hangover, a gloomy malice grew and became brutal—what a power they had lost! No one respects us, we have turned into servants. Stand! Be silent! Fear!
>
> And so, on February 24, 2022, at dawn, the triangular wheel collapsed with a crash that echoed around the world. Its new turn begins, and it is not known how long it will last and how many misfortunes it will bring.
>
> One thing is clear: life will not be the same. War brings blood, death, violence, and hatred. The purpose of this war is incomprehensible—how can one drive an entire country into a stall . . . ?
>
> The collective West will certainly draw conclusions and ask Russia to leave the banquet hall, take measures to reduce ties as much as possible, and depend as little as possible on the paranoid state.

---

22 For a detailed yet concise summary of the lead-up to the Russian war in Ukraine, see Lera Toropin's interview with David Marples, March 5, 2022, in *The Slavic Connexion*, podcast, https://www.slavxradio.com/ukraine. For more about the claim of de-Nazification, see Leonid Ragozin, "Putin's War in Ukraine: Russian Roulette," March 23, 2022, in *The Slavic Connexion*, podcast, https://www.slavxradio.com/ukraine-3.

> The American and European militaries will be strengthened. Ukraine, if it survives, will rally around nationalism. The Russian-language agenda will be closed.
>
> A map of Russian missile strikes on targets in Ukraine shows the scope of detailed planning for the operation. We still have much to learn—lists for arrests have surely been prepared, the composition of the new government has been assembled—everything is just as it was in 1946, in the countries of Eastern Europe.
>
> In the conquered territories, Russian television propaganda will begin to work, inside Russia itself, according to the laws of wartime, the Russian opposition will be equated with traitors.
>
> And there, you see, the borders can be closed. Fix the ruble, abolish changes of office as unnecessary, introduce coupons for soap and cereals . . .
>
> All for what? Who needs this insane war?
>
> "Russia, where are you going? Answer us."
>
> There is no answer.[23]

Many of the predictions in this post came true as a result of Putin's war in Ukraine, and the remaining prophesies are fated to follow as well. NATO and the European Union have found a raison d'être, after floundering and searching for a purpose since the fall of the USSR. Hatred has grown, most modern nations have turned against Russia, and Russia itself has turned against its own people, endangering Russophones in Ukraine and arresting Russians in Russia who protest the senseless carnage and destruction.[24] History is indeed repeating itself but with an even more bewildering refrain. Russian propaganda and

---

23 Novgorodsev, Facebook post, February 24, 2022, accessed March 27, 2022.

24 N.a., "Russian Forces 'Destroying Everything' in East Ukraine," Al-Jazeera, July 6, 2022, https://www.aljazeera.com/news/2022/7/6/russia-using-scorched-earth-tactics-in-eastern-ukraine. Russian troops have been indiscriminately killing civilians in regions that previously had been pro-Moscow and designated as separatist territory. These are Russian-dominated areas, so it is more than likely that not only are monuments to Russian culture being razed but also that ethnic Russian-speakers themselves are losing their lives. Those arrested in Russia for protesting the war include even survivors of the Siege of Leningrad. Robert Coalson, "Survivors of Nazi Siege," March 20, 2022, RFE/RL, https://www.rferl.org/a/russia-ukraine-invasion-mariupol-siege-leningrad-survivors/31765250.html.

disinformation, as Seva wrote in his post, has grown to unfathomable levels, separating families and friends and creating division globally.[25] Unfortunately, instead of combatting the propaganda in constructive ways, Western governments have not yet returned to diplomatic practices from the Cold War and instead are focused solely on crippling sanctions, blocking Russian imports, canceling Russian culture, and arming Ukrainians against Russia in this hot conflict. Perhaps shortwave radio is neither feasible nor the most efficient and effective method for combat in this new escalation of tensions. Yet there are other tools that Western governments have with which they can speak directly to people—tools such as podcasts, social media platforms, and perhaps especially cultural output in the form of music that are barely utilized—not in official capacities. Vladimir Putin is just another bloody speck in Russia's vast timeline. Kinetic war does not and cannot last forever, and regimes likewise are not eternal. What will the West do if, when Russia emerges from this war and from under the eventual rubble of Putinism, the majority of Russian people harbor only resentment and hatred of the West? "Winning hearts and minds" remains as crucial a goal as ever, perhaps even more so when the possibility of nuclear war has only grown. *Sound*craft should not be abandoned. As Seva and all broadcasters proved during the Cold War, sowing seeds to combat fear and misinformation, even when the ground is hard and hostile, will bear fruit—the overwhelming pro-American disposition of Russia and the Baltic states immediately after the collapse of the USSR shows as much.

The DJ Who "Brought Up" a Generation

Perhaps, then, the claim that a BBC radio presenter "brought down the USSR" may have merit, after all, though what Seva did is far more complicated than the simple dissolution of a system. He did not bring down the Soviet regime, he did not attack it. Rather, he focused on the most important aspect of any state: the people. He loved the people as if they were his children. The people in turn loved him for speaking to them openly and honestly, for making them laugh, for consciously or unconsciously employing the BBC's principle of educating the masses by bringing information right to Soviet kitchens. He essentially raised an

25 See Alex Kokcharov, "Truth Will Be Told," March 9, 2022, in *The Slavic Connexion*, podcast, https://www.slavxradio.com/ukraine-2.

entire generation. In a 2007 documentary on the World Service, Seva reflected on his work:

> Some people jokingly say that "you singlehandedly brought down the Soviet system," which of course is not true. But it is true in a sense that by talking direct to people and being honest with them, you liberate them, and you give them a whole spectrum of ideas.[26]

To reiterate: "[Seva] was our agent in a Western environment. Because of him, the 'West' was a big smile with the Russian language who understood our matters."[27] It is with great pathos and obvious nostalgia that those who were young in the late Soviet period recount their listening experiences—many say it was the most hope-filled time of their lives. As Alex Tatishchev said, concluding his own story, "I doubt if any NORIS member would say that our movement—what we did—wasn't the best thing that ever happened to them."[28]

Through the medium of radio, Seva made an incalculable difference in the Cold War. The community he inadvertently cultivated because of the rock he broadcast and the letters he read on air became the community that did eventually overwhelm and force the Soviet system to change. A jazz musician, a cultural patriot, a *stilyaga*, a "True Gentleman," a father figure and friend, Seva Novgorodsev won the hearts and minds of millions, granting listeners in the closed society of the Soviet Union the one thing they craved most: *freedom*. When asked in March 2019 how he would like to be remembered, Seva poignantly replied with a poem by Pushkin:

> "And long will my name be dear to people / Because with my lyre, I evoked good feelings / Because in my cruel age I praised Freedom / And mercy for the fallen summoned."
>
> That's how I'd like to be remembered.[29]

---

26 "London Calling: Inside BBC World Service," 2007, BBC, https://www.bbc.co.uk/programmes/b007rw2f/episodes/guide.

27 D. Tockman in discussion with author, May 2019.

28 A. Tatishchev, May 2019.

29 Novgorodsev, interview by Matthew Orr, March 28, 2019, in *The Slavic Connexion*, podcast.

Seva official portrait (Credit: seva.ru)

Acknowledgements

I have an endless list of people to thank because no project is a lone wolf achievement. First, I must thank two key people whom I met in the early stages of research, Sergey Pantsirev and Alexey (Alex) Tatishchev for their expertise, experience, and rich contributions without which this book could not have been written. Thank you to Anna Pantsireva, an amazing artist, for sharing with me her memories and intimate knowledge as well as being (along with Sergey) a wonderful translator and guide in Budapest, Moscow, and St. Petersburg. Thank you, Alex, for your incredible kindness and generosity, for being the principal organizer of meetings with NORIS members, and for sharing with me your story and amazing archive of *samizdat*, photos, and so much more.

Since this book is for all of the listeners, I shall attempt to list some of the wonderful people who lived through the fall of the USSR and told me their stories: Oleg Osetrov, Oleg Rusakov, Andrey Balakirev, Andrey Kulik, Igor Tolstenkov, Alexey Pribyl, Konstantin Zaitzev, Eugen Neumann, Yevgeny Ayrapetov, Georgy Beliaev, Dmitry Busygin, and Dmitry Tockman (a kindred spirit if I ever met one). A special thanks to the women listeners in Russia who showed me that Soviet-era radio and rock were not as heavily gendered as they seemed. I must also, with great sadness and gratitude, make mention of Vladimir Ivanov and his lovely wife Natasha. Vladimir, a videographer and Beatles fan, passed away on Monday, August 31, 2020, in Moscow. He was, as Seva himself put it, the "video chronicler" of the NORIS movement. Vladimir graciously opened his treasured archive of radio recordings, pictures, notebooks of album artwork, and more to me with unforgettable enthusiasm. I am forever indebted to him and Natasha for their hospitality while I was in Moscow.

Thank you to the many scholars and practitioners who gave so much to this endeavor. First and foremost, thank you to the director of the Center for Russian, East European, and Eurasian Studies at UT Austin, the incomparable Dr. Mary C. Neuburger, for her immense support and for bringing Seva and his wife Olga to Austin, Texas in March 2019 for a full week—an unforgettable experience. Next, I wish to express my heartfelt gratitude to Dr. Mark Pomar, former director of VOA's USSR Service and the superlative "voice" of experience in all things radio and public diplomacy. I am thankful for all the people of note with whom he has connected me. Next, thank you to Jeff and Gretchen

Trimble for meeting with me numerous times, keeping tabs on me in the birthing stages of the project, and also connecting me with helpful sources, including Eduard Gladkov and especially Olga Slobodskaya who generously answered my many questions about her life and time at the Leningrad Rock Club. I also wish to thank Dr. Thomas J. Garza at UT Austin for his genuineness, cultural expertise, and connecting me to Artemy Troitsky. To Artemy Troitsky, I am grateful for the hours spent in Moscow talking about radio, rock, and Russia—and also the connections to Boris Grebenshchikov and others. I am indebted.

Thank you to the following musicians: Andrei Solovyov (and by extension Oxana Budjko, who introduced me to him in the first place and facilitated my Russian visa), Boris Grebenshchikov, Randy Zimmerman, Jim Milne, Mike Steinel, and, especially, Sasha Titov and Joanna Stingray for providing such insightful answers to my questions—and, in Joanna's case, permission to use some of her amazing pictures.

Additional thanks to Bill Skundrich, who gave me two hours on a Saturday to talk about his time as radio presenter at VOA in the '80s and '90s and for sharing several pictures and personal accounts from listeners with me. Thank you to Marina Oeltjen, director of VOA Russian Service, at the time of writing this, for connecting me with so many people, including Mr. Skundrich, and sending much valuable information my way. Thank you to Yuri Felshtinsky for humoring my request for an interview and for being generous with his time and information. Thank you to Lyalya Kharitonova and Sarah Patton at the Hoover Institution and Maristella Feustle at the UNT Libraries. Additional thanks to Dr. Mark Zentner, Peter Pomerantsev, Tatiana Smorodinska (Middlebury College), and A. Ross Johnson (former director of RFE/RL), who sadly passed away in February 2021. Also, thanks go to Dr. Jeremi Suri whose teaching, encouragement, and podcast *This is Democracy* sparked my research topic. Finally, thanks to everyone at *The Slavic Connexion,* too many wonderful people to name, but in particular Matthew Orr and Thomas Rehnquist who willingly launched this crazy project with me in February 2019 while we were all still overloaded grad students.

On a personal note, thank you to my closest friends and family for their encouragement, in particular my sister Joanne, Charlie Harper, Chris Grall, Vandon Gibbs, Cara Keirstead, Audrius Rickus, and Lera Toropin. Eternal gratitude to my amazing children, Jasmine, Benjamin, and Jada, for always and unconditionally supporting me, and to my husband and editor in chief James Geraci who combed through this manuscript and provided the technical expertise to code the map for listener letters and NORIS cards. Finally, thank you to Olga whose sweetness and vivacious personality translate perfectly in any culture, and to Seva, whose life and story has irrevocably changed mine.

Bibliography

Secondary Sources

Andrew, Christopher, and Oleg Gordievsky. *KGB: The Inside Story.* New York: Harper Collins, 1990.

Applebaum, Anne. *Gulag: A History.* London: Penguin, 2003.

Benn, David Wedgwood. "How the FO tried to stifle the BBC." *New Statesman,* December 6, 1999. http://www.newstatesman.com/199912060009.

———. "Winning Hearts and Minds." *Gulf News,* December 4, 2004. https://gulfnews.com/uae/david-wedgwood-benn-winning-hearts-and-minds-1.340549.

Bergmeier, Horst J. P., and Rainer E. Lotz. *Hitler's Airwaves: The Inside Story of Nazi Radio Broadcasting and Propaganda Swing.* New Haven: Yale University Press, 1997.

Bourdeaux, Lorna. *Valeri Barinov: The Trumpet Call.* London: Marshall Morgan & Scott Ltd., 1985.

Coates, Stephen. *X-Ray Audio: The Strange Story of Soviet Audio on the Bone.* London: Strange Attractor Press, 2015.

Conquest, Robert. *The Great Terror: A Reassessment.* Oxford: Oxford University Press, 2008.

Crisell, Andrew. *An Introductory History of British Broadcasting.* London: Routledge, 2002.

Dale, Robert. "Rats and Resentment: The Demobilization of the Red Army in Postwar Leningrad, 1945–50." *Journal of Contemporary History* 45, no. 1 (2010): 113–33.

Eke, Steven. "BBC Russian Radio Hits off Switch." BBC News, March 23, 2011. https://www.bbc.com/news/world-europe-12820788.

Galeotti, Mark. "Poison, Protests, Prison: The Continued Saga of Alexei Navalny." February 3, 2021. In *The Slavic Connexion,* produced by Matthew Orr and Tom Rehnquiest. Podcast. MP3 audio, 47:79. https://www.slavxradio.com.

Gessen, Masha. *Dead Again: The Russian Intelligentsia after Communism.* London: Verso, 1997.

Glanville, Jo. *Radio Redux: Freedom on the Airwaves.* London: Sage Publications Ltd., 2010.

Gross, Jan., Kotkin, Stephen. *Uncivil Society: 1989 and the Implosion of the Communist Establishment.* New York: Random House, 2010.

Guback, Thomas H., and Steven P. Hill. *The Innovation of Broadcasting in the Soviet Union and the Role of V. I. Lenin.* Urbana: University of Illinois, Institute of Communication Research, 1972.

Guseva, Anna. "Genre and Stylistic Features of the Radio Programs of Seva Novgorodsev." Master's thesis, Saint Petersburg State University, 2017. http://hdl.handle.net/11701/9877.

Hickman, Tom. *What Did You Do in the War, Auntie?: The BBC at War 1939–45.* London: BBC Publications, 1996.

Jablonsky, Col. David. *Churchill: The Making of a Grand Strategist.* Carlisle, PA: US Army War College, 1990.

Kotkin, Stephen. *Magnetic Mountain.* Berkeley: University of California Press, 1995.

———. *Stalin: Waiting for Hitler, 1929–1941.* Harmondsworth: Penguin Press, 2017.

Lipovetsky, Mark. "Tricksters in Disguise: The Trickster's Transformations in the Soviet Film of the 1960s–70s." In *Charms of the Cynical Reason: Tricksters in Soviet and Post-Soviet Culture,* 193–230. Boston: Academic Studies Press, 2011.

Lovell, Stephen. "Broadcasting Bolshevik: The Radio Voice of Soviet Culture, 1920s–1950s." *Journal of Contemporary History* 48, no. 1 (2013): 78–97. http://www.jstor.org/stable/23488337.

———. "How Russia Learned to Listen: Radio and the Making of Soviet Culture." *Kritika: Explorations in Russian and Eurasian History* 12, no. 3 (August 13, 2011): 591–615. https://doi.org/10.1353/kri.2011.0040.

———. *Russia in the Microphone Age: A History of Soviet Radio, 1919–1970*. Oxford: Oxford University Press, 2015.

Lownie, Andrew. *Stalin's Englishman: Guy Burgess, the Cold War, and the Cambridge Spy Ring*. London: Macmillan, 2016.

Marochkin, Vladimir. "Interview with Late Soviet Rock Artist Vladislav Petrovsky." *Spetsial'noe Radio*, March 24, 2006. https://specialradio.ru/art/id212/.

McAdams, A. James. "An Obituary for the Berlin Wall." *World Policy Journal* 7, no. 2 (1990): 357–75. http://www.jstor.org/stable/40209151.

McKinlay, R. "To What Extent Did the BBC Russian Service Help Shape Youth Attitudes in the USSR in the 1970s and 1980s?" Master's thesis, University of London, 2017.

McLuhan, Marshall. *Understanding Media: The Extensions of Man*. McGraw-Hill Paperbacks. New York: McGraw-Hill, 1965.

Mytton, Graham. "Audience Research at the BBC External Services during the Cold War: A View from the Inside." *Cold War History* 11, no. 1 (February 2011): 49–67. doi.org/10.1080/14682745.2011.545597.

Nekola, Anna. "'More than Just a Music': Conservative Christian Anti-Rock Discourse and the U. S. Culture Wars." *Popular Music* 32, no. 3 (2013): 407–26. http://www.jstor.org/stable/24736782.

Nelson, Michael. *War of the Black Heavens: The Battles of Western Broadcasting in the Cold War*. Syracuse: Syracuse University Press, 1997.

Nicholas, Siân. "The People's Radio: The BBC and Its Audience, 1939–1945." In *Millions Like Us?: British Culture in the Second World War*, edited by Nick Hayes and Jeff Hill, 62–92. Liverpool: Liverpool University Press, 1999.

Oberdorfer, Don. *From the Cold War to a New Era: The United States and the Soviet Union, 1983–1991*. Baltimore: John Hopkins University Press, 1998.

Parta, R. Eugene, and A. Ross Johnson. *Cold War Broadcasting: Impact on the Soviet Union and Eastern Europe: A Collection of Studies and Documents*. Budapest: Central European University Press, 2010.

Peddie, Ian. *Popular Music and Human Rights: Two-volume set*. Farnham: Ashgate Publishing Group, 2011.

Pomerantsev, Peter. *This Is Not Propaganda: Adventures in the War Against Reality*. New York: Public Affairs, 2019.

Puddington, Arch. *Broadcasting Freedom: The Cold War Triumph of Radio Free Europe and Radio Liberty*. Lexington: University Press of Kentucky, 2000.

Raleigh, Donald J. *Soviet Baby Boomers: An Oral History of Russia's Cold War Generation*. Oxford: Oxford University Press, 2013.

Rawnsley, Gary D. *Radio Diplomacy and Propaganda: The BBC and VOA in International Politics, 1956–64*. London: Palgrave Macmillan, 1996.

Riordan, James, ed. *Soviet Youth Culture*. London: Palgrave Macmillan, 1989.

Ripmaster, Terry. *Willis Conover: Broadcasting Jazz to The World*. New York: iUniverse, 2007.

Risch, William Jay, ed. *Youth and Rock in the Soviet Bloc: Youth Cultures, Music, and the State in Russia and Eastern Europe*. Lanham: Lexington Books, 2014.

Roth-Ey, Kristin. *Moscow Prime Time: How the Soviet Union Built the Media Empire That Lost the Cultural Cold War*. Ithaca: Cornell University Press, 2011.

———. "Listening out, Listening for, Listening in: Cold War Broadcasting and the Late Soviet Audience." *The Russian Review* 79, no. 4 (October 2020): 556–77.

Schmelz, Peter J. *Such Freedom, if Only Musical: Unofficial Soviet Music during the Thaw*. New York: Oxford University Press, 2009.

Schwartz, Lowell H. *Political Warfare against the Kremlin: US and British Propaganda Policy at the Beginning of the Cold War*. London: Palgrave Macmillan, 2009.

Sheeran, Paul. *Cultural Politics in International Relations*. Farnham: Ashgate Publishing, 2001.

Starr, S. Frederick. *Red and Hot: The Fate of Jazz in the Soviet Union*. New York: Limelight, 2004.

Steinholt, Yngvar Bordewich. *Rock in the Reservation: Songs from the Leningrad Rock Club 1981–1986*. New York: Mass Media Music Scholars' Press, 2004.

Stourton, Edward. *Auntie's War*. London: Doubleday, 2017.

Taubman, William. *Gorbachev: His Life and Times*. New York: Simon & Schuster, 2017.

Taylor, Philip M. *British Propaganda in the Twentieth Century: Selling Democracy*. Edinburgh: Edinburgh University Press, 1999.

Tockman, D. "Interview with Seva Novgorodsev." *Rossiskaya Gazeta*, April 2018.

Troitsky, A. *Back in the USSR: The True Story of Rock in Russia*. London: Omnibus Press, 1987.

———. *Subkultura: Stories of Youth and Resistance in Russia 1815–2017*. London: The New Social, 2017.

Tusa, John. *Conversations with the World*. London: BBC Publications, 1990.

Vučetic, Radina. *Coca-Cola Socialism: Americanization of Yugoslav Culture in the Sixties*. Budapest: Central European University Press, 2018.

Webb, Alban. *London Calling: Britain, the BBC World Service and the Cold War*. London: Bloomsbury Academic, 2014.

Willis, David K. "How the British Broadcasting Corporation Keeps Its Balance." *Christian Science Monitor*, August 17, 1982. https://www.csmonitor.com/1982/0817/081733.html.

Wolf, René. *The Undivided Sky: The Holocaust on East and West German Radio in the 1960s*. Basingstoke: Palgrave Macmillan, 2010.

Wood, James. *History of International Broadcasting*. London: P. Peregrinus Ltd., 1992.

Yurchak, Alexei. *Everything Was Forever, until It Was No More: The Last Soviet Generation*. Princeton: Princeton University Press, 2005.

Zhuk, Sergei I. *Rock and Roll in the Rocket City: The West, Identity, and Ideology in Soviet Dniepropetrovsk, 1960–1985*. Baltimore: Johns Hopkins University Press, 2010.

Zubok, Vladislav M. *Zhivago's Children*. Cambridge, MA: Harvard University Press, 2009.

Primary Sources

Anderson, Jack, and Dale Van Atta. "Assassination in London." *Washington Post*, September 8, 1991. https://www.washingtonpost.com/archive/opinions/1991/09/08/assassination-in-london/e2fdc212-656d-46ff-9a6f-773da07ef875/.

"Anti-Soviet Rising Spread in South; Red Troops Rushed from Rumanian Border to Stem Revolution in Ukraine. Kronstadt Invites Reporters to See the Fighting." *New York Times*, March 16, 1921. http://timesmachine.nytimes.com/timesmachine/1921/03/16/107009958.html.

Batashev, Alexei. *Sovetskii dzhaz. Istoricheskii ocherk* [Soviet jazz: An historical essay]. Moscow: Muzyka, 1972.

"BBC Russian Service 'Warned' May be Blocked over 'Provocative Interview'." BBC Monitoring, August 5, 2014. https://advance-lexis-com.ezproxy.lib.utexas.edu/api/document?collection=news&id=urn:contentItem:5CV5-PN31-DYRV-31JG-00000-00&context=1516831.

McNaughton, Cathal. "Buried in Lead in Londongrad." *The Sunday Times* (London), December 10, 2006. https://advance-lexis-com.ezproxy.lib.utexas.edu/api/document?collection=news&id=urn:contentItem:4MJ4-D1V0-TX38-S3DY-00000-00&context=1516831.

"Concerning the NKVD's Monitoring of International Communications." December 28, 1939, History and Public Policy Program Digital Archive, RGASPI f.17 op.162 d.22 l.158-159. Translated by Gary Goldberg. https://digitalarchive.wilsoncenter.org/document/121878.

Conover, Willis. "Music USA #695-B, Hungarian Jazz Guests." Voice of America, November 21, 1956. University of North Texas University Libraries, UNT Digital Library, Denton, TX. https://digital.library.unt.edu/ark:/67531/metadc790677/m1/.

———. Interviewed by Harold Rogers. BBC, August 4, 1957. University of North Texas University Libraries, UNT Digital Library, Denton, TX. https://digital.library.unt.edu/ark:/67531/metadc800494/m1/.

———. Writings by Conover, "Russ 67". Box 17, Folder 31. Willis Conover Collection, 1930–1996, University of North Texas University Libraries, Denton, TX.

Danilov, I. "Seva-Seva Novgorodtsev, gorod Kiev, Bi-Bi-Si." *Sovetskaia molodyozh'*, July 10, 1990. https://seva.ru/media/?id=191.

Dimitrov, Georgi M., and Ivan Banac, eds. *The Diary of Georgi Dimitrov*. New Haven: Yale University Press, 2003.

Filinov, Yuri. "Barbarossa rock n' rolla" ["Barbarossa of Rock 'n' Roll"]. *Komsomol'skaia pravda*, September 16, 1984.

———. "Talanty i chinovniki." *Komsomol'skaia pravda*, November 23, 1988.

Golomstock, Igor. *A Ransomed Dissident: A Life in Art Under the Soviets*. London: Bloomsbury Publishing, 2018.

Gorodetskaya, A. "Seva Novgorodsev: Ot chekistov mozhno zhdat' chto ugodno." seva.re, January 10, 2020. https://seva.ru/media/?id=258.

Gromyko, Andrei. *Memoirs*. New York: Doubleday, 1990.

Keller, Bill. "Russia's Restless Youth." *New York Times*, July 26, 1987. https://www.nytimes.com/1987/07/26/magazine/russia-s-restless-youth.html.

Kennan Institute Russian History Audio Archive. Wilson Centre, Washington, DC.

Kennan, George F. "George Kennan's 'Long Telegram'" [February 22, 1946]. In *Foreign Relations of the United States, 1946*. Vol. 6: *Eastern Europe, The Soviet Union*, edited by Rogers P. Churchill and William Slaney, 296–709. Washington, DC: United States Government Printing Office, 1969.

Kennan, George F., and Frank Costigliola, eds. *The Kennan Diaries*. New York: W. W. Norton & Company, 2014.

Kremer, William. "Seva Novgorodsev: The DJ Who 'Brought down the USSR.'" BBC News, September 5, 2015. https://www.bbc.com/news/magazine-34157596.

"Kto on takoi?" ["Who is he really?"]. *Rovesnik* 9 (1982): 27–28. Also at Seva.ru. Accessed July 22, 2022. https://seva.ru/media/?id=1.

Lenin, Vladimir Ilyich, and Alexander Trachtenberg, eds. *Collected Works of V. I. Lenin: Completely Revised, Edited and Annotated.* Vols. 21–33. London: M. Lawrence, 1927.

Lisann, Maury. *Broadcasting to the Soviet Union: International Politics and Radio*. Praeger Special Studies in International Politics and Government. New York: Praeger, 1975.

Maisky, Ivan, and Gabriel Gorodetsky, eds. *The Maisky Diaries: Red Ambassador to the Court of St. James's, 1932–1943*. New Haven: Yale University Press, 2015.

Macfarlane, Jess. "BBC World Service in the 1990s." *Tuning In: Researching Diasporas at the BBC World Service* [digital project). London: The Open University, 2014. Accessed August 5, 2022. https://www.open.ac.uk/researchprojects/diasporas/sites/www.open.ac.uk.researchprojects.diasporas/files/BBC%20World%20Service%20in%20the%201990s.pdf.

Maisky, Ivan, and Gabriel Gorodetsky, eds. *The Complete Maisky Diaries: Volumes 1–3*. Translated by Tatiana Sorokina and Oliver Ready. New Haven: Yale University Press, 2017.

Molotov, Vyacheslav. *Molotov Remembers: Inside Kremlin Politics*. Chicago: Ivan R. Dee, Publisher, 1993.

Orr, Matthew, host. "Seva Novgorodsev—*Russkaya Sluzhba* BBC." April 9, 2019. In *The Slavic Connexion*, produced by Matthew Orr and Tom Rehnquist. Podcast. MP3 audio, 31:28. https://www.slavxradio.com/seva-in-russian.

———. Letters Received. Hoover Institution Archives, Stanford, California.

———. *Integral pokhozh na saksofon*. Saint Petersburg: Amphora, 2011.

Ogonëk Digital Archive. East View Information Services, Minnetonka, Minnesota. https://dlib-eastview-com.ezproxy.lib.utexas.edu/browse/udb/3030.

Orwell, George. *George Orwell Diaries*. Edited by Peter Davison. New York: Liveright, 2012.

Parta, R. Eugene. *Discovering the Hidden Listener: An Assessment of Radio Liberty and Western Broadcasting to the USSR during the Cold War: A Study Based on Audience Research Findings, 1970–1991*. Hoover Institution Press Publication, no. 546. Stanford: Hoover Institution Press, 2007.

Rosenstiel, Thomas B. "Captive Gorbachev Tuned in to the BBC, Voice of America." *Los Angeles Times*, August 23, 1991. https://www.latimes.com/archives/la-xpm-1991-08-23-mn-1029-story.html.

Rul, Konstantin. "Seva Novgorodsev, 'I Didn't Intend to Destroy the USSR—Only to Reveal Its Idiotism.'" *Opinion*, July 11, 2018. https://opinionua.com/en/2018/07/11/seva-novgorodsev-i-didnt-intend-to-destroy-the-ussr-only-to-josh-and-reveal-its-idiotism/.

"Russia in the Melting Pot," Public Record Office at Kew, FO 395/453.

Schmemann, Serge. "End of the Soviet Union: The Soviet State, Born of a Dream, Dies." *New York Times*, December 26, 1991. https://www.nytimes.com/1991/12/26/world/end-of-the-soviet-union-the-soviet-state-born-of-a-dream-dies.html.

Simonov, V. "Vsevolod Borisovich." *Rovesnik* 12 (1990). https://seva.ru/media/?id=9.

Slushaī͡ut radio. Kruglovskii detdom Kolpashevskoi komendatury. Russian Federation, Tomsk Oblast, Narym, 1930. Narym: n.p., 1930–1936. Photograph. Special Settlers in West Siberia in 1930s. Library of Congress. https://www.loc.gov/item/2018685583/.

Smirnov, Ilya. "Rock 'n' Gertsen." *Русская idea*, November 3, 2014. https://politconservatism.ru/experiences/rock-n-gertsen.

Stalin, Joseph V. "Soviet Union: Foreign Office Telegram to Moscow, No 855. Stalin to Prime Minister," July 20, 1941. FO 954/24B/346. The National Archives, Kew.

Stalin, Joseph V., Harry S. Truman, and C. R. Attlee. "The Big Three Report on the Potsdam Conference." *Current History* 9, no. 49 (1945): 240–50. http://www.jstor.org/stable/45306784.

Stingray, Joanna and Madison Stingray. *Red Wave: An American in the Soviet Music Underground.* Los Angeles: DoppelHouse Press, 2020.

Tolkunov, Dmitri. "Seva Novgorodsev: I Have Always Been Interested in the Spiritual and Intellectual Nature of My Listeners." *All Andorra*, April 29, 2019. https://all-andorra.com/seva-novgorodsev-i-have-always-been-interested-in-the-spiritual-and-intellectual-nature-of-my-listeners/.

Trotsky, Leon. "Speech at First All-Union Congress of the Society of Friends of Radio. March 1, 1926, Moscow." In *Collected Works of L. D. Trotsky*. Vol. 21. Moscow: Moscow State Publishing House, 1927.

Additional Sources

Bischof, Anna, and Zuzana Jürgens, eds. *Voices of Freedom—Western Interference? 60 Years of Radio Free Europe*. Veröffentlichungen Des Collegium Carolinum, Band 130. Göttingen: Vandenhoeck & Ruprecht, 2015.

Hale, Julian. *Radio Power: Propaganda and International Broadcasting*. Philadelphia: Temple University Press, 1975.

"Hungarian Refugee Opinion." Audience Analysis Section, Radio Free Europe, 02 January 1957. OSA 1956 Digital Archive. Open Society Archives at Central European University, Budapest. Accessed November 23, 2018. http://w3.osaarchivum.org/digitalarchive/hoover/index.html.

"'Ideological Sabotage' by the BBC Russian Service." *BBC Summary of World Broadcasts*, October 9, 1979. https://advance-lexis-com.ezproxy.lib.utexas.edu/api/document?collection=news&id=urn:contentItem:3S8G-Y3K0-000F-01HH-00000-00&context=1516831.

Lisann, Maury. *Broadcasting to the Soviet Union: International Politics and Radio*. Praeger Special Studies in International Politics and Government. New York: Praeger, 1975.

Lovell, Stephen. "Broadcasting Bolshevik: The Radio Voice of Soviet Culture, 1920s–1950s." *Journal of Contemporary History* 48, no. 1 (2013): 78–97.

McGuire, Bill. *Tales of an American Culture Vulture*. New York: iUniverse, 2003.

McLuhan, Marshall. *Understanding Media: The Extensions of Man*. New York: McGraw-Hill, 1965.

Saito, Yoshiomi. *The Global Politics of Jazz in the Twentieth Century: Cultural Diplomacy and "American Music."* New York: Routledge, 2019.

"Summary of Science Broadcasts to the U.S.S.R." BBC. Dora Winifred Russell papers. Internationaal Instituut voor Sociale Geschiedenis, Netherlands.

Index